THE COMPLETE STUDY GUIDE FOR SCORING HIGH

GARDENER
ASSISTANT GARDENER

by The ARCO EDITORIAL BOARD

arco 219 Park Avenue South
New York, N.Y. 10003

Third Edition B-2098

Published by ARCO PUBLISHING COMPANY, INC.
219 Park Avenue South, New York, N.Y. 10003

Library of Congress Catalog
Card Number 75-27588

Arco Catalog Number **ISBN 0-668-01340-0**

Printed in the United States of America

CONTENTS

HOW TO USE THIS INDEX
Slightly bend the right-hand edge of the book. This will expose the corresponding Parts which match the index, below.

PART

1

2

3

4

WHAT THIS BOOK WILL DO FOR YOU 7

How this book was prepared; what went into these pages to make them worth your while. How to use them profitably for yourself in preparing for your test. The essentials of successful study.

PART ONE
APPLYING AND STUDYING FOR YOUR JOB

OFFICIAL ANNOUNCEMENTS 11

Facts that foreshadow your test and help you do your best.

STUDYING AND USING THIS BOOK 13

How to study with maximum efficiency. Five basic steps in attacking each assignment. The techniques of learning . . . concentrating . . . taking notes . . . testing yourself . . . developing careful reading habits . . . analyzing your weaknesses—and correcting them.

HOW TO BE A MASTER TEST TAKER 19

Master each of these methods—they apply to question types you may meet on your exam. Practice them when testing yourself in this book to insure a top performance on your actual exam.

PART TWO
PREVIOUS EXAMS FOR PRACTICE

I. THE LATEST PREVIOUS EXAM **December 14, 1974** 27

This is the latest available civil service test for your job. After taking it you will have a fair indication of your present knowledge and ability. After completing this book, take the test again and measure your improvement.

II. PREVIOUS EXAM FOR PRACTICE **September 26, 1964** 42

Begin real training for the test you must take by testing yourself with this civil service exam which was actually given to candidates for your job. Adhere strictly to test instructions and conditions to get a measure of your present knowledge and ability.

III. PREVIOUS EXAM FOR PRACTICE 51

Another exam given at a different time for the very job you want. Even though you are somewhat familiar with the test instructions, follow them carefully. Don't relax. Now is the time to master them, so you don't puzzle over them during your actual test.

IV. PREVIOUS EXAM FOR PRACTICE 59

Another actual civil service exam for the job you want, and it may well be an accurate forecast of what you may find on your exam. Therefore, follow the directions carefully, read each question thoroughly, and be careful in recording your answers.

V. PREVIOUS EXAM FOR PRACTICE 59

This exam once given for the very civil service job you are seeking can be made even more useful if you follow this advice: take it when you are about halfway through your studies. This way you will be able to determine how much you have improved, and how much you will have to improve to get the score you want.

...continued on next page

CONTENTS continued

PART

1

2

3

4

VI. FINAL REVIEW EXAMINATION 77

Your score on this previous examination should tell you where you stand. If you're not satisfied, there's still time. Review, then take the test again, working for improvement over your other scores. A higher score now predicts a higher score on the actual test.

PART THREE
BASIC INFORMATION
DIRECTLY CONNECTED WITH THE JOB

GARDENER'S HANDBOOK 89

POINTERS ON MAKING GOOD LAWNS
14 steps necessary for making a good lawn. Renovating the lawn. Grasses for lawns . . . requirements of various grasses

GROWING ANNUAL FLOWERING PLANTS 94
General Cultural Suggestions: *Preparation of the soil. Water. Starting the plants. Hotbeds and coldframes. Pits. Plants for special soils or conditions. A chart listing the principle characteristics of some annual flowering plants.*

HERBACIOUS PERENNIALS 110
Adaptability of different kinds of plants. Table listing some herbaceous perennials suitable for use in the different sections of the United States. Index of common names, giving the corresponding scientific names.

CARE OF TREES 118
An analysis of the steps to follow in selecting, planting, and caring for trees. Interpretive science and related information. Shade and ornamental trees suitable for grounds. Care of Damaged Shade Trees: *Causes of wounds and how they may be avoided . . . injuries due to the weather. Man-made wounds. Animal-caused wounds . . . injuries inflicted by insects . . . injuries caused by plants. How wounds heal. Increasing tree vigor as an aid to healing. Complications that hinder healing. Wound Treatment: Procedure. Importance of prompt treatment . . . season. Tools and hardware needed. Shaping the wounds . . . removing branches and roots. Dressing the wounds.* Cases Requiring Special Handling: *Cavities. Cankers. Superficial bark wounds . . . slime flux. Girdling roots. Frost cracks.*

INSECTS AND DISEASES 149
General feeders. General methods of insect and disease control . . . how to prepare insecticides and fungicides for garden-pest control. A descriptive list of spray mixtures, dust mixtures, solutions, and poisoned baits. Fungicides . . . seed disinfectants . . . spraying and dusting . . . copper sprays. Copper dusts . . . sulfur dusts . . . DDT insecticides . . . table of measures. Proper quantities of sprays or dusts to apply . . . spraying and dusting equipment.

CONTENTS continued

PART

PART FOUR
BACKGROUND AND STUDY MATERIAL FOR THE EXAM
FINAL ADVICE

1

TECHNIQUES OF READING INTERPRETATION 161

2

Two aspects of success in reading interpretation. Causes of and cures for slow reading and poor comprehension. Ten success step to help you avoid reading traps. Using the "success steps" with a practice passage.

READING COMPREHENSION 166

3

Some helpful hints followed by steps to take and some traps to avoid in developing your ability to comprehend what you read. Reading passages, each followed by several statements or questions, to test your ability. Correct answers.

4

SUPERVISION QUIZZER 182

Complete Q and A guide for all ranks. Explanatory answers provide a concise review of all the important principles of supervision.

SUPERVISING UNSKILLED WORKERS 183

TRAINING AND RATING EMPLOYEES 195

ESTABLISHING DISCIPLINE 198

MAKING REPORTS 201

SAFEGUARDING EMPLOYEES 205

SUPERVISOR-SUPERIOR RELATIONSHIPS 209

TEST-TAKING MADE SIMPLE 214

Test-taking strategy for successful exam performance. How to prepare yourself emotionally, factually, physically. During the exam . . . budgeting your time . . . following directions. "Musts" for the master test-taker.

ARCO BOOKS 222

You'll want to consult this list of Arco publications to order other invaluable career books related to your field. The list also suggests job opportunities and promotions that you might want to go after with an Arco self-tutor.

WHAT THIS BOOK WILL DO FOR YOU

To get the greatest help from this book, please understand that it has been carefully organized. You must, therefore, plan to use it accordingly. Study this concise, readable book earnestly and your way will be clear. You will progress directly to your goal. You will not be led off into blind alleys and useless fields of study.

Arco Publishing Company has followed testing trends and methods ever since the firm was founded in 1937. We have specialized in books that prepare people for tests. Based on this experience it is our modest boast that you probably have in your hands the best book that could be prepared to help *you* score high. Now, if you'll take a little advice on using it properly, we can assure you that you will do well.

To write this book we carefully analyzed every detail surrounding the forthcoming examination . . .

* the job itself
* official and unofficial announcements concerning the examination
* all the available previous examinations
* many related examinations
* technical literature that explains and forecasts the examination.

As a result of all this (which you, happily, have not had to do) we've been able to create the "climate" of your test, and to give you a fairly accurate picture of what's involved. Some of this material, digested and simplified, actually appears in print here, if it was deemed useful and suitable in helping you score high.

But more important than any other benefit derived from this research is our certainty that the study material, the text and the practice questions are right for you.

The practice questions you will study have been judiciously selected from hundreds of thousands of previous test questions on file here at Arco. But they haven't just been thrown at you pell mell. They've been organized into the subjects that you can expect to find on your test. As you answer the questions, these subjects will take on greater meaning for you. At the same time you will be getting valuable practice in answering test questions. You will proceed with a sure step toward a worthwhile goal: high test marks.

Studying in this manner, you will get the feel of the entire examination. You will learn by "insight," by seeing through a problem as a result of experiencing *previous similar situations.* This is true learning according to many psychologists.

In short, what you get from this book will help you operate at top efficiency . . . make you give the best possible account of yourself on the actual examination.

CAN YOU PREPARE YOURSELF FOR YOUR TEST?

We believe, most certainly, that you *can* with the aid of this "self-tutor!"

It's not a "pony." It's not a complete college education. It's not a "crib sheet," and it's no HOW TO SUCCEED ON TESTS WITHOUT REALLY TRYING. There's nothing in it that will give you a higher score than you really deserve.

It's just a top quality course which you can readily review in less than twenty hours . . . a digest of material which you might easily have written yourself after about five thousand hours of laborious digging.

To really prepare for your test you must motivate yourself . . . get into the right frame of mind for learning from your "self-tutor." You'll have to urge *yourself* to learn and that's the only way people ever learn. Your efforts to score high on the test will be greatly aided by the fact that you will have to do this job on your own . . . perhaps without a teacher. Psychologists have demonstrated that studies undertaken for a clear goal . . . which you initiate yourself and actively pursue . . . are the most successful. You, yourself, want to pass this test. That's why you bought this book and embarked on this program. Nobody forced you to do it, and there may be nobody to lead you through the course. Your self-activity is going to be the key to your success in the forthcoming weeks.

Used correctly, your "self-tutor" will show you what to expect and will give you a speedy brush-up on the subjects peculiar to your exam. Some of these are subjects not taught in schools at all. Even if your study time is very limited, you should:

- Become familiar with the type of examination you will meet.
- Improve your general examination-taking skill.
- Improve your skill in analyzing and answering questions involving reasoning, judgment, comparison, and evaluation.
- Improve your speed and skill in reading and understanding what you read—an important part of your ability to learn and an important part of most tests.
- Prepare yourself in the particular fields which measure your learning.

This book will tell you exactly what to study by presenting in full every type of question you will get on the actual test. You'll do better merely by familiarizing yourself with them.

This book will help you find your weaknesses and find them fast. Once you know where you're weak you can get right to work (before the test) and concentrate your efforts on those soft spots. This is the kind of selective study which yields maximum test results for every hour spent.

This book will give you the *feel* of the exam. Almost all our sample and practice questions are taken from actual previous exams. Since previous exams are not always available for inspection by the public, these sample test questions are quite important for you. The day you take your exam you'll see how closely this book follows the format of the real test.

This book will give you confidence *now*, while you are preparing for the test. It will build your self-confidence as you proceed. It will beat those dreaded before-test jitters that have hurt so many other test-takers.

This book stresses the modern, multiple-choice type of question because that's the kind you'll undoubtedly get on your test. In answering these questions you will add to your knowledge by learning the correct answers, naturally. However, you will not be satisfied with merely the correct choice for each question. You will want to find out why the other choices are incorrect. This will jog your memory . . . help you remember much you thought you had forgotten. You'll be preparing and enriching yourself for the exam to come.

Of course, the great advantage in all this lies in narrowing your study to just those fields in which you're most likely to be quizzed. Answer enough questions in those fields and the chances are very good that you'll meet a few of them again on the actual test. After all, the number of questions an examiner can draw upon in these fields is rather limited. Examiners frequently employ the same questions on different tests for this very reason.

There are other things which you should know and which various sections of this book will help you learn. Most important, not only for this examination but for all the examinations to come in your life, is learning how to take a test and how to prepare for it.

PART ONE

Applying and Studying For Your Exam

GARDENER - ASSISTANT GARDENER

OFFICIAL ANNOUNCEMENTS

Here's a fairly good example of the kind of official statements issued to describe your test and your job. Read it all rather carefully because there are clues here as to the kind of test you'll be taking and how you have to prepare yourself. In writing this book we have examined quite a number of these announcements and have guided ourselves accordingly. We urge that you read and understand all such statements that are issued to you, personally. They will undoubtedly contain facts that foreshadow your test.

GARDENER
New York City Civil Service Commission

Before you can be appointed as a Gardener, you MUST meet the following minimum requirements and you must receive a passing mark on the written test, the physical test, and the medical test. Exam weight 100, 70% required.

MINIMUM REQUIREMENTS: (a) Two years of full-time, paid experience in gardening work; or (b) a satisfactory equivalent combination of education and experience. Thirty credits in gardening, agriculture or a related field from an accredited college or community college will be accepted in place of one year of experience. Gardening work must include experience in each of the following: planting, cultivating and caring for trees, plants, shrubs and lawns. All candidates must have at least one year of experience as described above.

The minimum requirements must be met by the last day for receipt of applications. All candidates who file applications will be summoned for the written test prior to a determination of whether or not they meet the minimum requirements. The experience papers of passing candidates only will be evaluated.

Eligibles will be required to pass a qualifying medical test and a qualifying physical test prior to appointment. Eligibles will be evaluated on the basis of the following medical standard:

1. A candidate may be rejected for any current illness, disease, abnormality, injury, or other liability or condition which will impair his ability to perform the duties of the class of positions.

2. Alcohol and Drugs -- Excessive use of alcohol or abusive use of drugs or chemicals, which interferes with sensorium or other functions, rejects.

3. Infectious or Communicable Diseases -- Presence of, in an infectious or communicable stage, rejects.

Medical evidence to allow participation in the physical test may be required, and the Department of Personnel reserves the right to exclude from the physical test any eligible who, upon examination of such evidence, is apparently medically unfit. Eligibles will take the physical test at their own risk of injury, although every effort will be made to safeguard them.

Candidates will be required to complete satisfactorily the following physical tests:

1. AGILITY -- Rise from a supine position, scale a vault box 3 feet high, sprint 3 yards to a maze of obstacles and dodge through, proceed through a tunnel approximately 4 yards in length and sprint back approximately 10 yards to the finish line within 25 seconds.

2. STRENGTH -- Lift a 50 pound barbell, using both hands, from the floor to shoulder level and then return it to the floor under control.

PROMOTION TO GARDENER
New York City Civil Service Commission

Before you can be promoted to Gardener, you MUST meet the following minimum requirements and you must receive a passing mark on the written test. Exam weight 85, 70% required.

MINIMUM REQUIREMENTS: (a) Six months of full-time, paid experience in gardening work; or (b) a satisfactory equivalent. Fifteen credits in gardening, agriculture or a related field from an accredited college will be accepted in place of six months of experience. Gardening work must include experience in each of the following: planting, cultivating and caring for trees, plants, shrubs and lawns.

The minimum requirements must be met by the date of the written test. All candidates who file an application will be summoned to the written test prior to a determination of whether or not they meet the minimum requirements. The experience papers of passing candidates only will be evaluated.

STUDYING AND USING THIS BOOK

Even though this course of study has been carefully planned to help you get in shape by the day your test comes, you'll have to do a little planning on your own to be successful. And you'll also need a few pointers proven effective for many other good students.

SURVEY AND SCHEDULE YOUR WORK

Regular mental workouts are as important as regular physical workouts in achieving maximum personal efficiency. They are absolutely essential in getting top test scores, so you'll want to plan a test-preparing schedule that fits in with your usual program. Use the Schedule on the next page. Make it out for yourself so that it really works with the actual time you have at your disposal.

There are five basic steps in scheduling this book for yourself and in studying each assignment that you schedule:

1. SCAN - the entire job at hand.
2. QUESTION - before reading.
3. READ - to find the answers to the questions you have formulated.
4. RECITE - to see how well you have learned the answers to your questions.
5. REVIEW - to check up on how well you have learned, to learn it again, and to fix it firmly in your mind.

Scan

Make a survey of this whole book before scheduling. Do this by reading our introductory statements and the table of contents. Then leaf through the entire book, paying attention to main headings, sub-headings, summaries, and topic sentences. When you have this bird's eye view of the whole, the parts take on added meaning, and you'll see how they hang together.

Question

As you scan, questions will come to your mind. Write them into the book. Later on you'll be finding the answers. For example, in scanning this book you would naturally change the headline STUDYING AND USING THIS BOOK into *What don't I know about studying? What are my good study habits? How can I improve them? How should I go about reading and using this book?* Practice the habit of formulating and writing such questions into the text.

Read

Now, by reviewing your questions you should be able to work out your schedule easily. Stick to it. And apply these five steps to each assignment you give yourself in the schedule. Your reading of each assignment should be directed to finding answers to the questions you have formulated and will continue to formulate. You'll discover that reading with a purpose will make it easier to *remember* the answers to your questions.

Recite

After you have read your assignment and found the answers to your questions, close the book and recite to yourself. For example, if your question here was "What are the five basic steps in attacking an assignment?" then your answer to yourself would be scan, question, read, recite, and review. Thus, you check up on yourself and "fix" the information in your mind. You have now seen it, read it, said it, and heard it. The more senses you use, the more you learn.

Review

Even if you recall your answers well, review them in order to "overlearn." "Overlearning" gives you a big advantage by reducing the chances of forgetting. Definitely provide time in your schedule for review. It's the clincher in getting ahead of the crowd. You'll find that "overlearning" won't take much time with this book because the text portions have been written as concisely and briefly as possible. You may be tempted to stop work when you have once gone over the work before you. This is wrong because of the ease with which memory impressions are bound to fade. Decide for yourself what is important and plan to review and overlearn those portions. Overlearning rather than last minute cramming is the best way to study.

Your Time is Limited—Schedule Your Study

SUBJECT SCHEDULE

1. SCOPE OF EXAMINATION

Test Subjects	No. of Questions	Percentage of Total (Weight)
Total:		100 percent

2. YOUR KNOWLEDGE OF SUBJECT

Test Subjects	Poor	Fair	Good	Very Good	Excellent

3. DIVIDING YOUR STUDY TIME

Test Subjects	Total Hours	Hours Per Week
Total:		

Total number of weeks for study ....

Hours per week ....

Total number of hours ....

The SUBJECT SCHEDULE is divided into three parts: 1. Scope of Examination; 2. Your Knowledge of Subject; and 3. Dividing Your Study Time. To use your schedule, put down in part 1 all the subjects you will face on your test, the number of questions in each subject, and the "weight," or percentage, given to each subject in the total make-up of the test.

In part 2, again fill in all the test subjects and, with a check mark, rate yourself *honestly* as to your knowledge of each subject.

At the top of part 3, put down the number of weeks you will be able to devote to your studying. Determine the number of hours you will study each week and multiply that figure by the number of weeks to give you the total hours of study.

Again fill in the subjects. Then, take the weight given to each test subject (in part 1) and average it against your knowledge of that subject (as checked in part 2) to arrive at the number of hours you should allow for study of that subject out of your total study hours. In Chapter 2, under the heading "10. Total Time Allowed For Each Subject," you will find a more detailed explanation of how to divide your study time.

After you have fixed the total number of hours to be devoted to each subject, divide them by the number of weeks of study to arrive at the total weekly hours you will study each subject.

Plan to study difficult subjects when you can give them your greatest energy. Some people find that they can do their best work in the early morning hours. On the other hand, it has been found that forgetting is less when study is followed by sleep or recreation. Plan other study periods for those free times which might otherwise be wasted . . . for example lunch or when traveling to and from work.

Plan your schedule so that not more than 1½ or 2 hours are spent in the study of any subject at one sitting. Allow at least a half-hour for each session with your book. It takes a few minutes before you settle down to work.

You will find that there is enough time for your study and other activities if you follow a well-planned schedule. You will not only be able to find enough time for your other activities, but you will also accomplish more in the way of study and learning. A definite plan for study increases concentration. If you establish the habit of studying a subject at the same time each day, you will find that less effort is required in focusing your attention on it.

Where To Study

SELECT A ROOM THAT WILL BE AVAILABLE EACH DAY AT THE SAME TIME. THIS WILL HELP YOU CONCENTRATE.

USE A DESK OR TABLE WHICH WILL NOT BE SHARED SO THAT YOU CAN "LEAVE THINGS OUT". IT SHOULD BE BIG ENOUGH TO ACCOMMODATE ALL YOUR EQUIPMENT WITHOUT CRAMPING YOU. ELIMINATE ORNAMENTS AND OTHER DISTRACTIONS.

SELECT A ROOM WHICH HAS NO DISTRACTIONS. KEEP IT THAT WAY.

PROVIDE FOR GOOD AIR CIRCULATION IN YOUR STUDY ROOM.

KEEP THE TEMPERATURE AROUND 68°.

PROVIDE ADEQUATE LIGHTING . . . USE A DESK LAMP IN ADDITION TO OVERHEAD LIGHTS.

NOISE DISTRACTS SO KEEP RADIO AND TV TURNED OFF.

ARRANGE TO HAVE A PERMANENT KIT OF NECESSARY STUDY EQUIPMENT . . . PEN, PENCIL, RULER, SHEARS, ERASER, NOTEBOOK, CLIPS, DICTIONARY, ETC.

Study On Your Own

As a general rule you will find it more beneficial to study with this book in your room, alone. There are times, however, when two or more individuals can profit from team study. For example, if you can't figure something out for yourself, you might get help from a friend who is also studying for this test. Review situations sometimes lend themselves to team study if everyone concerned has already been over the ground by himself. Sometimes you can gain greater understanding of underlying principles as you volley ideas back and forth with other people. Watch out, though, that you don't come to lean on the others so much that you can't work things out for yourself.

PROVEN STUDY SUGGESTIONS

1. Do some work every day in preparation for the exam.
2. Budget your time—set aside a definite study period for each day during the week.
3. Study with a friend or a group occasionally—the exchange of ideas will help all of you. It's also more pleasant getting together.
4. Answer as many of the questions in this book as you can. Some of the questions that you will get on your actual test will be very much like some of the questions in this book.
5. Be physically fit. Eat the proper food—get enough sleep. You learn better and faster when you are in good health.
6. Take notes.
7. Be an active learner. Participate. Try harder.

TECHNIQUES OF EFFICIENT STUDY

DO NOT ATTEMPT SERIOUS STUDY WHILE IN TOO RELAXED A POSITION.

AVOID SERIOUS STUDY AFTER A HEAVY MEAL.

DO SOMETHING WHILE STUDYING . . . MAKE NOTES, UNDERLINE, FORMULATE QUESTIONS.

BEGIN CONCENTRATING AS SOON AS YOU SIT DOWN TO STUDY. DON'T FOOL AROUND.

MAKE TIME FOR STUDY BY ELIMINATING NEEDLESS ACTIVITIES AND OTHER DRAINS ON YOUR PRECIOUS TIME.

MAKE UP YOUR OWN ILLUSTRATIONS AND EXAMPLES TO CHECK ON YOUR UNDERSTANDING OF A TOPIC.

FIND SOME PRACTICAL APPLICATION OF YOUR NEWLY ACQUIRED KNOWLEDGE.

RELATE NEWLY ACQUIRED KNOWLEDGE TO WHAT YOU KNEW BEFORE.

CONSCIOUSLY TRY TO LEARN, TO CONCENTRATE, TO PAY ATTENTION.

LOOK UP NEW WORDS IN YOUR DICTIONARY.

Concentrating

Most students who complain that they don't know how to concentrate deserve no sympathy. Concentration is merely habit and ought to be as readily acquired as any other habit. The way to begin to study is simply to begin.

Don't wait for inspiration or for the mood to strike you, nor should you permit yourself to indulge in thoughts like, "This chapter is too long" or "I guess I could really let that go until some other time."

Such an attitude throws an extra load on your mental machinery, and by making you work against a handicap, makes it harder for you to begin.

Reading aloud is a good device for those whose minds wander while studying. Articulating "subvocally" for a few moments is another tonic for drifting thoughts. If this doesn't work, write down the point you happen to be dealing with when your mind "goes off track."

Do your studying alone, and you'll find it much easier to concentrate. If you are certain you need help on doubtful or difficult points, check these points and list them; you can go back or ask about them later. In the meantime, proceed to the next point.

A "little tenseness" is a good thing because it helps you keep alert while studying. Do without smoking, or newspapers, or magazines, or novels which may lead you into temptation. Studying in one place all the time also helps.

Boiling it all down, the greatest asset for effective studying is plain, garden variety "common sense" and will power.

Grasshoppers Never Learn

Don't be a "skipper." Jumping around from one part of your course to another may be more interesting, but it won't help you as much as steady progress from page one right through the book.

Studying and learning takes more than just reading. The "text" part of your course can be a valuable tool in test-preparation if you use it correctly. Introductions to the various sections of your book must be "studied." Reread the paragraph that gives you trouble. Be certain that you understand it before you pass on to the next one. Many persons who have been away from school for a long time, and those people who have a habit of reading rapidly, find that it helps if they hold a piece of white paper under the paragraph they are reading, covering the rest of the page. That helps you concentrate on the facts you are absorbing. Keep a pen or pencil in your hand while reading, and underline important facts. Put a question mark after anything that isn't quite clear to you, so that you can get back to it. Summarize ideas in the margins of your book. You'll be surprised how much easier it is to remember something once you have written it down, and expressed it in your own words.

Taking Notes

Although your "self-tutor" has done a great deal for you in summarizing the information that is essential to success on the test, it's still worth your while to do some notetaking. Your notes, which can be made either in a separate notebook or in the margins of this book, will help you concentrate; are a form of self-recitation; will provide you with concise outlines for review before the test; will help you identify basic and essential materials; will help you retain what you learn, with greater accuracy for a longer period of time; and will help you learn better because they require thinking and active participation on your part.

The following suggestions will help you take the kind of notes that will be of greatest use to you on the test:

RECORD ESSENTIAL FACTS AND AVOID TOO MUCH DETAIL. JOT DOWN CLUES.

ADOPT AN ACTIVE MEANING-SEEKING ATTITUDE. STICK TO BASIC SIGNIFICANCE.

USE YOUR OWN WORDS. BUT BE BRIEF.

DON'T HURRY. WRITE READABLY AND ACCURATELY. YOU'LL BE READING THEM AGAIN.

BE NEAT. WRITE TITLES AND LABELS. DON'T BE SPARING OF PAPER.

USE A SINGLE LOOSELEAF NOTEBOOK SO THAT YOU CAN RE-ORGANIZE AND COMBINE NOTES.

TAKE NOTES IN ALL LEARNING SITUATIONS RELATING TO THIS TEST.

DON'T COPY VERBATIM.

REVIEW YOUR NOTES OF THE PREVIOUS DAY BEFORE STARTING THE CURRENT ASSIGNMENT.

USE QUESTION MARKS IN THE MARGINS OF THE BOOK FOR VAGUE OR DIFFICULT PASSAGES WHICH MAY BE CLARIFIED AS YOU READ ON. YOU MAY WANT TO COME BACK TO THEM TO BE SURE YOU UNDERSTAND THEM.

TRY TO DO SOME FOLLOW UP WORK ON UNDERLINED SECTIONS.

SOME SUGGESTED SYMBOLS FOR MAKING NOTES IN THIS BOOK.

|, ( ), [ ] A vertical line in the margin, or a bracket, or parenthesis around a sentence or group of sentences is used to indicate an important idea or ideas.

— Underlining is used to indicate especially important materials, specific points to be consulted during reviews.

O A circle around a word may be used to indicate that you are not familiar with the word, and that you will come back later to look it up in the dictionary.

√ E The letter "E" or a check mark (√) in the margin may be used to mark materials that are important and likely to be used in the examination.

1 , 2 , 3 , 4 Arabic numerals, circled or uncircled may be placed before a word or at the beginning of a sentence to indicate a series of facts, ideas, important dates, etc.

D The letter "D" may be used to indicate your disagreement with a passage or a statement.

Keep in mind that effective notetaking is vital to learning. If your notes are effective, your learning is likely to be effective.

Test Yourself Frequently

The major part of your course consists of study questions and answers prepared by experts. Try to answer every question in the book as you reach it. Each study session should end with a self-test.

Develop Careful Reading Habits

While present-day examinations seldom have "trick" questions, the men who make up examinations often frame questions so that careful reading is necessary to understand the question fully and to give the proper answer. Use this book as a personal reading-improver. Rephrase every question in your own words before you answer, to be sure that you really understand what is being asked.

Don't Try to Memorize

It is true that the same questions often reappear on examinations of the same kind, but it would not be worthwhile to try to memorize the hundreds of questions in your book. After all, the *scope* of any examination is fairly limited. Using your book as a self-tester will show you the fields in which you may be weak or strong. The questions and answers will help put you into the important examination-taking frame of mind, and give you an excellent idea of the different types of information about which you will be questioned on your test.

Be Tough With Yourself

One error made by many persons who are preparing for examinations is to give themselves too much of a break. They will peek at the book answer to a question and excuse themselves on the grounds that if they had "really" been taking a test, they would have been more careful and would have given the correct answer. Don't let yourself get away with that!

You have to be a stern teacher to get the most out of any program of self-study. When you test yourself, be as tough as if the test-taker were someone you didn't know. Don't let yourself get away with an "almost right" answer. Today there is keen competition on most tests, and the habits you develop while preparing for your test will show up on the examination in the form of earned or lost percentage points. Mark yourself rigidly. Be honest in appraising your weaknesses, and try to correct them before you sit down to take the real test.

And don't take anything for granted. Even if you find yourself scoring 100% in some area of your test, don't relax too much. When you find that you have answered a question correctly, use that as a lever for self-improvement. Ask yourself *why* your answer was correct. Try to think of other forms in which the same question could have been asked. Try to frame your own questions that are "harder" or more demanding than the ones you can answer easily.

You may find that some sections of this book are difficult, just as some portions of the test will be more difficult than others. Don't worry about it. Don't panic. Remember that the test is a competitive one . . . that your score is relative to the scores of all the other competitors. What's hard for you will be just as hard (or harder) for them.

When the going gets rough you're on notice to study more carefully. You've discovered one of your weaknesses. You're ahead of the game because you have the opportunity of strengthening yourself. Concentrate on your weak spots and you won't be caught off balance by the test questions.

On the other hand don't permit yourself to be lulled into a false sense of security when you discover material which is very easy for you. Don't quit studying—just give the easy portions less time. Adjust your schedule and use the time you pick up in this way to work where it is most needed.

This technique of devoting as much time and thought as is required by each job (and no more) should be applied to the actual test, with one caution. The easy questions should be answered as rapidly as you can, as you come to them. But if a question appears very difficult and likely to take a lot of time to answer, defer spending too much time on it. Continue on, giving the quick, easy answers. Then go back and use the time remaining to answer the slow, hard ones.

Scissors and Glue for Review

One helpful form of review, as your examination date approaches, is this: Cut out individual questions from your book. Paste them on slips of paper, and mark the correct answers on the back of each question.

Then, whenever you have a few minutes to spare, you can shuffle the questions around and find out whether you have the correct answers in your mind. This is especially helpful in dealing with questions of the "information" type which are basically tests of how well you remember important information and facts.

Another good learning technique is to have someone read the questions and suggested answers to you. "Hearing" will serve as a memory aid after you have read and studied the material.

Analyze Your Weaknesses—And Correct Them

One purpose of this course is to familiarize you with the types of questions you will face and to prepare you for them. Perhaps its more important purpose is to help you find your own weaknesses and to correct them before the examination.

Every time you give the incorrect answer to a practice question you should ask yourself, "Why?" Be honest with yourself and you'll soon discover the subjects in which you're weak. Devote extra time to these subjects and you will have taken giant steps to test success.

We have analyzed test failures and have found time after time that many persons who are perfectly able to pass a test fail it simply because of their weakness in such basic subjects as arithmetic or vocabulary.

If you find that you have such a problem, be brave. Put in the extra effort each day.

GARDENER - ASSISTANT GARDENER

HOW TO BE A MASTER TEST TAKER

It's really quite simple. Do things right . . . right from the beginning. Make successful methods a habit by practicing them on all the exercises in this book. Before you're finished you will have invested a good deal of time. Make sure you get the largest dividends from this investment.

SCORING PAPERS BY MACHINE

A typical machine-scored answer sheet is shown below, reduced from the actual size of 8¼ x 11 inches. Since it's the only one that reaches the office where papers are scored, it's important that the blanks at the top be filled in completely and correctly.

The chances are very good that you'll have to mark your answers on one of these sheets. Consequently, we've made it possible for you to practice with them throughout this book.

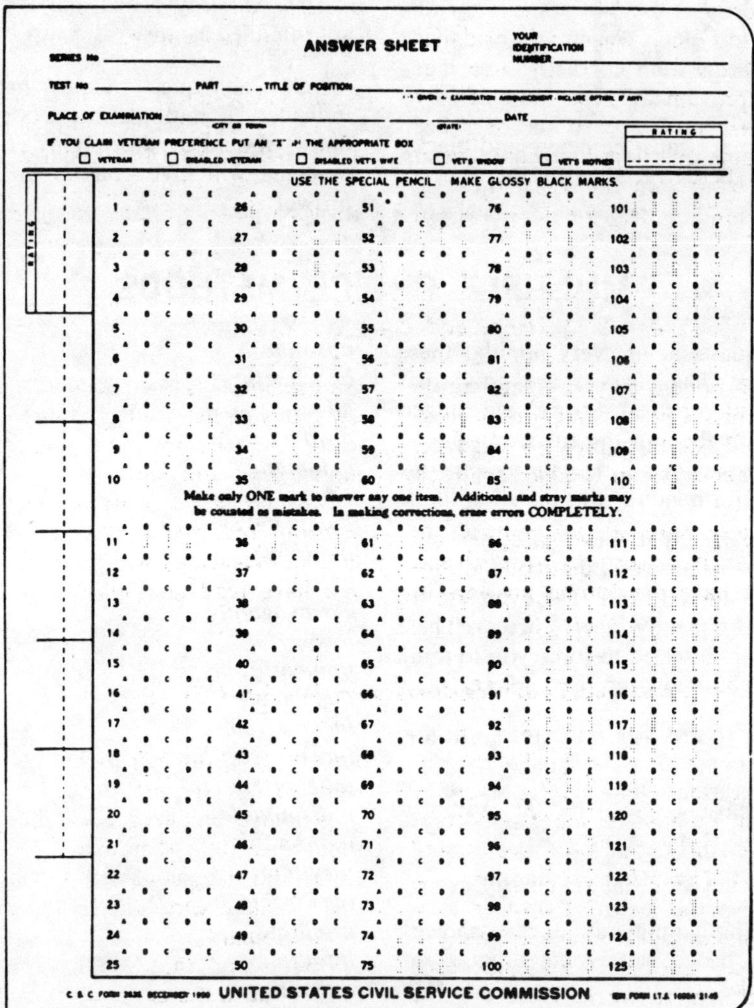

ANSWER SHEET

SERIES No ______ YOUR IDENTIFICATION NUMBER ______

TEST No ______ PART ______ TITLE OF POSITION ______

PLACE OF EXAMINATION ______ (CITY OR TOWN) ______ (STATE) DATE ______

RATING

IF YOU CLAIM VETERAN PREFERENCE, PUT AN "X" IN THE APPROPRIATE BOX

☐ VETERAN ☐ DISABLED VETERAN ☐ DISABLED VET'S WIFE ☐ VET'S WIDOW ☐ VET'S MOTHER

USE THE SPECIAL PENCIL. MAKE GLOSSY BLACK MARKS.

Make only ONE mark to answer any one item. Additional and stray marks may be counted as mistakes. In making corrections, erase errors COMPLETELY.

UNITED STATES CIVIL SERVICE COMMISSION

FOLLOW DIRECTIONS CAREFULLY

It's an obvious rule, but more people fail for breaching it than for any other cause. By actual count there are over a hundred types of directions given on tests. You'll familiarize yourself with all of them in the course of this book. And you'll also learn not to let your guard down in reading them, listening to them, and following them. Right now, before you plunge in, we want to be sure that you have nothing to fear from the answer sheet and the way in which you must mark it; from the most important question forms and the ways in which they are to be answered.

HERE'S HOW TO MARK YOUR ANSWERS ON MACHINE-SCORED ANSWER SHEETS:

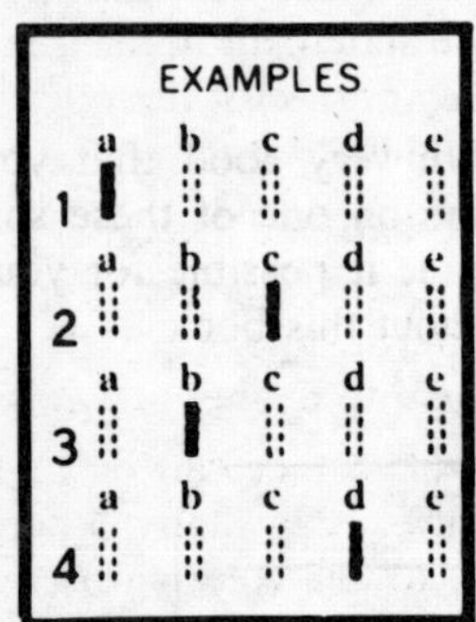

Make only ONE mark for each answer. Additional and stray marks may be counted as mistakes. In making corrections, erase errors COMPLETELY. Make glossy black marks.

(a) Each pencil mark must be heavy and black. Light marks should be retraced with the special pencil.

(b) Each mark must be in the space between the pair of dotted lines and entirely fill this space.

(c) All stray pencil marks on the paper, clearly not intended as answers, must be completely erased.

(d) Each question must have only one answer indicated. If multiple answers occur, all extraneous marks should be thoroughly erased. Otherwise, the machine will give you *no* credit for your correct answer.

MULTIPLE CHOICE METHODS

Multiple choice questions are very popular these days with examiners. The chances are good that you'll get this kind on your test. So we've arranged that you practice with them in the following pages. But first we want to give you a little help by explaining the best methods for handling this question form.

You know, of course, that these questions offer you four or five possible answers, that your job is to select *only* the *best* answer, and that even the incorrect answers are frequently *partly* correct. These partly-true choices are inserted to force you to think . . . and prove that you know the right answer.

USE THESE METHODS TO ANSWER MULTIPLE CHOICE QUESTIONS CORRECTLY:

1. Read the item closely to see what the examiner is after. Reread it if necessary.
2. Mentally reject answers that are clearly wrong.
3. Suspect as being wrong any of the choices which contain broad statements hinging on "cue" words like

absolute
absolutely
all
always
axiomatic
categorical
completely
doubtless
entirely
extravagantly
forever
immeasurably
inalienable
incontestable
incontrovertible
indefinitely
indisputable
indubitable
inevitable
inexorable
infallible
infinite
inflexible
inordinately
irrefutable
inviolable
never
only
peculiarly
positive
quite
self-evident
sole
totally
unchallenged
unchangeable
undeniable
undoubtedly
unequivocal
unexceptionable
unimpeachable
unqualified
unquestionable
wholly
without exception

If you're unsure of the meanings of any of these words, look them up in your dictionary.

4. A well-constructed multiple choice item will avoid obviously incorrect choices. The good examiner will try to write a cluster of answers, all of which are plausible. Use the clue words to help yourself pick the *most* correct answer.
5. In the case of items where you are doubtful of the answer, you might be able to bring to bear the information you have gained from previous study. This knowledge might be sufficient to indicate that some of the suggested answers are not so plausible. Eliminate such answers from further consideration.
6. Then concentrate on the remaining suggested answers. The more you eliminate in this way, the better your chances of getting the item right.
7. If the item is in the form of an incomplete statement, it sometimes helps to try to complete the statement before you look at the suggested answers. Then see whether the way you have completed the statement corresponds with any of the answers provided. If one is found, it is likely to be the correct one.
8. Use your head! Make shrewd inferences. Sometimes with a little thought, and the information that you have, you can reason out the answer. We're suggesting a method of intelligent guessing in which you can become quite expert with a little practice. It's a useful method that may help you with some debatable answers.

NOW, LET'S TRY THESE METHODS OUT ON A SAMPLE MULTIPLE-CHOICE QUESTION.

1. Leather is considered the best material for shoes chiefly because
   (A) it is waterproof
   (B) it is quite durable
   (C) it is easily procurable
   (D) it is flexible and durable
   (E) it can be easily manufactured in various styles.

Here we see that every one of the answer statements is plausible: leather is waterproof if treated properly; it is relatively durable; it is relatively easily procurable; it bends and is shaped easily, and is, again, durable; it constantly appears in various styles of shoes and boots.

However, we must examine the question with an eye toward identifying the key phrase which is: *best* for shoes *chiefly*.

Now we can see that (A) is incorrect because leather is probably not the *best* material for shoes, simply because it is waterproof. There are far better waterproof materials available, such as plastics and rubber. In fact, leather must be treated to make it waterproof. So by analyzing the key phrase of the question we can eliminate (A).

(B) seems plausible. Leather is durable, and durability is a good quality in shoes. But the word *quite* makes it a broad statement. And we become suspicious. The original meaning of *quite* is completely, wholly, entirely. Since such is the case we must reject this choice because leather is *not completely* durable. It does wear out.

(C) Leather is comparatively easy to procure; but would that make it *best* for shoes? And would that be the *chief* reason why it is used for making shoes? Although the statement in itself is quite true, it does not fit the key phrase of the question and we must, reluctantly, eliminate it.

(D) is a double-barreled statement. One part, the durability, has been suggested in (B) above. Leather is also quite flexible, so both parts of the statement would seem to fit the question.

(E) It is true that leather can be manufactured in various styles, but so can many other materials. Again, going back to the key phrase, this could be considered one, but not the *chief* reason why it is *best* for shoes.

So, by carefully analyzing the *key* phrase of the question we have narrowed our choices down to (D). Although we rejected (B) we did recognize that durability is a good quality in shoes, but only one of several. Since flexibility is also a good quality, we have no hesitation in choosing (D) as the correct answer.

The same question, by slightly altering the answer choices, can also call for a *negative* response. Here, even more so, the identification of the key phrase becomes vital in finding the correct answer. Suppose the question and its responses were worded thus:

2. Leather is considered the best material for shoes chiefly because
   (A) it is waterproof
   (B) it is easily colored
   (C) it is easily procurable
   (D) it can easily be manufactured in various styles
   (E) none of these.

We can see that the prior partially correct answer (B) has now been changed, and the doubly-correct answer eliminated. Instead we have a new response possibility (E), "none of these."

We have analyzed three of the choices previously and have seen the reason why none of them is the *chief* reason why leather is considered the *best* material for shoes. The two new elements are (B) "easily colored," and (E) "none of these."

If you think about it, leather *can* be easily colored and often is, but this would not be the chief reason why it is considered *best*. Many other materials are just as easily dyed. So we must come to the conclusion that *none* of the choices is *completely* correct—none fit the key phrase. Therefore, the question calls for a negative response (E).

We have now seen how important it is to identify the key phrase. Equally, or perhaps even more important, is the identifying and analyzing of the key *word*—the qualifying word—in a question. This is usually, though not always, an adjective or adverb. Some of the key words to watch for are: *most, best, least, highest, lowest, always, never, sometimes, most likely, greatest, smallest, tallest, average, easiest, most nearly, maximum, minimum, chiefly, mainly, only, but* and *or*. Identifying these key words is usually half the battle in understanding and, consequently, answering all types of exam questions.

Rephrasing the Question

It is obvious, then, that by carefully analyzing a question, by identifying the key phrase and its key words, you can usually find the correct answer by logical deduction and, often, by elimination. One other way of examining, or "dissecting," a question is to restate or rephrase it with each of the suggested answer choices integrated into the question.

For example, we can take the same question and rephrase it.

(A) The chief reason why leather is considered the best material for shoes is that it is waterproof.

or

(A) Because it is waterproof, leather is considered the best material for shoes.

or

(A) Chiefly because it is waterproof, leather is considered the best material for shoes.

It will be seen from the above three new versions of the original statement and answer that the question has become less obscure because it has been, so to speak, illuminated from different angles. It becomes quite obvious also in this rephrasing that the statement (A) is incorrect, although the *original* phrasing of the question left some doubt.

The rules for understanding and analyzing the key phrase and key words in a question, and the way to identify the *one* correct answer by means of intelligent analysis of the important question-answer elements, are basic to the solution of all the problems you will face on your test.

In fact, perhaps the *main* reason for failing an examination is failure to *understand the question*. In many cases, examinees *do* know the answer to a particular problem, but they cannot answer correctly because they do not understand it.

METHODS FOR MATCHING QUESTIONS

In this question form you are actually faced with multiple questions that require multiple answers. It's a difficult form in which you are asked to pair up one set of facts with another. It can be used with any type of material . . . vocabulary, spatial relations, numbers, facts, etc.

A typical matching question might appear in this form:

Directions: Below is a set of words containing ten words numbered 1 to 10, and twenty other words divided into five groups labeled Group A to Group E. For each of the numbered words select the word in one of the five groups which is most nearly the same in meaning. The letter of that group is the answer for that numbered item.

Although this arrangement is a relatively simple one for a "matching" question, the general principle is the same for all levels of difficulty. Basically, this type of question consists of two columns. The elements of one of the columns must be matched with some or all of the elements of the second column.

1. fiscal
2. deletion
3. equivocal
4. corroboration
5. tortuous
6. predilection
7. sallow
8. virtuosity
9. scion
10. tenuous

Group A
indication ambiguous
excruciating thin

Group B
confirmation financial
phobia erasure

Group C
fiduciary similar
yellowish skill

Group D
theft winding
receive procrastination

Group E
franchise heir
hardy preference

Correct Answers

1. B
2. B
3. A
4. B
5. D
6. E
7. C
8. C
9. E
10. A

There are numerous ways in which these questions may be composed, from the simple one shown above to the most difficult type of arrangement. In many cases the arrangement of the question may be so complicated that more time may be spent upon the comprehension of the instructions than on the actual question. This again, points up the importance of fully and quickly understanding the instructions before attempting to solve any problem or answer any question.

Several general principles apply, however, when solving a matching question. Work with one column at a time and match each item of that column against all the items in the second column, skipping around that second column looking for a proper match. Put a thin pencil line through items that are matched so they won't interfere with your later selections. (This is particularly important in a test that tells you to choose any item only once. The test gets real tricky, however, when you are asked to choose an item more than once.)

Match each item very carefully—don't mark it unless you are certain—because if you have to change any one, it may mean changing three or four or more, and that may get you hopelessly confused. After you have marked all your *certain* choices, go over the unmarked items again and make a *good* guess at the remaining items, if you have time.

USE CONTROLLED ASSOCIATION when you come to an item which you are not able to match. Attempt to recall any and all facts you might have concerning this item. Through the process of association, a fact recalled might provide a clue to the answer.

TRUE-FALSE TACTICS

True-false questions may appear on your test. Because they are easier to answer they are used less frequently than multiple-choice questions. However, because examiners find that they are easier to prepare, here are some suggestions to help you answer them correctly.

I. Suspect the truth of broad statements hinging on those *all or nothing* "cue" words we listed for you in discussing multiple-choice questions.

II Watch out for "spoilers" . . . the word or phrase which negates an otherwise true statement.

Vegetation is sparse on the Sahara desert where the climate is hot and humid. T F

III. Statements containing such modifiers as *generally, usually, most,* and similar words are usually true.

IV. If the scoring formula is "Rights minus Wrongs", don't guess. If you know it's true, mark it T. If you don't know it's true, ask yourself "What have I learned that would make it false?" If you can think of nothing on either side, omit the answer. Of course, if the R-W formula is not being used it is advisable to guess if you're not sure of an answer.

V. Your first hunch is usually best. Unless you have very good reason to do so, don't change your first answer to true-false questions about which you are doubtful.

Single-Statement Question

The basic form of true-false question is the "single-statement" question; i.e., a sentence that contains a single thought, such as:

1. The Statue of Liberty is in New York T F

The same statement becomes slightly more difficult by including a negative element

2. The Statue of Liberty is not in New York T F

or, more subtly:

3. The Statue of Liberty is not in Chicago T F

or, by adding other modifiers:

4. The Statue of Liberty is sometimes in New York T F

5. The Statue of Liberty is always in New York T F

Even from these very simple and basic examples of a "single-statement" true-false question it can be seen that a *complete understanding* of the subject area as well as of the phrasing of the question is essential before you attempt to answer it. Careless or hasty reading of the statment will often make you miss the *key* word, especially if the question appears to be a very simple one.

An important point to remember when answering this type of question is that the statement must be *entirely true* to be answered as "true"; if even just a *part* of it is false, the answer must be marked "false."

Composite-Statement Question

Sometimes a true-false question will be in the form of a "composite statement," a statement that contains more than one thought, such as:

6. The Statue of Liberty is in New York, and Chicago is in Illinois T F

Some basic variations of this type of composite-statement question are these:

7. The Statue of Liberty is in New York, and Chicago is in Michigan T F
8. The Statue of Liberty is not in New York and Chicago is in Illinois T F
9. The Statue of Liberty is not in New York and Chicago is in Michigan T F

Of the four questions above, only question 6 is true. Each of the other statements (7 , 8 , 9), is false because each contains at least *one* element that is false.

It can be seen from the above that in a composite statement *both* elements, or "substatements," must be true in order for the answer to be "true." Otherwise, the answer must be "false."

This principle goes for all composite statements that are, or can be, connected by the word "and," even if the various "thoughts" of the statement seem to be entirely unrelated.

We have seen how to handle a composite statement that consists of *unrelated* substatements. Finally, we will examine a composite true-false statement which consists of *related* elements:

10. The Golden Gate Bridge is in San Francisco, which is not the capital of California. T F
11. The Golden Gate Bridge is in San Francisco, the capital of California. T F
12. The Golden Gate Bridge is not in San Francisco, the capital of California. T F
13. The Golden Gate Bridge is not in San Francisco, which is not the capital of California. T F

Again, only the first composite statement (10) is true. All the rest are false because they contain at least one false substatement.

PART TWO

Previous Exams for Practice

DIRECTIONS FOR ANSWERING QUESTIONS

For each question read all the choices carefully. Then select that answer which you consider correct or most nearly correct. Write the letter preceding your best choice next to the question

Should you want to answer on the kind of answer sheet used on machine-scored examinations, we have provided several such facsimiles. Tear one out if you wish, and mark your answers on it . . . just as you would do on an actual exam.

In machine-scored examinations you should record all your answers on the answer sheet provided. Don't make the mistake of putting answers on the test booklet itself.

On some machine-scored exams you are instructed to "place no marks whatever on the test booklet."

In other examinations you may be instructed to mark your answers in the test booklet. In such cases you should be careful that no other marks interfere with the legibility of your answers.

It is always best NOT to mark your booklet unless you are sure that it is permitted.

It is most important that you learn to mark your answers clearly and in the right place.

To help you understand the procedure, the following sample item is given:

SAMPLE O: The sum of 5 and 3 is

(A) 11 (B) 8 (C) 9 (D) 2 (E) 10.

The sum of 5 and 3 is 8, so that the acceptable answer is shown thus on your answer sheet:

	A	B	C	D	E
SAMPLE O	‖	█	‖	‖	‖

Practice Using Answer Sheets

Alter numbers to match the practice and drill questions in each part of the book.
Make only ONE mark for each answer. Additional and stray marks may be counted as mistakes.
In making corrections, erase errors COMPLETELY. Make glossy black marks.

	A	B	C	D	E
1	⁞	⁞	⁞	⁞	⁞
2	⁞	⁞	⁞	⁞	⁞
3	⁞	⁞	⁞	⁞	⁞
4	⁞	⁞	⁞	⁞	⁞
5	⁞	⁞	⁞	⁞	⁞
6	⁞	⁞	⁞	⁞	⁞
7	⁞	⁞	⁞	⁞	⁞
8	⁞	⁞	⁞	⁞	⁞
9	⁞	⁞	⁞	⁞	⁞
0	⁞	⁞	⁞	⁞	⁞

	A	B	C	D	E
1	⁞	⁞	⁞	⁞	⁞
2	⁞	⁞	⁞	⁞	⁞
3	⁞	⁞	⁞	⁞	⁞
4	⁞	⁞	⁞	⁞	⁞
5	⁞	⁞	⁞	⁞	⁞
6	⁞	⁞	⁞	⁞	⁞
7	⁞	⁞	⁞	⁞	⁞
8	⁞	⁞	⁞	⁞	⁞
9	⁞	⁞	⁞	⁞	⁞
0	⁞	⁞	⁞	⁞	⁞

	A	B	C	D	E
1	⁞	⁞	⁞	⁞	⁞
2	⁞	⁞	⁞	⁞	⁞
3	⁞	⁞	⁞	⁞	⁞
4	⁞	⁞	⁞	⁞	⁞
5	⁞	⁞	⁞	⁞	⁞
6	⁞	⁞	⁞	⁞	⁞
7	⁞	⁞	⁞	⁞	⁞
8	⁞	⁞	⁞	⁞	⁞
9	⁞	⁞	⁞	⁞	⁞
0	⁞	⁞	⁞	⁞	⁞

	A	B	C	D	E
1	⁞	⁞	⁞	⁞	⁞
2	⁞	⁞	⁞	⁞	⁞
3	⁞	⁞	⁞	⁞	⁞
4	⁞	⁞	⁞	⁞	⁞
5	⁞	⁞	⁞	⁞	⁞
6	⁞	⁞	⁞	⁞	⁞
7	⁞	⁞	⁞	⁞	⁞
8	⁞	⁞	⁞	⁞	⁞
9	⁞	⁞	⁞	⁞	⁞
0	⁞	⁞	⁞	⁞	⁞

	A	B	C	D	E
1	⁞	⁞	⁞	⁞	⁞
2	⁞	⁞	⁞	⁞	⁞
3	⁞	⁞	⁞	⁞	⁞
4	⁞	⁞	⁞	⁞	⁞
5	⁞	⁞	⁞	⁞	⁞
6	⁞	⁞	⁞	⁞	⁞
7	⁞	⁞	⁞	⁞	⁞
8	⁞	⁞	⁞	⁞	⁞
9	⁞	⁞	⁞	⁞	⁞
0	⁞	⁞	⁞	⁞	⁞

TEAR OUT ALONG THIS LINE AND MARK YOUR ANSWERS AS INSTRUCTED IN THE TEXT

GARDENER

I. THE LATEST PREVIOUS EXAM

"A thousand mile journey begins with a single step." So here's the most recent, available civil service test for your job. It's a reliable indicator of what you're up against, and what you have to study. Get right to work on it. Follow all the instructions carefully, just as though it were the actual test. If you have time, after you've completed the book, you may want to take this test again to compare results and measure your improvement.

DATE OF EXAM: December 14, 1974

The time allowed for the entire examination is 3 hours. In order to create the climate of the test to come, that's precisely what you should allow yourself . . . no more, no less. Use a watch and keep a record of your time, especially since you may find it convenient to take the test in several sittings.

In answering the questions on this examination, assume that you are a Gardener with responsibility for supervising a crew of workers.

1. What is a mulch?

   (A) A fertilizer which is high in nitrogen.
   (B) A material spread upon the surface of the soil to conserve moisture and inhibit weed growth.
   (C) A chemical compound which is sprayed on the foliage of plants to prevent wilting.
   (D) A mixture of coarse gravel, stones, and broken rock used for drainage in the bottom of flower pots and planting tubs.

2. A good permanent grass seed mixture for a dry, shady lawn area is

   (A) 2 parts Merion Blue grass, 1 part Kentucky Blue grass
   (B) 1 part Merion Blue grass, 2 parts Rhode Island or Colonial Bent grass
   (C) 1 part chewing fescue, 1 part Illahee fescue, 1 part Pennlawn fescue
   (D) 2 parts Perennial Rye grass, 1 part Italian Rye grass.

3. Which of the following is the best cutting height for the average lawn in the New York City area in hot weather?

   (A) 1/4"   (B) 1/2"   (C) 1"   (D) 2"

4. Earthworms are most likely to

(A) make good soil from poor soil
(B) make good soil into even better soil
(C) ruin good soil
(D) indicate a lack of organic matter in the soil.

5. Before turning over a power rotary lawn mower to clean the underside and cutting blade you should

(A) adjust the carburetor idle setting to low speed
(B) allow the engine to cool for at least 10 minutes
(C) remove the high-tension wire from the spark plug
(D) adjust the caburetor setting to full choke.

6. A 10-6-4 fertilizer contains

(A) 4% nitrogen
(B) 10% potassium
(C) 6% potassium
(D) 6% phosphorus

7. Which of the following is generally the best pH range for a lawn soil?

(A) pH 2 - 3.5
(B) pH 3 - 4.5
(C) pH 6 - 6.5
(D) pH 8 - 10.5.

8. Peat moss is best used as

(A) a mulch
(B) an organic soil amendment
(C) a fertilizer
(D) a substitute for lime.

9. What does pH indicate?

(A) The amount of nitrogen in the soil.
(B) The amount of moisture in the soil.
(C) The acidity or alkalinity of the soil.
(D) The amount of organic matter in the soil.

10. In order to promote dense growth on all parts of a hedge, it is best to prune it so that the

(A) top is wider than the bottom
(B) bottom is wider than the top
(C) top and bottom are of equal width
(D) top and bottom are narrower than the middle.

11. When should shrubs that bloom in the spring such as Weigela and Lilac generally be pruned?

(A) As soon as they are finished blooming.
(B) Just before they bloom.
(C) While they are blooming.
(D) When they are still dormant.

12. Assume that you wish to cut a large limb off a tree trunk. In order to do this without damage to the tree, the minimum number of separate saw cuts which should usually be made is

(A) 1 (B) 2 (C) 3 (D) 4.

13. The best method of controlling infestations of scale insects on young trees is by

(A) dusting the trees with a good fungicide
(B) removing and burning affected limbs and branches
(C) digging up and destroying the trees
(D) spraying the trees with dormant oil.

14. In a slat house for shading plants, the direction in which the roof slats should run is

(A) an east-west direction
(B) a north-south direction
(C) a northeast by southwest direction
(D) a northwest by southeast direction.

15. Which one of the following plants is a monocotyledon?

(A) begonia (B) geranium (C) phlox (D) iris

16. You are in charge of a small lawn area of 1850 sq. ft. You are asked to apply lime on this lawn at the rate of 46 pounds per 1000 sq. ft. The number of pounds of lime you will need to cover the entire area of the lawn is most nearly

(A) 85 lbs. (B) 86 lbs. (C) 87 lbs. (D) 89 lbs.

17. A Kentucky Blue grass lawn requires 3 lbs. of actual nitrogen per 1000 square feet. How many pounds of 10-6-4 fertilizer will be needed to fertilize a 5000 sqare-foot lawn of Kentucky Blue grass?

(A) 15.5 lbs. (B) 150 lbs. (C) 555 lbs. (D) 50 lbs.

18. You need to fill a 32 oz. bottle with a solution containing 10% malathion, but all you have is a gallon of 50% malathion solution. How many ounces of the 50% malathion solution and how many ounces of water should you put in the bottle?

(A) 3.2 oz. of 50% malathion solution and 28.8 oz. of water.
(B) 6.4 oz. of 50% malathion solution and 25.6 oz. of water.
(C) 9.6 oz. of 50% malathion solution and 22.4 oz. of water.
(D) 12.8 oz. of 50% malthion solution and 19.2 oz. of water.

19. The term "hardiness" is most often used to refer to the

(A) tensile strength of the plant's stem and branches
(B) ability of plants to endure low temperatures
(C) amount of wind force the plant can withstand
(D) length of time that plant can survive without water.

20. Which one of the following is <u>not</u> a method of plant propagation?

(A) Layering
(B) Budding
(C) Chlorosis
(D) Division

21. Clematis, wisteria, and ampelopsis are all

(A) indoor foliage plants
(B) outdoor annuals
(C) grown from bulbs planted each fall
(D) ornamental climbing plants.

22. In attaching a scion to a stock you should use which one of the following methods?

(A) Whip or tongue
(B) Tack weld
(C) Pintle and gudgeon
(D) Clinch or rivet and burr

23. "Pinching" as performed by a gardener is a method of

(A) grafting
(B) pruning
(C) propagation
(D) pollination.

24. In a project involving the laying of sod, the soil was properly cultivated, fertilized, and the turf laid and rolled in the approved fashion. Water was periodically applied in ample quantity. After a few days the grass began to die around the edges of each rectangular piece of sod. The best method of avoiding such a problem is probably to

(A) add more fertilizer to the soil before the turf is laid
(B) apply lime before and after the sod has been laid
(C) brush a dressing of sandy loam into the joints between the sods
(D) water the sod only in bright sunlight.

25. A label on a plant was marked as follows:

Abies nobilis glauca
Pinaceae

The name of this plant reveals that

(A) the species is Abies, the genus is nobilis, the family is glauca, and the variety is Pinaceae
(B) the family is Abies, the variety is nobilis, the genus is glauca, and the species is Pinaceae
(C) the genus is Abies, the family is nobilis, the species is glauca, and the variety is Pinaceae
(D) the genus is Abies, the species is nobilis, the variety is glauca, and the family is Pinaceae.

26. A small deciduous tree in leaf has just been dug from the ground and transplanted into a tub and then watered until the soil is saturated. It quickly shows symptoms of severe wilting. In trying to save this tree, which of the following would be the least acceptable remedy?

(A) Remove some of the foliage, either by removing some of the leaves or some of the smaller branches with their foliage
(B) Wet the plant's foliage and then place a plastic bag over the entire tree and place it either in a shady place or a darkened room
(C) Remove the tree from the tub and remove all the soil from the roots and then place the plant in a pail of water so the roots are completely submerged
(D) Place the tree under the constant mist of a fine water spray.

27. A certain broad-leaf evergreen tree had many flowers in the spring but it bore no fruit in the fall. The next spring a close examination of the flowers revealed only stamens and no pistils. The probable reason for the failure of the tree to fruit is that the

(A) flowers were deformed
(B) tree was a male
(C) tree was a female and there was no male in the vicinity
(D) tree was planted too far north and the cold weather prevented it from fruiting.

28. Which one of the following trees would be least desirable for planting in a shady area?

(A) dogwood
(B) pine
(C) hemlock
(D) holly

29. Brown patches are noticed in a sunny lawn area in the summer. A close examination reveals numerous brown insects around the grass roots in the patches about 1/6" long with white markings on their backs. These insects most likely are

(A) aphids
(B) scale insects
(C) chinch bugs
(D) leaf hoppers

30. Many diseases of lawn grasses can be treated effectively with

(A) Benomyl (Benlate)
(B) 2,4-D
(C) DDT
(D) Rotenone

31. Of the following the best way to reduce the acidity of soil is to apply

(A) limestone
(B) flowers of sulfur
(C) aluminum sulfate
(D) water

32. The most effective of the following actions to take to stop erosion of soil on steep embankments is to

(A) break the flow of water on the embankment
(B) dig several water channels from the top of the embankment to the bottom
(C) rototill the embankment
(D) spray the embankment with 2,4-D

33. A complete fertilizer contains

(A) nitrogen, phosphorus, and iron
(B) calcium, potassium, and sulfur
(C) nitrogen, phosphorus, and potassium
(D) calcium, carbon, and nitrogen.

34. Plants produce seeds by means of

(A) pollination and fertilization
(B) cultivation and grafting
(C) hybridization and air-layering
(D) rooting and hydrogenation

35. If a tree is to be replanted in a heavy clay-loam soil with questionable drainage it would be best to plant the tree

(A) three inches deeper than it was planted before
(B) six inches deeper than it was planted before
(C) at the same level as before and back-fill with sand
(D) slightly higher in the soil than it was planted before.

36. Suckers are most likely to develop from

(A) buds
(B) roots
(C) shoots
(D) leaf cuttings

37. All of the following are piercing-sucking insects except

(A) white fly
(B) leaf hopper
(C) lace bug
(D) black vine weevil.

38. Knowing and using good horticultural books for reference is important in gardening work. Which of the following is a good horticultural book?

(A) Hortus Second by Liberty Hyde Bailey
(B) Plant Location in Theory and in Practice by Melvin Greenhut
(C) How Green Was My Valley by Richard Llewellyn
(D) The Greening of America by Charles Reich.

39. The pine bark aphid is a pest of pines such as the Eastern White Pine (Pinus strobus). A superior-type emulsifiable oil spray can be applied during the early spring when the tree is still dormant. Which of the following conditions are best for applying the spray?

(A) There is no wind, the day temperature is 50°F. or higher, the night temperature is above the mid 30's, no rain is predicted
(B) A slight wind is predicted, the day temperature does not exceed 48°F., the night temperature is predicted to fall below freezing
(C) A slight wind is predicted, the day temperature and the night temperature are both above 85°F., and the day is misty
(D) The aphids start to move.

40. An excellent fungicide which not only has historical significance but is still highly recommended for control of certain fungus diseases contains copper sulfate, hydrated lime, and water. This fungicide is called

(A) Ferbam
(B) Bordeaux mixture
(C) Solution C.S.H.L.
(D) Captan

41. A heavy mulch is <u>least</u> desirable for

(A) iris
(B) rhododendrons
(C) azaleas
(D) newly planted trees.

42. You have noticed that a number of older leaves fall each year from a pine tree. This phenomenon is probably due to

(A) root rot
(B) insufficient fertilizer
(C) natural aging of the needles
(D) insufficient water.

43. The best time to sow grass seed in New York City is

(A) mid-August to mid-September
(B) mid-March to mid-April
(C) late April to mid-May
(D) late May to early June.

44. In order to maintain natural growth, the best of the following methods of pruning forsythia is to remove

(A) half of the top growth
(B) only the apical buds
(C) up to one-third of the older stems
(D) all growth over two feet.

45. Which one of the following trees can be safely pruned in spring when sap is flowing?

(A) Acer saccharium - Sugar Maple
(B) Ulmus species - Elms
(C) Cladrastis lutea - Yellow-wood
(D) Pinus thumbergii - Japanese Black Pine

46. Of the following the best way to treat trees or shrubs with dead and diseased branches is to

(A) leave them alone
(B) prune to remove 1/3 of older wood
(C) prune back to healthy wood
(D) spray with 2,4-D

47. Anthracnose disease of Platanus species (Plane trees) is more prevalent in wet spring weather. This disease is caused by a

(A) beetle
(B) fungus
(C) mildew
(D) gas leak

48. Peat moss is frequently used in gardening to change soil conditions. Which of the following is the best definition of peat moss?

(A) A short, slow-growing plant
(B) Completely decomposed animal life
(C) Partially decomposed plant life
(D) A type of wood

49. A sprayer which has been used to spray insecticides and will be used for this purpose in the future should never be used to apply

(A) fungicides
(B) miticides
(C) malathion
(D) herbicides.

50. It is especially important that an excess of fertilizer not be applied to the soil because of the possibility of root damage. This is due to the fact that fertilizer is

(A) an acid
(B) a base
(C) a salt
(D) an alkalai.

51. Of the following, the best time to apply fertilizer to lawn grasses is usually when the

(A) soil is moist and the grass is wet
(B) grass is dry and the soil is moist
(C) soil and the grass are dry
(D) soil is dry and the grass is wet.

52. Assume that a child's rope swing has been attached to a tree by tying the rope securely around the lowest limb. Of the following it is most important that

(A) girdling of the limb at the point of attachment of the rope does not eventually occur
(B) only a natural fiber rope is used
(C) the rope be lengthened as the tree grows in height
(D) as the limb grows in length the swing be moved back toward the trunk to adjust for linear growth.

53. An established lawn which requires watering during dry periods should be watered

(A) lightly twice a day in the morning and again at dusk
(B) lightly once a day in the morning unless the humidity is above 90%
(C) thoroughly to a depth of at least 4 inches early in the day
(D) thoroughly to a depth of 4 inches in the morning and again at dusk.

54. A Rhododendron shows severe yellowing of leaves. The problem is due to an iron deficiency. To correct this deficiency, it is most effective to apply

(A) iron carbide
(B) iron pyrites
(C) iron chelate
(D) iron oxide.

55. The color of the flower of some species of plants is distinctly affected by soil alkalinity or acidity as well as the amount of aluminum or iron in the soil. When the soild is neutral or alkaline the flower color is pinker, whereas under acid soil conditions the flower color is bluer. Which one of the following plants is best known to exhibit his response?

(A) Rosa species - Roses
(B) Hydrangea macrophylla (hortensis) - House Hydrangea
(C) Chrysanthemum morifolium - Florist and Garden Chrysanthemums
(D) Begonia semperflorens - wax or fibrous-rooted begonias.

56. Which one of the following terms refers to a method in which trees or shrubs can be trained into a special shape or form?

(A) Abscission
(B) Layering
(C) Pricking-out
(D) Espalier

57. Which one of the following is <u>not</u> a shrub?

(A) Pieris japonica
(B) Abelia grandiflora
(C) Acer platanoides
(D) Viburnum japonicum

58. You have just been told by your supervisor that your crew members must use a new method for accounting for the time spent on specific jobs. Some members of your crew complain to you that the previous method was better. Of the following the best action to take <u>first</u> is to

(A) find out specifically to what your crew objects
(B) suggest to your crew members that they are correct and that management does not really understand the effect of the change
(C) tell your crew to try the new method and that if they still feel that way in a few weeks they can go back to the old method.
(D) take a vote among your crew to determine which method to use.

59. Complaining to your crew about working conditions is

(A) advisable; since it makes you "one of the boys"
(B) advisable; since it allows you to get your feelings out in the open
(C) inadvisable; since it permits the crew to depend more on the attitudes and approval of their supervisor
(D) inadvisable; since it brings attention to problems but does not resolve them.

60. Asking your crew for their suggestions on better gardening methods is

(A) inadvisable; they may feel that you lack self-confidence
(B) inadvisable; it is poor practice to become too friendly with those you supervise
(C) advisable; it makes the men feel they have a hand in decision making
(D) advisable; those who make the suggestions can be held responsible for results.

61. For you, as a supervisor, to explain Parks Department objectives for the year ahead to a new employee is

(A) inadvisable; the new employee may leave before the year is up
(B) inadvisable; the new employee has nothing to do with the goals of the department
(C) advisable; it may enable the new employee to do the job with less training
(D) advisable; it may give the new employee a sense of personal involvement and motivation.

62. When a new Laborer reports for duty for the first time, which of the following should be discussed with him first?

(A) Departmental rules and regulations that relate to his employment
(B) The priorities that he should assign to his work
(C) The latest techniques of getting the technical work done
(D) The recognition of what constitues an error in his work and its consequences.

63. While you are trimming some shrubs in the park, a woman comes up to you and tells you that her civic club is running a benefit for the handicapped and that it would be wonderful if the Parks Department would donate some flowers to this worthy cause. You do not know how this type of situation has been handled in the past. Of the following, the best action for you to take is to tell the woman that

(A) (A) you are sure the Parks Department will be happy to donate flowers, and take you name and address
(B) you have nothing to do with Parks Department policy and cannot make that decision
(C) you are not sure what the Parks Department policy is but you think she is wasting her time trying to get flowers from the Parks Department
(D) you are not sure what Parks Department policy is but that you will tell her how to get more information.

64. One of your crew members has made an error in the care of bulbs, resulting in the loss of many expensive bulbs. Of the following, the best way to handle this situation initially is to

(A) write a memo on the care of bulbs and post it where your crew can refer to it
(B) call your crew together and discuss the proper care of bulbs
(C) speak privately to the crew member who make the error and discuss his error and proper care of bulbs with him
(D) tell the crew member who made the error you will not report him at present, but if this type of error occurs again you will recommend his dismissal.

65. It has been brought to your attention that several expensive tools are missing from the tool cabinet. Since this had never before been a problem, the cabinet was always left unlocked. Of the following, the best way to handle this situation is to

(A) lock the cabinet, and give keys to all your crew members, making them all responsible for the tools
(B) lock the cabinet, and make one of your crew members responsible for the key to the cabinet and the tools inside
(C) announce to your crew members that if a tool is missing they will all have to be charged an appropriate amount towards the purchase of a new tool
(D) assign each crew member a particular tool and have him use this device exclusively.

66. Of the following, the best reason for the practice of requiring your crew members to sign in and out for lunch is that

(A) the crew members are more productive when they are more strictly controlled
(B) it enables the supervisor to regulate the time and working hours of the crew members more directly
(C) it will prevent crew members from leaving the work area during their lunch period
(D) the supervisor will find out the preferred lunch period of each individual crew member.

67. While pruning some shrubs, a crew member under your supervision trips over what he thinks was a loose cobblestone. After checking to make sure he has suffered no injury, of the following the most advisable action for you to take next is to

(A) tell him to be more careful in the future
(B) determine what actually caused the accident
(C) post safety rules where they can be seen by all crew members
(D) assign him to a different type of work at another location.

68. One of the crew members under your supervision tells you that the lawn mower he has been using has just broken down. Of the following, the best reason for you to try operating the mower yourself is to

(A) test the worker's knowledge with his performance on the job
(B) keep the machines in need of repair in service as long as possible
(C) show that supervisors can do the work of the crew members
(D) determine whether a minor adjustment will bring the machine to operating condition.

69. You have just explained to your most competent crew member a complicated root-pruning procedure that you wish him to follow. He tells you that he is a little uncertain about it and is not sure he can handle it. Of the following, the best action for you to take is to

(A) show him how much confidence you have in him by leaving him alone to do the job
(B) have another crew member work with him to make sure that the job is done correctly
(C) stay with him while he does the job to assure yourself that he knows how to do it correctly
(D) drop the assignment until such time as he indicates that he is ready for it.

70. While you are replanting some flowers, a man comes up to you and starts berating you for the condition of the park. Of the following, the best way to handle this situation is to

(A) suggest that he write to the Parks Department about his complaints
(B) ask the man to leave and call for a police officer if he does not
(C) explain to the man that those who use the park are primarily responsible for its condition
(D) tell him that his opinions about the conditions of the park are wrong.

71. Gardeners should be courteous to the public primarily because

(A) someone might report them if they are not
(B) this might earn them a merit increase
(C) a good relationship between the Department and the public is important
(D) this makes for better morale among their crew members.

72. Assume that you have been asked to evaluate the performance of one of your crew members. The one of the following which should be given the least consideration when making this evaluation is the employee's attitude towards

(A) his co-workers
(B) the organization
(C) his friends
(D) you.

Answer questions 73 through 75 on the basis of the following report.

To: John Greene
General Park Foreman

Date: May 5, 1974

From: Earl Jones
Gardener

Subject:

On May 3rd, as I was finishing a job six feet from the boathouse, I observed that the hole which had been filled in last week was now not level with the ground around it. This seems to be a hazardous condition because it might cause pedestrians to fall into it. I therefore suggest that this job be re-done as soon as possible.

73. This report should be considered poorly written mainly because

(A) it does not give enough information to take appropriate action
(B) too many different tenses are used
(C) it describes no actual personal injury to anyone
(D) there is no recommendation in the report to remedy the situation.

74. It is noted that the subject of the report has been left out. Which of the following statements would be best as the Subject of this report?

(A) Observation made by Earl Jones, Gardener
(B) Deteriorating condition of Park grounds
(C) Report of dangerous condition near boathouse
(D) A dangerous walk through the Park

75. In order for John Greene to take appropriate action, additional information should be added to the report giving the

(A) exact date the repair was made
(B) exact location of the hole
(C) exact time the observation was made
(D) names of the crew who previously filled in the hole.

Questions 76 through 80 are based on the Fact Situation and the Repair Request Report form below. Read the Fact Situation carefully and examine the blank report form. Questions 76 through 80 ask how the report form should be filled in based on the information given in the Fact Situation.

FACT SITUATION

"John Smith is a Gardener, permanently assigned to the greenhouse in Queens. On Tuesday morning he arrives at the greenhouse at 8 a.m. and sees that seven panes of glass in the west wing of the greenhouse have been broken. Since several large rocks are found on the greenhouse floor, it appears that the panes of the windows have been broken by vandals. It is necessary to repair the windows immediately due to the cold weather. In order to arrange for the repair, John Smith must complete the following "Repair Request Report."

REPAIR REQUEST REPORT

1. Date of Request ______________ 2. Time ____________

3. Location of Needed Repair ______________________

4. Type of Repair Requested ________________________

5. Reason for Request ____

____

6. Signed ____________________ 7. Title ___________

8. Additional Comments ____

____

76. Which of the following should be entered in Blank 4?

(A) Rock removal
(B) Broken glass
(C) Window pane replacement
(D) Heater installation.

77. Based on the information given in the Fact Situation, it is impossible to fill in which one of the following blanks?

(A) Blank 1
(B) Blank 3
(C) Blank 5
(D) Blank 7

78. Which of the following would it be most appropriate to include in Blank 8?

(A) "John Smith was on time for work on January 10, 1974."
(B) "It seems that the windows were broken by vandals."
(C) "The weather forecast for the next few days is unknown."
(D) "Identity of vandals is unknown."

79. Of the following the best way for John Smith to show his supervisor that the Repair Request Report was properly filled out is to

(A) personally deliver the Report to the repair crew
(B) have two signatures instead of one required in Blank 6
(C) show his supervisor a duplicate copy of the Report
(D) in Blank 8 include the dimensions of the panes of glass needed.

80. It is necessary to emphasize the need to have the repair made quickly. The proper blank on the form to show the urgency of this request is

(A) Blank 2 (C) Blank 7
(B) Blank 3 (D) Blank 8.

Correct Answers For The Foregoing Questions

(Please try to answer the questions on your own before looking at our answers. You'll do much better on your test if you follow this rule.)

1.B	11.A	21.D	31.A	41.A	51.B	61.D	71.C
2.C	12.C	22.A	32.A	42.C	52.A	62.A	72.C
3.D	13.D	23.B	33.C	43.A	53.C	63.D	73.A
4.B	14.B	24.C	34.A	44.C	54.C	64.C	74.C
5.C	15.D	25.D	35.D	45.D	55.B	65.B	75.B
6.D	16.A	26.C	36.A	46.C	56.D	66.B	76.C
7.C	17.B	27.B	37.D	47.B	57.C	67.B	77.A
8.B	18.B	28.B	38.A	48.C	58.A	68.D	78.B
9.C	19.B	29.C	39.A	49.D	59.D	69.C	79.C
10.B	20.C	30.A	40.B	50.C	60.C	70.A	80.D

TEST____________________ PART__________

DATE__________

RATING

(Slightly reduced from standard size used with many tests)

USE THE SPECIAL PENCIL. MAKE GLOSSY BLACK MARKS.

1 A B C D E	26 A B C D E	51 A B C D E	76 A B C D E	101 A B C D E
2 A B C D E	27 A B C D E	52 A B C D E	77 A B C D E	102 A B C D E
3 A B C D E	28 A B C D E	53 A B C D E	78 A B C D E	103 A B C D E
4 A B C D E	29 A B C D E	54 A B C D E	79 A B C D E	104 A B C D E
5 A B C D E	30 A B C D E	55 A B C D E	80 A B C D E	105 A B C D E
6 A B C D E	31 A B C D E	56 A B C D E	81 A B C D E	106 A B C D E
7 A B C D E	32 A B C D E	57 A B C D E	82 A B C D E	107 A B C D E
8 A B C D E	33 A B C D E	58 A B C D E	83 A B C D E	108 A B C D E
9 A B C D E	34 A B C D E	59 A B C D E	84 A B C D E	109 A B C D E
10 A B C D E	35 A B C D E	60 A B C D E	85 A B C D E	110 A B C D E

Make only ONE mark for each answer. Additional and stray marks may be counted as mistakes. In making corrections, erase errors COMPLETELY.

11 A B C D E	36 A B C D E	61 A B C D E	86 A B C D E	111 A B C D E
12 A B C D E	37 A B C D E	62 A B C D E	87 A B C D E	112 A B C D E
13 A B C D E	38 A B C D E	63 A B C D E	88 A B C D E	113 A B C D E
14 A B C D E	39 A B C D E	64 A B C D E	89 A B C D E	114 A B C D E
15 A B C D E	40 A B C D E	65 A B C D E	90 A B C D E	115 A B C D E
16 A B C D E	41 A B C D E	66 A B C D E	91 A B C D E	116 A B C D E
17 A B C D E	42 A B C D E	67 A B C D E	92 A B C D E	117 A B C D E
18 A B C D E	43 A B C D E	68 A B C D E	93 A B C D E	118 A B C D E
19 A B C D E	44 A B C D E	69 A B C D E	94 A B C D E	119 A B C D E
20 A B C D E	45 A B C D E	70 A B C D E	95 A B C D E	120 A B C D E
21 A B C D E	46 A B C D E	71 A B C D E	96 A B C D E	121 A B C D E
22 A B C D E	47 A B C D E	72 A B C D E	97 A B C D E	122 A B C D E
23 A B C D E	48 A B C D E	73 A B C D E	98 A B C D E	123 A B C D E
24 A B C D E	49 A B C D E	74 A B C D E	99 A B C D E	124 A B C D E
25 A B C D E	50 A B C D E	75 A B C D E	100 A B C D E	125 A B C D E

GARDENER

II. PREVIOUS EXAM FOR PRACTICE

Test yourself now with this civil service exam which was actually given to candidates for your job. Adhere strictly to the test instructions and conditions. You will get a measure of your present knowledge and ability . . . and you will begin real training for the test you must take. You will also discover where your weaknesses lie and can thus concentrate your study in those areas.

DATE OF EXAM: September 26, 1964

The time allowed for the entire examination is 3 hours. In order to create the climate of the test to come, that's precisely what you should allow yourself . . . no more, no less. Use a watch and keep a record of your time, especially since you may find it convenient to take the test in several sittings.

1. For best growth, azaleas require a soil that is

   (A) neutral (B) either alkaline or neutral (C) alkaline (D) acid.

Questions 2 to 6 give the names of shrubs. Column I gives suggested times for pruning shrubs. For each shrub in questions 2 to 6, select from Column I the best time to prune it and blacken the appropriate space on your answer sheet.

2. Buddleja
3. Common lilac
4. peegee hydrangea
5. rose of sharon
6. Vanhoutte's spirea

<u>Column I</u>

(A) Prune in spring after flowering

(B) Prune in fall after flowering.

7. Which one of the following is the <u>least</u> acceptable procedure when transplanting trees?

   (A) Prune the top back about one fourth. (B) Root prune a large tree for at least one growing season before it is transplanted. (C) Transplant in the spring or the fall. (D) Transplant only large trees because they can withstand the shock of transplanting better.

8. When a deciduous shrub is dug with a ball of earth for transplanting from one location to another, the size of the ball of earth should usually be about

   (A) twice the spread of the branches (B) $1\frac{1}{2}$ times the spread of the branches (C) equal to the spread of the branches (D) one-half the spread of the branches.

Questions 9 to 12 give the names of 4 pairs of shrubs. Classify each pair of shrubs according to the scheme shown in Column II, and then blacken the proper space on your answer sheet.

9. mountain laurel - fragrant viburnum
10. mountain adromeda - Pfitzer juniper
11. dwarf japanese yew - pyramidal arborvitae
12. sweet mockorange - snowhill hydrangea

Column II

(A) both shrubs are deciduous
(B) both shrubs are evergreen
(C) one shrub is deciduous and one shrub is evergreen

Questions 13 to 17 give the names of 5 shrubs. Classify each shrub according to height as in Column III, and blacken the proper space on your answer sheet.

13. Shrub Althea
14. Slender deutzia
15. Tartarian honeysuckle
16. Japanese adromeda
17. Thunberg spirea

Column III

(A) low shrub - about 3 feet in height
(B) medium shrub - about 5 feet in height
(C) tall shrub - about 8 feet or more in height

18. Which of the following is true about California privet but not about Japanese Barberry?

(A) It is suitable for use as a hedge material. (B) It requires little clipping for a neat appearance. (C) It grows very tall. (D) It is thorny.

19. Outdoor fall planting is not recommended for

(A) dahlias (B) hyacinths (C) lilies-of-the-valley (D) tulips.

20. A characteristic of plants classified as annuals is that they usually

(A) grow well on any soil (B) grow well only on considerably acid soil
(C) are shade-loving (D) are sun-loving.

21. The recommended spacing between sweet pea plants is

(A) over 24 inches (B) 18 - 24 inches (C) 6 - 12 inches
(D) 1 - 4 inches.

22. To say that a seed is viable, means that it

(A) is subject to fungus disease (B) is subject to insect damage
(C) can take root and grow (D) can not grow in moist soils.

Each of questions 23 to 26 gives the name of a mulch which may be classified under one of the headings in Column IV. For each mulch, select the heading from Column IV under which it is most correctly classified and blacken the proper space on your answer sheet.

Column IV

(A) acid mulch

(B) non-acid mulch

23. corn cobs

24. decayed pine needles

25. grass clippings

26. peat moss

27. A characteristic of Merion Kentucky blue grass is that it

(A) is highly susceptible to leafspot (B) needs heavy watering daily (C) will thrive on close cutting (D) germinates quickly.

28. Fertilization of bluegrass and fescue grasses in the summer is

(A) desirable because the usual dryness of this season requires increased feeding to offset the shortage of moisture (B) not desirable because there is more chance of burning the grass (C) desirable because this is the period of their most active growth (D) not desirable because they are semi-dormant and fertilization will stimulate weed growth.

Questions 29 to 33 give the names of 5 lawn grasses. For each grass, select the statement from Column V that is most applicable and blacken the proper space on your answer sheet.

Column V

(A) used mainly for golf course putting greens

(B) best grass for sunny places in good soil

(C) suitable for moist, shady areas

(D) turns brown in fall till mid-spring

(E) best grass for dry soil, sun or shade

29. Kentucky bluegrass

30. red fescue

31. rough bluegrass

32. bentgrass

33. Meyer Zoysia

Each of questions 34 to 37 gives the name of a weed. For each weed, select the best weed killer from Column VI and blacken the proper space on your answer sheet.

Column VI

(A) 2,4-D

(B) 2,4,5 - TP (Silvex)

(C) Endothal

34. chickweed

35. dandelion

36. plantain

37. speedwells (Veronica)

38. Just before seeding a new lawn on average soil, a 5-10-5 fertilizer should be applied at the rate of

(A) 100 pounds for every 1,000 square feet (B) 75 pounds for every 1,000 square feet (C) 40 pounds for every 1,000 square feet (D) 20 pounds for every 1,000 square feet.

In areas where it is difficult to establish and maintain grass, such as on slopes and in deep shade, the planting of a ground cover plant is recommended. Questions 39 to 41 give the names of 3 ground cover plants. Select from Column VII the descriptive statement that is most applicable to each one, and blacken the appropriate space on your answer sheet.

39. English ivy

40. Japanese pachysandra

41. myrtle

Column VII

(A) small, dark green, glossy leaves; violet blue flowers
(B) trailing evergreen vine
(C) spreads by suckers; greenish-white flowers; plants about 8 inches high
(D) a bunch-growing member of the lily family; 8-12 inches high; purple to white flowers

42. Serious and widespread diseases of lawn grasses are caused mostly by
(A) algae (B) bacteria (C) crab grass (D) fungi.

43. Anthracnose is a type of
(A) worm (B) insect pest (C) lawn grass (D) fungus disease.

Each of questions 44 to 47 gives the name of an insect which may be classified under one of the headings in Column VIII. For each insect, select the heading from Column VIII under which it is most correctly classified and blacken the proper space on your answer sheet.

44. aphid

45. grasshopper

46. lady beetle (lady bug)

47. syrphid fly

Column VIII

(A) insect beneficial to plants
(B) insect injurious to plants
(C) insect neither beneficial nor injurious to plants

Each of questions 48 to 51 gives the name of a fumigant or an insecticide which may be classified under one of the headings in Column IX. For each fumigant or insecticide, select the heading from Column IX under which it is most correctly classified and blacken the proper space on your answer sheet.

48. arsenate of lead

49. chloropicrin

50. pyrethrum

51. rotenone

Column IX

(A) a plant insecticide non-poisonous to man
(B) a plant insecticide poisonous to man
(C) a soil fumigant which should not be used on plants

52. A disadvantage of DDT is that it

(A) is not effective against sucking insects (B) is not effective against chewing insects (C) destroys the roots of most flowering plants (D) destroys the natural enemies of various mites.

53. A characteristic of chlordane is that it

(A) does not act as a contact poison (B) does not act as a stomach poison (C) has long-lasting effects (D) is slow-acting.

54. For a soil test, it is best to dig the samples of soil in the

(A) early spring (B) summer (C) early fall (D) winter.

55. The symbol used to indicate soil acidity is

(A) AC (B) Hp (C) pH (D) SA.

56. Loam is a type of soil that

(A) contains no organic matter (B) is coarser than clay (C) is coarser than sand (D) is usually unfertile.

57. A poor way to improve the structure of a sandy soil is to add

(A) compost (B) humus (C) organic matter (D) sand.

58. As compared to a sandy soil, a characteristic of a clay soil is that it is

(A) able to hold less water (B) harder to work when wet (C) quicker in drying out in the spring (D) quicker to warm up in the spring.

59. A characteristic of compost is that it

(A) decreases slightly the amount of plant nutrient in the soil (B) decreases slightly the humus content of the soil (C) improves soil texture in flower gardens (D) is naturally free of weed seeds.

60. An advantage of a commercial fertilizer over an animal manure is that a commercial fertilizer

(A) has a higher percentage of plant nutrients (B) adds to the organic content of the soil (C) greatly increases bacterial activity in the soil (D) will not burn plant roots.

61. A disadvantage in using raw bone meal as a fertilizer is that

(A) it increases the soil acidity over a period of years (B) it is unsafe for use on most plants (C) its nitrogen content is very slowly available to plants (D) its phosphorus content is very slowly available to plants.

62. What is the action of superphosphate applied to the soil as a top dressing?

(A) It does not penetrate the soil. (B) It penetrates the soil very slowly. (C) It penetrates the soil moderately fast. (D) It penetrates the soil very quickly.

63. The addition of which one of the following will be <u>least</u> likely to make the soil more acid?
(A) aluminum sulphate (B) lime (C) oak leafmold (D) sawdust.

64. Which one of the following is <u>not</u> alkaline in its reaction?
(A) ammonium phosphate (B) calcium nitrate (C) cyanamide
(D) wood ashes.

65. Which one of these statements about a 4-12-4 fertilizer is true?
(A) The first number shows the percentage of phosphorus. (B) The first number shows the percentage of potassium. (C) The last number shows the percentage of potash. (D) The second number shows the percentage of nitrogen.

66. A good <u>organic</u> source of nitrogen is
(A) ammonium sulphate (B) nitrate of soda (C) bone meal (D) dried blood.

67. The one of the following which is <u>not</u> a source of potash is
(A) steamed bone meal (B) wood ashes (C) potassium chloride
(D) potassium sulphate.

68. Urea is a form of
(A) iron (B) nitrogen (C) phosphorus (D) potassium.

69. To hold an electric hedge cutter with both hands when using it is considered
(A) good procedure because it lessens the severity of electric shocks
(B) poor procedure because it increases the likelihood of receiving electric shocks (C) good procedure because it reduces the chance of an accident
(D) poor procedure because it slows up the work.

70. Reel power mowers as contrasted with rotary power mowers
(A) are easier to control (B) cause fewer accidents (C) cost less
(D) cut closer to trees.

71. A gardener stands a 24 foot ladder against an upright tree trunk. To safely use the ladder, the distance between the base of the tree trunk and the foot of the ladder should be approximately
(A) 8 inches (B) 2 feet (C) 3 feet (D) 6 feet.

72. Compared with the hydraulic sprayer, the mist blower
(A) causes more loss of spray material from dripping (B) is always preferred in areas inaccessible to heavy equipment (C) is less affected by windy weather (D) requires greater skill by the operator.

73. A Gardener notices that one of his crew members does not get along with the rest of the crew. The best thing for the Gardener to do would be to
(A) ignore the situation since it probably won't affect work output
(B) tell his men they must get along with each other if they don't want to be transferred (C) try to find the reason for the trouble to see if the differences can be settled (D) write a report to his supervisor and await instructions.

74. A Gardener supervising a group of men on a work project spoke to them one morning, just before lunch, about the importance of getting back to work on time after lunch. He turned to one of the men and said: "Bill, you have been particularly guilty of coming back late from lunch." The Gardener's action was <u>not</u> good because

(A) he could have taken care of the problem better and with less waste of time by issuing a written order to the men (B) he should have named at least one other man who was guilty of this violation (C) he should not have criticized one of his men in front of the other men (D) this was not a proper subject to talk about to his men at a group meeting.

75. Suppose that as a Gardener you are in charge of several men. Warning your men that they will be penalized if they do poor work is

(A) good practice because it is only fair that they know what the penalties are for neglect of duty (B) poor practice because then you will actually have to penalize them if they don't do good work (C) good practice because they will try to do better work (D) poor practice because they should be encouraged to do good work without such warnings.

76. If you are training a new member of your crew to use a piece of equipment, it would probably be <u>least</u> important for you to

(A) give him a set of written instructions on use of the equipment (B) give him an actual demonstration in using the equipment (C) watch him using the equipment the first time (D) check him frequently to see how he is progressing.

77. Your supervisor gives you a letter of complaint from a citizen and tells you to "look into this and get the facts." It would be a good idea for you, as a <u>first</u> step, to

(A) interview the person who wrote the letter at his home (B) speak to the people in your Department who have knowledge of the matter complained about (C) turn this over to one of your men who is not very busy (D) write the person a letter telling him that the matter he complains about is being looked into and will be settled to his satisfaction.

78. Suppose that an Assistant Gardener whom you supervise has an accident on the job and is hurt. In your written report of this accident to your own superior it is <u>least</u> important for you to include information about

(A) the Assistant Gardener's attitude toward other employees (B) the tool used when the accident happened (C) what you plan to do to prevent such accidents in the future (D) when the accident happened.

79. Just before the end of a new Assistant Gardener's probationary period, his supervisor, the Gardener, turned in a report to the foreman on the new employee's work and record during the probationary period. In his report, the Gardener did not make any recommendation whether the new employee should be kept on after his probationary period. The Gardener's action was

(A) bad because it is the Gardener's responsibility to make a recommendation whether the new employee should be kept on after the probationary period
(B) good because he should be impartial to all new employees (C) bad because the new employee will not know if he is going to be kept on the job or not (D) good because it is the job of "higher-ups" to decide if new employees should be kept on after the end of probation.

80. Suppose that your supervisor has asked you to investigate some new gardening procedure and give him a written report with a recommendation whether the new procedure should be used in the Park Department. It would probably be best for you to put your recommendation

(A) any place in the report where you can fit it in without too much trouble
(B) at the end of the report after you have given the facts of your investigation
(C) in the middle of the report (D) on a separate attached sheet.

Correct Answers For The Foregoing Questions

(Please try to answer the questions on your own before looking at our answers. You'll do much better on your test if you follow this rule.)

1.D	11.B	21.C	31.C	41.A	51.A	61.D	71.D
2.B	12.A	22.C	32.A	42.D	52.D	62.B	72.D
3.A	13.C	23.B	33.D	43.D	53.C	63.B	73.C
4.B	14.A	24.A	34.B	44.B	54.A	64.A	74.C
5.B	15.C	25.B	35.A	45.B	55.C	65.C	75.D
6.A	16.B	26.A	36.A	46.A	56.B	66.D	76.A
7.D	17.B	27.C	37.C	47.A	57.D	67.A	77.B
8.D	18.C	28.D	38.C	48.B	58.B	68.B	78.A
9.C	19.A	29.B	39.B	49.C	59.C	69.C	79.A
10.B	20.D	30.E	40.C	50.A	60.A	70.B	80.B

Practice Using Answer Sheets

DIRECTIONS: Read each question or statement. When you have decided the statement is true or false, blacken the corresponding space on this sheet with a No. 2 pencil. Make your mark as long as the pair of lines, and completely fill the area between the pair of lines. If you change your mind, erase your first mark COMPLETELY. Make no stray marks; they may count against you.

SAMPLE	
1. CHICAGO IS A CITY	1 T F
2. PHILADELPHIA IS A STATE	2

SCORES

1 ____ 5 ____
2 ____ 6 ____
3 ____ 7 ____
4 ____ 8 ____

1 T F	2 T F	3 T F	4 T F	5 T F	6 T F	7 T F	8 T F
9	10	11	12	13	14	15	16
17	18	19	20	21	22	23	24
25 T F	26 T F	27 T F	28 T F	29 T F	30 T F	31 T F	32 T F
33	34	35	36	37	38	39	40
41	42	43	44	45	46	47	48
49 T F	50 T F	51 T F	52 T F	53 T F	54 T F	55 T F	56 T F
57	58	59	60	61	62	63	64
65	66	67	68	69	70	71	72
73 T F	74 T F	75 T F	76 T F	77 T F	78 T F	79 T F	80 T F
81	82	83	84	85	86	87	88
89	90	91	92	93	94	95	96
97	98	99	100				
				101 T F	102 T F	103 T F	104 T F
105 T F	106 T F	107 T F	108 T F	109	110	111	112
113	114	115	116	117	118	119	120
121	122	123	124	125	126	127	128
129 T F	130 T F	131 T F	132 T F	133 T F	134 T F	135 T F	136 T F
137	138	139	140	141	142	143	144
145	146	147	148	149	150	151	152
153 T F	154 T F	155 T F	156 T F	157 T F	158 T F	159 T F	160 T F
161	162	163	164	165	166	167	168
169	170	171	172	173	174	175	176
177 T F	178 T F	179 T F	180 T F	181 T F	182 T F	183 T F	184 T F
185	186	187	188	189	190	191	192
193	194	195	196	197	198	199	200
201 T F	202 T F	203 T F	204 T F	205 T F	206 T F	207 T F	208 T F
209	210	211	212	213	214	215	216
217	218	219	220	221	222	223	224
225 T F	226 T F	227 T F	228 T F	229 T F	230 T F	231 T F	232 T F
233	234	235	236	237	238	239	240
241	242	243	244	245	246	247	248
249 T F	250 T F	251 T F	252 T F	253 T F	254 T F	255 T F	256 T F
257	258	259	260	261	262	263	264
265	266	267	268	269	270	271	272
273 T F	274 T F	275 T F	276 T F	277 T F	278 T F	279 T F	280 T F
281	282	283	284	285	286	287	288
289	290	291	292	293	294	295	296
297	298	299	300				

TEAR OUT ALONG THIS LINE AND MARK YOUR ANSWERS AS INSTRUCTED IN THE TEXT

III. PREVIOUS EXAM FOR PRACTICE

Now here's another examination held on another date, but again, quite similar to yours. So you have another opportunity to test and sharpen your skills. The instructions are similar. By this time you should be more familiar with them. But don't relax. Follow them closely. On your actual exam you don't want to waste time puzzling out instructions which you can learn to recognize now without penalty.

The time allowed for the entire examination is 2½ hours. In order to create the climate of the test to come, that's precisely what you should allow yourself . . . no more, no less. Use a watch and keep a record of your time, especially since you may find it convenient to take the test in several sittings.

DIRECTIONS: For each of the following statements, mark T if the statement is True, and F if it is False.

1. Fence posts sunk into the soil need no wood preservative below the soil line because the earth itself is a natural preservative.

2. An assistant gardener who sees a man drop papers on a lawn, should say nothing and pick the papers up himself in order to keep the goodwill of the public.

3. One reason for wrapping newly planted trees with burlap cloth when they are over 2 inches in diameter is to cut down on loss of water through the bark of the tree.

4. When a large branch is cut from a tree-like shrub, the cut should usually be left open to the healing powers of the air.

5. If you find that a lawn area your foreman has sent you to mow has just been mowed by another assistant gardener, you should say nothing about this and mow the lawn anyway.

6. A sandy soil usually holds water longer than a clay soil.

7. Pole pruners are used mainly for sawing down posts.

8. A fan-shaped bamboo rake is a good rake for gathering leaves on a lawn.

9. If your foreman asks you to help a gang of Park Department laborers who are digging a trench, you should refuse to do so because digging is not one of the duties of an assistant gardener.

10. Before using a chisel which has "mushroomed" from constant use, an assistant gardener should lay the chisel on a hard piece of steel and hammer the "mushroomed" edges until they disappear.

11. If you wish to dig up a plant from one place in order to plant it in another place, you should do this on a sunny day so that the roots receive some of the sunlight they seldom get.

12. Lime is usually added to the soil to make the soil more acid.

13. The leaf is usually the part of the plant that makes food for the plant.

14. Gasoline is one of the safest cleaning liquids to use for greasy, dirty, metal equipment.

15. An assistant gardener should work steadily but slowly so that there will be enough work to go around.

16. When a dump truck brings brush to a spot to be burned, the truck should usually dump the brush at a place some distance from the fire rather than right on the fire.

17. If the sod you are cutting to plant in another place seems to be infected with fungus, you should report this to your foreman as soon as possible.

18. The best trees for planting on streets are those with roots that can get into sewers for water.

19. To let the sunlight get to the lower branches, a hedge should usually be trimmed so that it is wider at the top than at the bottom.

20. To help grass on a lawn become deep rooted, it is better to soak the lawn with water when the lawn needs it than to water it lightly every day.

21. If you should overhear several teen-agers plotting a gang fight in the park to which you are assigned, you should notify your foreman so that he can take action.

22. Most northern grasses should usually be cut much shorter than usual in a summer drought because shorter grass leaves require less water.

23. You notice that a mechanic working in the park is doing his work in a way you consider inefficient. You, as the assistant gardener, should report this mechanic for inefficiency.

24. A newly planted bed of lawn seed should be watered with a fine spray rather than a heavy spray to keep from washing the seed away.

25. A scythe is mainly used to trim hedges.

26. If you see a child annoying squirrels in the park in which you work, you should call a policeman to arrest the child.

27. A sickle is mainly used to cut tall grass and weeds.

Your answers to questions 28 to 36 must be based only on the information given in the following paragraph and not on any other information you may have.

"Plant reproduction is called propagation. Methods of propagation can be divided into two classes, those methods which depend on seed and those depending on the use of buds. Buds are the small swellings on plant stems from which shoots, clusters of leaves, or flowers develop. Propagation by seed is called sexual, while propagation by buds is called asexual. Asexual propagation depends primarily upon the activity of the cambium. This is a layer of very thin tissue consisting entirely of young, easily broken cells filled with protoplasm, the basic stuff found in all living things. This cambium layer forms new plant tissues under the proper circumstances. It plays an important part in growth, in healing, and in asexual reproduction. When a bud is cut from a parent plant and inserted into water, sand, or other material suitable for starting growth, the cambium promotes root formation on the bud. When a branch is cut from one tree and grafted onto another of the same kind, the cambium from the branch unites with that of the tree and develops an additional protective covering. Propagation by asexual rather than sexual means is used because it is the most certain means of producing an offspring closely resembling the parent."

28. One example of propagation by sexual means is the growing of a plant from a bud.
29. Several forms of growth can develop from buds which are on a plant stem.
30. The cambium layer is made up of tough cells which help protect the tree.
31. A special quality of the cambium layer is that it will form new plant tissues under any circumstances.
32. Cambium activity is important in asexual reproduction.
33. All living animals have protoplasm in them.
34. Roots may start to grow from a bud cut from a parent plant only when the bud is placed in sand.
35. When a branch from one tree is grafted onto another tree of the same kind, the cambium of the first tree joins with that of the second tree.
36. The surest way of obtaining plants which look very much like the parent plant is to grow such plants from the seeds of the parent.

Your answers to questions 37 to 41 must be based only on the information given in the following paragraph and not on any other information you may have.

"The soil around young trees and shrubs is often cultivated the first two or three years in order to insure a good start. Cultivation helps to control and eliminate weeds but has no other value in stimulating plant growth. Deep cultivation is done in the spring. As the growing season progresses, cultivation should be gradually shallower. This method may result in the destruction of feeding roots formed the previous year in the same cultivated areas, but it does not disturb the carrier roots from which the feeding roots came. If the tree or shrub is not cultivated for a few years, however, these feeding roots grow into carrier roots with feeding roots growing mainly from their ends. When cultivation is resumed after such an interval, extra precaution must be taken not to prune the carrier roots too severely. Injurious results of severe root pruning may be partially offset by a correspondingly severe pruning of the top at the time of root pruning."

37. Cultivating the earth around young trees for the first two or three years helps plant growth by letting air get to the roots.

38. Even though the method of cultivating a young tree may be the right one, some feeding roots of the tree may be destroyed.

39. Cultivation of young trees at the beginning of the growing season should be more shallow than cultivation late in the growing season.

40. If several seasons of growth of a tree have gone by without cultivation, some feeding roots grow into carrier roots.

41. Cutting a lot from the top of a tree makes up partly for the bad effects of cutting a lot from the roots.

Your answers to questions 42 to 46 must be based only on the information given in the following paragraph and not upon any other information you may have.

"Low shrubs need no guys to maintain their position. But newly planted trees and tree-like shrubs, unless they are staked or guyed at once, may be pushed out of alignment by the wind or other forces. When pulled by a wire back to a vertical position, such trees continue to exert a force against the pull. In such cases not only will all the strain usually be put on one stake or guy wire but, most important, air pockets may form around the roots. To best maintain the stability of the tree, the tension on all stakes and guy wires should be approximately equal at the time of planting. Although the tension on individual wires will then vary with the conditions met later, the position of the tree is not likely to be affected."

42. To keep the wind from bending low shrubs, they should be staked or guyed right after planting.

43. If a tree pushed out of line is then pulled straight by one wire, the chances are that the tree will snap back out of line if the wire is cut.

44. The most important result of guying straight a tree which has been knocked out of line is that most of the strain is usually put on one guy wire.

45. Straightening out a tree after it has been pushed from its vertical position helps to remove air pockets around the roots.

46. If three guy wires are used to support a small tree after planting, the tension on one guy wire should be approximately one third of the total tension on all three guy wires.

Your answers to questions 47 to 50 must be based only on the information in the following paragraph and not upon any other information you may have.

"Sun often injures trees by burning their trunks and main branches. Especially susceptible to such injury are those trees growing in well-cultivated orchards. In the Northern Hemisphere such injury usually occurs on the south side although it often also occurs on the east side, less often on the west and never on the north side. The damage is sometimes confined to these exposed bark areas, but such limitation to exposed bark areas only is seldom found. When the tissues in the inner bark are destroyed, the downward flow of plant food is impeded and the roots to which these tissues lead are deprived of nourishment."

47. One method of protecting trees from sun injury is to cultivate well the orchard in which they grow.

48. In the United States, one side of the tree on which sun injury usually occurs is the north side.

49. Sun damage to trees is sometimes restricted to the outer bark of the tree.

50. Root nourishment depends on the downward flow of plant food in the inner bark.

Your answers to questions 51 to 53 must be based only on information given in the following paragraph and not upon any other information you may have.

"The belt should always be taut when clutch is fully engaged and at no other time. To check the belt for proper tension, first start the engine, and then bear down lightly on the handle of the mower in order to raise the mower wheels off the ground. While in this position, engage the clutch; then stop the engine by shorting the sparkplug with the stop switch, leaving the clutch engaged. If the belt is not taut, loosen the nut which holds the countershaft pedestal in order to make the countershaft pedestal movable. Then slide the countershaft pedestal to the back to tighten the belt. Sliding the countershaft pedestal forward loosens the belt."

51. The only time the belt should be tight is when the clutch is engaged completely.

52. In testing the belt for correct tension the clutch should be engaged after the mower wheels are raised off the ground.

53. To make the belt looser, tighten the nut holding the countershaft pedestal.

Your answers to questions 54 to 60 must be based only on information given in the following paragraph and not upon any other information you may have.

"The soil around actively growing delphiniums should receive a thorough soaking at least once a week. Delphiniums can be transplanted either in the autumn or in the spring. The fine and fibrous root system of these plants facilitates their removal. Since delphiniums are among the first herbaceous plants to start growth in the spring, autumn transplanting is generally recommended because the plants then undoubtedly suffer less shock. If the work is done with extreme care it is possible to move quite large plants when they are just coming into bloom. Large plants must be lifted with a generous quantity of earth in order that the root system remain intact. The use of a plastic spray will prevent wilting if applied before the plants are moved."

54. Delphiniums must be watered more than once a week.

55. Delphiniums are difficult to remove because of their thick, tough roots.

56. Delphiniums start growth earlier in the spring than many other herbaceous plants.

57. Delphiniums experience more shock from transplanting in the spring than in the fall.

58. To keep the root system together when large delphiniums are moved, a large amount of earth should be taken up with the roots.

59. One way of preventing a delphinium from wilting when moved is to apply a plastic spray to the plant beforehand.

60. Large delphinium plants are most easily moved at the time they are beginning to bloom.

61. "Formal shearing destroys the plant's individuality." In this sentence, the word 'formal' means nearly the same as 'irregular'.

62. "The entire tree is covered with a film which is flexible, colorless, and lasting." In this sentence, the word 'flexible' means nearly the same as 'tough'.

63. "All of the equipment is mobile." In this sentence, the word 'mobile' means nearly the same as the word 'movable'.

64. "Just enough asphalt adheres to make a mat." In this sentence, the word 'adheres' means nearly the same as the word 'sticks'.

65. "Efforts at proper maintenance were nullified by this act." In this sentence, the word 'nullified' means nearly the same as 'brought to nothing'.

66. Saying that a hose is "perforated" is another way of saying that a hose is "bent".

67. "Do not injure the foliage of a plant" means nearly the same as "do not injure the plant's roots".

68. "Pulverizing" soil is breaking it down into very small bits.

69. Humus is the part of the soil which is very often called clay in gardening practice.

70. "Aerating" a turf area is nearly the same as "sodding" the area.

71. "To mechanically agitate" means nearly the same as "to seed by mechanical power".

72. "To eliminate hand pumping" means nearly the same as "to do away with hand pumping".

73. "Discarding a ladder with a cracked rung" means nearly the same as "repairing a ladder with a cracked rung".

74. A "projecting" stub is usually a stub which sticks out.

75. A "nitrogen deficiency" in the soil is an over supply of nitrogen in the soil.

76. Saying that a soil has a heavy "texture" is nearly the same as saying that the soil has a deep color.

77. A "neutral" soil is one in which no useful plants will grow.

78. A plant which is "dormant" is usually in an inactive period of growth.

79. Saying that sun is "detrimental" to ferns is nearly the same as saying that sun is harmful to ferns.

80. "Vendors are permitted only in certain park areas." In this sentence, the word 'vendors' means nearly the same as 'sellers'.

81. Residents of New York City pay a general federal sales tax.

82. The largest zoo in New York City is located in Bronx Park.

83. The Police Commissioner of the City of New York is Michael J. Murphy.

84. The proposed new City Charter would give the Mayor more power than he now has.

85. The New York City governmental body which makes local laws for New York City is commonly known as the Legislature.

86. The man defeated by Mayor Wagner in the last democratic primary contest was Arthur Levitt.

87. All parks in New York State located outside New York City are state parks.

88. The New York City License Department issues all licenses in the City of New York.

89. A Secretary General of the United Nations, Dag Hammarskjold , died while trying to negotiate peace in the Congo.

90. The New York City Aquarium is located in Battery Park, Manhattan.

91. If 100 pounds of a certain artificial fertilizer does a job equal to that done by 1 ton of a certain kind of manure, then 125 pounds of this fertilizer should do the same job as 1½ tons of the manure.

92. If an assistant gardener digs up an average of 73 square yards of lawn area per hour, then the total area dug up in eight hours by this assistant gardener should be 574 square yards.

93. From a total of 245 shrubs in a nursery, 56 shrubs are taken away the first day and 62 shrubs are brought into the nursery on the second day. The number of shrubs in the nursery at the beginning of the third day should be 251.

94. An assistant gardener finished 1/3 of a job on the first day, 1/2 of the job on the second day, and the balance on the third day. The part of the job done by the assistant gardener on the third day was equal to the part done on the first day.

95. If there are 231 cubic inches in a gallon, then in 1/3 of a gallon there are 77 cubic inches.

96. If 12½% of a total force of 8,080 employees are laborers, then there are 1,010 laborers in this force.

97. If a bill for gardening materials lists $15.40 for rose bushes, $78.45 for lawn seed, $24.15 for fertilizer and $27.10 for bulbs and corms, then the total cost of these items is $145.10.

98. An assistant gardener must distribute a certain number of plants equally among a certain number of parks. To find the number of plants to give to each park, he should divide the number of parks by the number of plants.

99. A lawn 47 feet wide and 93 feet long has an area of 4,471 square feet.

100. If 14 out of a total of 114 shrubs are evergreens, then 14% of the total are evergreens.

Correct Answers For The Foregoing Questions

(Please try to answer the questions on your own before looking at our answers. You'll do much better on your test if you follow this rule.)

1.F	14.F	27.T	40.T	53.F	65.T	77.F	89.T
2.F	15.F	28.F	41.T	54.F	66.F	78.T	90.F
3.T	16.T	29.T	42.F	55.F	67.F	79.T	91.F
4.F	17.T	30.F	43.T	56.T	68.T	80.T	92.F
5.F	18.F	31.F	44.F	57.T	69.F	81.F	93.T
6.F	19.F	32.T	45.F	58.T	70.F	82.T	94.F
7.F	20.T	33.T	46.T	59.T	71.F	83.T	95.T
8.T	21.T	34.F	47.F	60.F	72.T	84.T	96.T
9.F	22.F	35.T	48.F	61.F	73.F	85.F	97.T
10.F	23.F	36.F	49.T	62.F	74.T	86.T	98.F
11.F	24.T	37.F	50.T	63.T	75.F	87.F	99.F
12.F	25.F	38.T	51.T	64.T	76.F	88.F	100.F
13.T	26.F	39.F	52.T				

GARDENER

IV. PREVIOUS EXAM FOR PRACTICE

Please don't trust us. Have faith in yourself. Be your own exam analyst. As you take this civil service test (which was given for the very job you seek) note down the different subjects covered by the various questions. This exam may very well provide an accurate forecast of the test you'll take. Individual questions may even be similar. Certainly the same subjects, the same types of questions can be expected. Have you scheduled study for each of these subjects? Check back to the chapter on Studying . . . and make sure you do!

The time allowed for the entire examination is 3 hours. In order to create the climate of the test to come, that's precisely what you should allow yourself . . . no more, no less. Use a watch and keep a record of your time, especially since you may find it convenient to take the test in several sittings.

1. It is not an important function of phosphorus in the soil to help

   (A) good root development (B) make the soil alkaline (C) produce an abundance of fruits and seeds (D) the formation of strong cell walls.

2. An element necessary for the nutrition of plants which is normally obtained from the soil, rather than from water or the atmosphere, is

   (A) carbon (B) hydrogen (C) oxygen (D) nitrogen.

3. "Fresh manure should never be used where it will come in direct contact with the root formation of the plants." The most important reason for this is that the

   (A) manure is liable to cause severe burning (B) manure may drain the soil and dehydrate the roots (C) nitrogen content of the manure may have harmful effects (D) nutrient value of the manure has not yet reached its maximum.

4. "Beginning to grow from a seed to a plant" is a description of

   (A) cultivating (B) germinating (C) propagating (D) transplanting.

5. Which one of these is a deficiency disease in plants?

   (A) black rot (B) chlorosis (C) leaf spot (D) mildew.

6. The best way of improving the structure of sandy soils is by

   (A) autumn spading or plowing (B) frequent watering (C) the addition of large quantities of organic matter (D) the use of inorganic fertilizers.

7. In gardening, to "drill" seed means to

(A) pack it into the earth by rolling (B) rake it into the soil (C) scatter it by hand or machine (D) sow it in rows.

8. "Lime should never be used in combination with animal manures or with nitrogenous fertilizers." The most important reason for this is that it would cause

(A) lime-induced chlorosis (B) the acidity of the soil to increase to a point which is not favorable for plant growth (C) the alkalinity of the soil to increase to a point which is not favorable for plant growth (D) the rapid release of ammonia.

9. Which one of these materials will increase the water-holding capacity of the soil most?

(A) bonemeal (B) lime (C) peat (D) potash.

10. The addition of humus to the soil does <u>not</u>

(A) increase its water holding capacity (B) modify soil structure (C) prevent leaching of soluble plant foods (D) slow up bacterial action.

11. An advantage of leaving grass clippings on the lawn is that it

(A) helps maintain the humus supply in the soil (B) prevents the grass roots from becoming too wet (C) protects the roots from the drying effects of wind and sun (D) tends to make the soil more compact.

12. Which one of the following is <u>least</u> important for satisfactory growth of lawn grasses?

(A) iron (B) nitrogen (C) phosphorus (D) potash.

13. Moss in a lawn is usually a sign of

(A) bad soil drainage (B) low soil fertility (C) poor soil texture (D) soil acidity.

14. The best time for sowing lawn grasses is usually the

(A) early autumn (B) early spring (C) late winter (D) summer.

15. Which one is <u>not</u> usually a cause of brown spots in a lawn?

(A) burning from unequal distribution of fertilizer (B) excessive soil acidity (C) fungus diseases (D) unfavorable weather conditions.

16. Which one of the following statements about crabgrass is <u>not</u> true?

(A) it is an annual (B) it is killed by the first light frost (C) its seed germinates in the fall (D) it thrives in the full sun.

17. A disadvantage of using rotted manure as a lawn fertilizer is that it

(A) increases the number of soil bacteria (B) often brings weed seeds into the lawn (C) often burns the roots of grass (D) usually burns the blades of grass.

18. A chemical effective for the control of crabgrass is

(A) chlordane (B) corrosive sublimate (C) dieldrin (D) potassium cyanate.

19. Kentucky bluegrass does <u>not</u>

(A) germinate more slowly than many other permanent lawn grasses (B) prefer a cool climate (C) require abundant moisture (D) require a highly acid soil.

20. The grass which must usually be established by means of stolons is

(A) creeping bent (B) Kentucky bluegrass (C) perennial ryegrass (D) redtop.

21. Lawns should be rolled lightly

(A) at least twice during the summer (B) before the frost sets in (C) during the winter (D) not more than once or twice during the spring.

22. Which one of these grasses is <u>least</u> suitable for use in a mixture for a dry, shady location?

(A) chewings fescue (B) colonial bent (C) Kentucky bluegrass (D) redtop.

23. In the planting of a new lawn, the best way to add lime to a highly acid soil is

(A) in one application after growth has started (B) in one application before seeding (C) in several applications after growth has started (D) in several applications before seeding.

24. "Organic fertilizers which are to be applied to lawns should supply nitrogen from a number of sources." This recommendation should be followed mainly because it will

(A) avoid the chance of poor nutrition due to poor products if the nitrogen is supplied from only one source (B) avoid the danger of delayed nitrogen burn since the nitrogen will be released over a period of time (C) make it possible to apply the fertilizer at any time of the year (D) make the soil neutral.

25. A characteristic of bent grasses is that they

(A) are less subject to attacks from fungus diseases than most other lawn grasses (B) are not tolerant of soil acidity (C) can stand close mowing (D) do well on dry soils.

Each of questions 26 to 30 gives the botanical or scientific name of some common plant material. For each one, select the correct common name from Column I and blacken the proper space on your answer sheet.

		Column I
26.	ilex	(A) firethorn
27.	ligustrum	(B) holly
28.	lonicera	(C) honeysuckle
29.	pyracantha	(D) lilac
30.	syringa	(E) privet

31. The chief purpose of the process of the "heeling-in" of shrubs is to

(A) improve their form (B) keep their roots from drying out (C) prevent the invasion of weeds (D) promote their natural increase in number.

32. Of the following, the best time for transplanting deciduous trees and shrubs is generally

(A) early spring (B) early summer (C) late summer (D) mid-winter.

33. Which best describes foliar feeding?

(A) leaves getting food from the rest of the plant (B) leaves making food for the rest of the plant (C) leaves taking in food for the rest of the plant (D) roots taking in food for the rest of the plant.

34. Which one of these shrubs has a preference for lime?

(A) azalea (B) firethorn (C) pieris (floribunda) (D) rhododendron.

35. Which one of the following groups of shrubs is most likely to provide blooms throughout the spring?.

(A) catawba rhododendron, sweet pepperbush, swamp rose (B) hydrangea, rose of sharon, golden bells (C) witch hazel (hamamelis), flowering quince, golden bells (D) witch hazel (hamamelis), rose of sharon, catawba rhododendron.

36. Which one of these is an evergreen shrub?

(A) cornus paniculata (gray dogwood) (B) rhododendron catawbiense (C) spiraea thunbergi (D) viburnum tomentosum.

37. Which one of the following is best to put in the bottom of a hole dug for planting a bare-rooted tree?

(A) complete fertilizer (B) fresh manure (C) lime (D) topsoil.

38. Which one of these will grow best in a wet location?

(A) Japanese barberry (berberis thunbergi) (B) rugosa rose (C) sweet pepper bush (clethra alnifolia) (D) wayfaring tree (viburnum lantana)

39. Pruning is <u>not</u> usually done in order to

(A) control the structure of a tree or shrub (B) improve the appearance of a plant (C) increase the height to which a plant grows (D) increase the quantity and quality of flowers and fruit.

40. For most evergreen hedges, the best season of the year for clipping is

(A) spring (B) summer (C) autumn (D) winter.

Each of questions 41 to 45 gives the name of a bulb, corm, or tuber which may be classified under one of the headings in Column II. For each one, select the heading from Column II under which it is most correctly classified and blacken the proper space on your answer sheet.

		Column II
41.	begonia	(A) spring-flowering
42.	caladium	(B) summer-flowering
43.	colchicum	(C) autumn-flowering
44.	hyacinth	
45.	narcissus	

46. Which one is most likely to be needed by perennials during periods when there is a great deal of rain?

(A) calcium (B) ground limestone (C) sulphate of ammonia (D) super phosphate.

47. "Pinching back" is the

(A) nipping out of a terminal bud of a plant to help the plant become bushy
(B) pruning of leaves which have shrivelled from an early frost
(C) removal of leaves of a plant close to the main stem
(D) shrivelling of the leaf tips of a plant from fungus infection.

48. Clumps of some perennials must be divided after a few years in order for them to continue to thrive. A perennial which should be lifted and divided <u>every</u> year is

(A) chrysanthemum (B) hardy aster (C) peony (D) phlox.

49. It is recommended that a good complete fertilizer be applied to perennials twice a year. The best time to make this application is in

(A) early spring before active growth and in late summer (B) early summer and in the fall (C) spring after active growth and in early summer (D) spring after active growth and in late summer.

Each of questions 50 to 53 gives the name of a plant which may be classified under one of the descriptions of color of blooms in Column III. For each plant, select the description from Column III which best describes the usual color of bloom and blacken the proper space on your answer sheet.

		Column III
50.	Cockscomb	(A) blue or pink
51.	Forget-me-not	(B) greenish-yellow
52.	Mignonette	(C) white
53.	Sweet alyssum	(D) yellow to crimson

54. Of the following annuals, the one which will best tolerate poor quality soil is

(A) gypsophila (B) petunia (C) rocket larkspur (D) zinnia.

55. The one of the following plants which is a biennial is

(A) candytuft (B) canterbury bells (C) marigold (D) snapdragon.

56. The one of the following plants which is most suitable as a ground cover is

(A) creeping charlie (B) ground ivy (C) Japanese honeysuckle
(D) Japanese pachysandra.

57. Of the following plants used for ground cover, the one which is evergreen is

(A) candytuft (iberis sempervirens) (B) forget-me-nots (myosotis palustris semperflorens) (C) lemon thyme (thymus citriodorus) (D) wall pepper (sedum acre).

58. "Hedges under trees are usually unsatisfactory." The chief reason for this is that

(A) diseased trees may result in diseased hedges (B) the landscape becomes too monotonous (C) the tree roots are competing with the hedges for nourishment (D) trimming the hedge becomes more difficult.

59. The one of the following plants which generally requires more than one trimming a year when used as a hedge is

(A) arborvitae (B) hemlock (C) privet (D) yew.

60. Of the following, the main advantage in using Euonymus alatus (winged burningbush) as a hedge is that it

(A) grows best in shade (B) grows to a maximum height of 3 feet (C) produces bright-red flowers in July and August (D) requires no clipping.

61. Of the following, the best shape for a formal, clipped hedge is

(A) taller than it is wide (B) wider at the bottom than at the top (C) wider at the top than at the bottom (D) wider than it is tall.

Each of questions 62 to 65 gives the name of a shrub which may be classified under one of the heights of growth in Column IV. For each shrub, select the height in Column IV which best describes its normal height of growth and blacken the proper space on your answer sheet.

		Column IV
62.	Beauty Bush (Kolkwitzia amabilis)	(A) $1\frac{1}{2}$ to 3 feet
63.	Garden lilac (Syringa vulgaris)	(B) 4 to 8 feet
64.	Mountain andromeda (Pieris floribunda)	(C) 8 to 15 feet
65.	Vanhoutte spirea (Spiraea Vanhouttei)	

66. Dieldrin is a chemical used most frequently

(A) as a dormant spray in early spring (B) as a fungicide (C) to arrest spore production (D) to grub-proof lawns.

67. Snow mold is a type of

(A) coldframe used during winter snow (B) fungus disease (C) soil rich in humus (D) winter grass.

Each of questions 68 to 73 gives the name of a chemical compound used in gardening which may be classified under one of the headings in Column V. For each chemical compound, select the heading from Column V under which it is most correctly classified and blacken the proper space on your answer sheet.

		Column V
68.	actidione	(A) antibiotic
69.	captan	(B) organic fungicide
70.	carolate	(C) systemic fungicide
71.	demeton	(D) systemic insecticide
72.	fermate	
73.	sodium selenate	

74. In gardening, arsenate of lead is most commonly used as a

(A) contact insecticide (B) fungicide (C) soil conditioner (D) stomach poison.

Each of questions 75 to 80 gives the name of an insect which may be classified under one of the headings in Column VI. For each insect, select the heading from Column VI under which it is most correctly classified and blacken the proper space on your answer sheet.

		Column VI
75.	aphid	(A) insect with chewing mouth parts
76.	beetle	(B) insect with sucking mouth parts
77.	caterpillar	
78.	grasshopper	
79.	leaf-hopper	
80.	scale	

81. When used in pruning, the pruning saw with teeth on both edges is

(A) best for removing large limbs (B) best for removing small limbs
(C) likely to cause injury to the worker, no matter how careful he is
(D) likely to wound the tree when used in close quarters.

82. Of the following statements about the standard steel rake, the one that is most correct is that it is

(A) easier to use than any other rake (B) suitable for all raking duties
(C) the least expensive rake on the market (D) used particularly for working the soil.

83. The common garden hoe, when used for weeding, should be handled as a

(A) chopping or slicing tool (B) digging tool (C) drawing tool
(D) pushing and pulling tool.

84. In gathering leaves and twigs, the large wooden rake should be used with

(A) brush strokes, like a broom (B) long sliding strokes, the teeth being lifted only to clear the debris (C) push and pull strokes, avoiding tearing the sod (D) pushing strokes in two directions, at right angles, over the whole planted area.

85. Thoroughly coating the inside of the galvanized iron tank of a hand sprayer with black asphaltum will

(A) add elements beneficial to plant life to the contents of the sprayer
(B) increase the efficiency of the sprayer (C) lengthen the life of the tank
(D) purify the water going through the tank.

86. If a garden tool becomes very dull, a new edge is best developed by using

(A) a carborundum wheel (B) a file (C) an oilstone (D) a whetstone.

87. A pointed tool used to make holes in soft ground for planting bulbs or setting small plants is known as a

(A) dibble (B) hand cultivator (C) spiker (D) spud.

88. The main reason why pruning shears should be kept sharp is to prevent

(A) extra tension between blade cutting edges (B) rust from forming on the blades (C) the user's hand from being pinched (D) unnecessary damage to the plant when pruning.

89. Of the following, the tool that is most useful in firming newly laid sod is the

(A) half-moon edger (B) sod beater (C) sod-cutting iron (D) spading fork.

90. Before storing a power lawn mower at the end of the season, it is wise to

(A) drain the crankcase and fill with fresh oil (B) fill the gasoline tank
(C) remove the air filter (D) rinse the oil filter in gasoline, but leave the oil in.

91. Suppose that you are promoted to gardener. You find that some of the tools given you need either repair or replacement. You should

(A) delay the operations requiring the use of these tools and work only on other jobs until your supervisor becomes aware of the situation (B) report the condition of your tools to your supervisor immediately (C) wait until you are sure of your job before you complain about any conditions of work (D) work with the equipment you have as best you can and wait until the end of the budget year to report your equipment needs.

92. Suppose you notice that two assistant gardeners under your supervision get into arguments whenever they work together on a job. You should first

(A) find out what is causing the arguments between them (B) recommend that one of the employees be transferred from your supervision (C) report the situation to your foreman (D) warn both that if this happens again you will have to take severe disciplinary action.

93. In a report requesting replacement of inadequate gardening tools, it would be least important to include

(A) a recommendation as to the types of tools to be purchased (B) the reason why the tools cannot be used any longer (C) the titles of employees who will be using these tools (D) the types of tools needing replacement.

94. Suppose that an employee working for you falls off a truck and suffers a head injury. You should

(A) give the employee first aid and call a doctor (B) immediately call a taxi and send the employee home (C) send the employee to the borough office for examination (D) send the employee to the nearest police precinct to report the accident and for first aid treatment.

95. Suppose that a temporary assistant gardener is assigned to you to help with a particular summer project in one of the City parks. The first day on the job he returns from his lunch hour one-half hour late. You should

(A) dismiss the employee since there is no point in training an obviously poor worker (B) explain the rules of the Department to him and warn him not to repeat this action (C) overlook the action since this is only a temporary worker (D) suspend the employee for the day with proper salary deduction.

96. If you find that the crew of men you supervise tend to be careless in the use of tools, you should

(A) ask that you be given another crew to work with (B) call each man aside and talk to him privately about this (C) call the men together at a meeting to discuss the problem (D) personally issue all tools yourself.

97. As gardener, you are assigned to be in charge of a number of temporary workers who are to report to you the following day for a special assignment. You find that you cannot be present that day because of urgent personal business. You should

(A) assign an experienced assistant gardener to substitute for you (B) contact the temporary workers and advise them to report the day after (C) leave written instructions for the workers as to how to proceed with the job (D) report the facts to your supervisor and await further instructions.

98. Of the following, the best way for a gardener to get the co-operation of his subordinates is to

(A) set low standards of work performance (B) be informal and make friends with his workers (C) be fair and co-operative himself (D) be easy going in applying Department rules and regulations.

99. Of the following, the most important reason for a gardener to regularly check the work of the employees under him is to

(A) be able to give the employees a service rating at the end of the year (B) increase the output of these employees (C) let the men see that he is interested in their progress (D) make sure that the work is being performed satisfactorily.

100. When assigning work to his employees, a gardener should

(A) be sure to give the same amount of work to each (B) consider each employee's individual ability and special skills (C) give the most work to the employee who usually shirks his responsibilities (D) give the simple jobs to those who have been in the Department the longest.

Correct Answers For The Foregoing Questions

(Please try to answer the questions on your own before looking at our answers. You'll do much better on your test if you follow this rule.)

1.B	14.A	27.E	40.A	53.C	65.B	77.A	89.B
2.D	15.B	28.C	41.B	54.B	66.D	78.A	90.A
3.A	16.C	29.A	42.B	55.B	67.B	79.B	91.B
4.B	17.B	30.D	43.C	56.D	68.A	80.B	92.A
5.B	18.D	31.B	44.A	57.A	69.B	81.D	93.C
6.C	19.D	32.A	45.A	58.C	70.C	82.B	94.A
7.D	20.A	33.C	46.C	59.C	71.D	83.A	95.B
8.D	21.D	34.B	47.A	60.D	72.B	84.B	96.C
9.C	22.C	35.C	48.B	61.B	73.D	85.C	97.D
10.D	23.D	36.B	49.C	62.B	74.D	86.A	98.C
11.A	24.B	37.D	50.D	63.C	75.B	87.A	99.D
12.A	25.C	38.C	51.A	64.A	76.A	88.D	100.B
13.B	26.B	39.C	52.B				

TEST____________________ PART____________

DATE____________

RATING

(Slightly reduced from standard size used with many tests)

USE THE SPECIAL PENCIL. MAKE GLOSSY BLACK MARKS.

A B C D E	A B C D E	A B C D E	A B C D E	A B C D E
1	26	51	76	101
2	27	52	77	102
3	28	53	78	103
4	29	54	79	104
5	30	55	80	105
6	31	56	81	106
7	32	57	82	107
8	33	58	83	108
9	34	59	84	109
10	35	60	85	110

Make only ONE mark for each answer. Additional and stray marks may be counted as mistakes. In making corrections, erase errors COMPLETELY.

A B C D E	A B C D E	A B C D E	A B C D E	A B C D E
1	36	61	86	111
12	37	62	87	112
13	38	63	88	113
14	39	64	89	114
15	40	65	90	115
16	41	66	91	116
17	42	67	92	117
18	43	68	93	118
19	44	69	94	119
20	45	70	95	120
21	46	71	96	121
22	47	72	97	122
23	48	73	98	123
24	49	74	99	124
25	50	75	100	125

TEAR OUT ALONG THIS LINE AND MARK YOUR ANSWERS AS INSTRUCTED IN THE TEXT

V. PREVIOUS EXAM FOR PRACTICE

Plan to test yourself somewhere around the midpoint of your studies with this real civil service examination. People now working in the job you want were successful on this examination. You're bound to do well, also, if you've followed our advice so far . . . if you have by now taken soundings in all the different exam subjects covered by this book. You should be developing a picture of your strengths and weaknesses. And you should begin to concentrate on your weak points. Test yourself analytically and clarify your self-knowledge.

The time allowed for the entire examination is 2½ hours. In order to create the climate of the test to come, that's precisely what you should allow yourself . . . no more, no less. Use a watch and keep a record of your time, especially since you may find it convenient to take the test in several sittings.

DIRECTIONS: For each of the following statements, mark T if the statement is True, and F if it is False.

1. A bed of leaves or straw on the surface of the ground around plants helps to keep down loss of moisture from the soil.
2. An evergreen tree is one which does not shed its leaves each year.
3. All insects are harmful to plant life.
4. Hedges should never be used as a border around walks and other landscaped areas.
5. When hedges are pruned it is considered good practice to cut them wider at the top than at the bottom in order to allow light to reach the bottom branches.
6. Leaves mixed with the soil will in time rot and add plant food to the soil.
7. The usual reason why a tree guard is placed around a young tree is to protect the tree from possible injury.
8. During periods of hot weather it is desirable to give lawns a light watering.
9. The fall is usually the best time to sow lawn grass seed.
10. If a plant loses its leaves in the fall of every year it shows that the plant has not been planted properly.
11. Sandy soils drain quickly and dry rapidly.
12. Animal manures added to the soil improve the condition of the soil.

13. It is often hard to grow grass under a tree because the roots of the tree take away most of the water and plant food from the grass.

14. Any rust found on garden tools during the summer should be removed the following spring.

15. An assistant gardener should know the tool best suited for each type of work so that the work involved will be made easier.

16. After use in gardening, tools should be stored in a cellar or basement because the dampness there is good for the metal parts.

17. As a help in keeing a good edge on tools, earth and grass clippings should be removed from the tools immediately after they are used.

18. A four-pronged spading fork is a good tool for digging up a garden area.

19. Chemicals used to kill plant insects usually can be applied only in a dissolved liquid form.

20. If a growing plant is to be moved from one spot to another it is good practice to first dig the new hole before digging up the plant that is to be moved in order to lessen the drying out of the roots.

21. Rapidly running water from an unattended hose can cause soil to wash off sloping planted areas.

22. An assistant gardener who comes late to work often, should expect his superiors to pay no attention to this lateness if his work is excellent.

23. It is all right for an assistant gardener to give members of the public parts of plants growing in city parks provided he cuts off the parts very carefully.

24. An assistant gardener at work who sees a person throwing rubbish on the ground in a park should pay no attention as this is a matter for the Sanitation Department.

25. If your superior gives you an assignment which you do not like you should try to do a good job anyway.

26. If you know in advance that you will not be able to report for work next Thursday you should tell your superior immediately rather than wait to telephone him on the day of your absence.

Your answers to questions 27 to 29 must be based only on the information given in the following paragraph and not upon any other information you may have.

"It has long been customary to wrap damp sphagnum moss, peat moss or wood shavings around the roots and crowns of plants to prevent loss of moisture from living tissues during storage or in transit. The use of these materials have two major disadvantages. They make heavy, bulky packages which adds to the cost in mail-order shipping. And, in the case of dormant stock, if the moisture content of the packing is too high the plants may prematurely start into new growth."

27. It has been customary to wrap sphagnum moss around the roots and crown of plants to prevent loss of moisture during storage or in transit.

28. A cost factor in mail-order shipping is the bulkiness of the package.

29. Plants cannot start into new growth if the moisture content of the packing is too high.

Your answers to questions 30 to 35 must be based only on the information given in the following paragraph and not upon any other information you may have.

"Lawn mowers as well lawns suffer when the grass is cut too short. There is much more dust and dirt on the base of the blades of grass, near the soil, than there is higher up. This grit wears away the blades and the strike bar and quickly dulls them. Other bad practices are leaving the mower out overnight and failing to wipe the cutting edges dry after each mowing. A couple of dewy nights, a session with wet grass, and the sharp edge has rusted. The simple measure of wiping an oily rag across the edges of the blades and the cutting bar will prevent rusting of these important surfaces."

30. When the grass is cut too short the lawn mower suffers.

31. There is more dirt on the base of a blade of grass than there is higher up.

32. The blades and the strike bar of a lawn mower are sharpened by the grit of the soil.

33. It is bad practice to leave the mower out overnight.

34. After each mowing the cutting edges of a mower should be wiped dry.

35. Wiping the edges of the blades and the cutting bar with an oily rag will not prevent rusting.

Your answers to questions 36 to 42 must be based only on the information given in the following paragraph and not upon any other information you may have.

"There are many organic fertilizers that can be used not only to add nutrients to the soil, but also to help build up humus content and thus increase its water-holding capacity. The organic fertilizers are those derived entirely from animal or vegetable sources, while inorganic kinds are chemical. The most readily available, complete organic fertilizers are the manures and these alone do not contain enough nutrients to satisfy a garden for a whole season. Application of one or more kinds of manure to the soil is excellent in the spring and again in the fall."

36. Organic fertilizers can be used to help build up the humus content of the soil.

37. Nutrients cannot be added to the soil through the use of organic fertilizers.

38. Inorganic fertilizers are chemical ones.

39. The organic fertilizers are derived from vegetable or animal sources.

40. The manures are the most readily available complete, organic fertilizer.

41. The manures contain enough nutrients to satisfy a garden for a whole season.

42. Application of manure to the soil is excellent in the spring and in the fall.

Your answers to questions 43 to 55 must be based only on the information given in the following paragraph and not upon any other information you may have.

"If roses are to bloom well they should not be neglected. Of the several measures to be taken, watering is one of the most important. A weekly soil soaking is recommended. Moisture should go down to the roots of the plants, where it is vitally needed, to a depth of about six inches. Taking the nozzle off the hose and letting water trickle into the soil is one way to do this.

"A four-inch layer of mulch on the surface of the soil will protect the roots of the rose plants against heat, cold and draught. Suitable mulches for roses include partly rotted stable manure, peat moss, compost, and even grass clippings. Peat moss is best worked lightly into the surface of the soil; otherwise, it is apt to form a crust.

"Rose plants are susceptible to black spot, mildew and the ravages of insects. It is advisable, therefore, to dust or spray rose plants at least once a week. Regular applications are necessary, covering both upper and under sides of the foliage. A well-nourished rose plant is more likely to resist disease than a weakened one. Any of the well-balanced commercially prepared rose food will stimulate growth and bloom. It should be applied around the base of the plants at intervals of about three weeks and watered in well. It is not advisable to fertilize rose plants after September first."

43. Watering of roses is the least important of the measures to be taken to insure good rose bloom.

44. Moisture should go down around the rose plant to a depth of about three inches.

45. Removing the nozzle from the hose and letting the water trickle into the soil is a method of getting water to the roots of the plants.

46. The roots of rose plants will be protected against heat, cold and draught by a four-inch layer of mulch on the surface of the soil.

47. Grass clippings are not suitable as a mulch for roses.

48. Peat moss which is not worked into the surface of the soil is apt to form a crust.

49. Rose plants are susceptible to black spot and mildew.

50. Rose plants should not be dusted or sprayed more than once a month.

51. It is necessary to apply a spray or dust on the under side of the foliage only.

52. A rose plant is more likely to resist disease if it is well nourished.

53. A well-balanced commercially prepared rose food will stimulate growth and bloom of the rose plant.

54. The rose food should be applied to the plant once during the growing season.

55. Rose plants should be fertilized up to November 1st.

Your answers to questions 56 to 62 must be based only on the information given in the following paragraph and not upon any other information you may have.

"In dry weather, after a few minutes of light sprinkling, the surface soil may become muddy and the inexperienced gardener is fooled into believing that enough water has been applied. Actually the water may not even reach the roots. The roots may be in an almost powdery dry earth below a thin layer of mud from which the water quickly evaporates. Deep roots thus get no benefit while shallow roots are attracted to the upper surface of the soil and are worse off than if no sprinkling had been done. Sprinkling should always be continued on any one spot until the soil has become drenched. The best time of the day to sprinkle is toward or during the evening because usually the air is cooler and evaporation losses will be reduced to a minimum.

56. A few minutes of light sprinkling in dry weather may make the surface of the soil become muddy.

57. After a few minutes of light sprinkling in dry weather the water may not even reach the roots.

58. Deep roots get no benefit from a light sprinkling.

59. Shallow roots are better off with a light sprinkling than with no sprinkling.

60. Sprinkling should not be continued on any one spot for so long that the soil becomes drenched.

61. The best time of day to sprinkle is toward or during evening.

62. The least amount of evaporation loss occurs during the evening because the air is usually cooler then.

63. "Some plants are grown for the decorative value of their leaves." In this sentence, the word 'decorative' means nearly the same as 'ornamental'.

64. "They made a circular flower garden." In this sentence, the word 'circular' means nearly the same as 'square'.

65. "The gardener was a conscientious worker." In this sentence, the word 'conscientious' means nearly the same as 'lazy'.

66. "A decaying branch is dangerous to the life of a tree." In this sentence, the word 'decaying' means nearly the same as 'rotting'.

67. "Shearing helps keep the plants in the shape required." In this sentence, the word 'shearing' means nearly the same as 'watering'.

68. "Some shrubs have vigorous growth and early flowering." In this sentence, the word 'vigorous' means nearly the same as 'weak'.

69. "The lawn retained its healthy green color." In this sentence, the word 'retained' means nearly the same as 'kept'.

70. "The soil is combined with an acid plant food." In this sentence, the word 'combined' means nearly the same as 'mixed'.

71. "Gardening can be tiring without the right tools." In this sentence, the word 'tiring' means nearly the same as 'amusing'.

72. "With the ground saturated the roots may die." In this sentence, the word 'saturated' means nearly the same as 'soaked'.

73. "Air can penetrate freely if holes are made in the soil." In this sentence, the word 'penetrate' means nearly the same as 'escape'.

74. "With some plants flowers precede the growth of leaves." In this sentence, the word 'precede' means nearly the same as 'follow'.

75. "The gardener anticipated frost." In this sentence, the word 'anticipated' means nearly the same as 'expected'.

76. "Tools are assembled when the job is finished." In this sentence, the word 'assembled' means nearly the same as 'cleaned'.

77. "Part of the area was set aside for a miniature rock garden." In this sentence, the word 'miniature' means nearly the same as 'beautiful'.

78. "Cheap tools are seldom durable." In this sentence, the word 'durable' means nearly the same as 'long lasting'.

79. "Concrete walks are maintained clean easily." In this sentence, the word 'maintained' means nearly the same as 'kept'.

80. "Each morning the assistant gardener was punctual in reporting to work." In this sentence, the word 'punctual' means nearly the same as 'prompt'.

81. "The landscaping work was a prolonged task." In this sentence, the word 'prolonged' means nearly the same as 'difficult'.

82. "A transparent removable cover was placed over the flower bed." In this sentence, the word 'transparent' means nearly the same as 'wooden'.

83. The present New York City sales tax is three per cent.

84. The Comptroller of the City of New York is appointed by the Mayor.

85. The President of the City Council is elected by a majority vote of the members of the City Council.

86. A good part of the money needed to run the city government comes out of taxes on real estate.

87. The population of New York City is less than 7 million.

88. An anti-polio vaccine has been developed by Dr. Jonas E. Salk.

89. The Police Commissioner of New York City is Robert Moses.

90. New York City is made up of six boroughs.

91. An auto use tax must be paid by all car owners living in New York City for each car owned.

92. Income taxes are collected by both the United States Government and the New York State Government.

93. A member of the local law-making body is known as an Alderman.

94. If a group of assistant gardeners planted 1,278 plants in zone A, 1,262 plants in zone B, 1,020 plants in zone C and 793 plants in zone D, then the total number of plants planted by this group in these 4 zones was between 4,450 to 4,500.

95. If an assistant gardener assigned to a job does 1/3 of the work on Monday, 1/3 of the work on Wednesday and the remainder on Friday, then the part of the work done by him on Friday is 1/3 of the whole job

96. If an assistant gardener can dig up 150 square yards of lawn area every 3 hours, then in 5 hours he can dig up 350 square yards of lawn area.

97. If a gardener rejects 12 spades out of a total shipment of 48, then the number of spades that he rejected is 25 per cent of the total.

98. If 4 assistant gardeners planted a total of 60 shrubs a day for a period of 22 days, then the total number of shrubs planted by these 4 in these 22 days was between 1,300 and 1,400.

99. If a park department spent $14.50 for rose bushes, **$76,15 for lawn seed, $20.00** for lime and $36.80 for **tulip bulbs, then the total amount of money spent by the** department for these items **was $137.45.**

100. If 165 plants are **distributed equally among 15 parks, then each park will get 11 plants.**

Correct Answers For The Foregoing Questions

(Please try to answer the questions on your own before looking at our answers. You'll do much better on your test if you follow this rule.)

1.T	14.F	27.OMIT	40.T	53.T	65.F	77.F	89.F
2.T	15.T	28.T	41.F	54.F	66.T	78.T	90.F
3.F	16.F	29.F	42.T	55.F	67.F	79.T	91.OMIT
4.F	17.T	30.T	43.F	56.T	68.F	80.T	92.T
5.F	18.T	31.T	44.F	57.T	69.T	81.F	93.F
6.T	19.F	32.F	45.T	58.T	70.T	82.F	94.F
7.T	20.T	33.T	46.T	59.F	71.F	83.T	95.T
8.F	21.T	34.T	47.F	60.F	72.T	84.F	96.F
9.T	22.F	35.F	48.T	61.T	73.F	85.F	97.T
10.F	23.F	36.T	49.T	62.T	74.F	86.T	98.T
11.T	24.F	37.F	50.F	63.T	75.T	87.F	99.F
12.T	25.T	38.T	51.F	64.F	76.F	88.T	100.T
13.T	26.T	39.T	52.T	65.F	77.F	89.F	

Practice Using Answer Sheets

DIRECTIONS: Read each question or statement. When you have decided the statement is true or false, blacken the corresponding space on this sheet with a No. 2 pencil. Make your mark as long as the pair of lines, and completely fill the area between the pair of lines. If you change your mind, erase your first mark COMPLETELY. Make no stray marks; they may count against you.

SAMPLE

1. CHICAGO IS A CITY — 1 T F
2. PHILADELPHIA IS A STATE — 2 T F

SCORES

1 ______ 5 ______
2 ______ 6 ______
3 ______ 7 ______
4 ______ 8 ______

1 T F	2 T F	3 T F	4 T F	5 T F	6 T F	7 T F	8 T F
9	10	11	12	13	14	15	16
17	18	19	20	21	22	23	24
25 T F	26 T F	27 T F	28 T F	29 T F	30 T F	31 T F	32 T F
33	34	35	36	37	38	39	40
41	42	43	44	45	46	47	48
49 T F	50 T F	51 T F	52 T F	53 T F	54 T F	55 T F	56 T F
57	58	59	60	61	62	63	64
65	66	67	68	69	70	71	72
73 T F	74 T F	75 T F	76 T F	77 T F	78 T F	79 T F	80 T F
81	82	83	84	85	86	87	88
89	90	91	92	93	94	95	96
97	98	99	100				
				101 T F	102 T F	103 T F	104 T F

105 T F	106 T F	107 T F	108 T F	109	110	111	112
113	114	115	116	117	118	119	120
121	122	123	124	125	126	127	128
129 T F	130 T F	131 T F	132 T F	133 T F	134 T F	135 T F	136 T F
137	138	139	140	141	142	143	144
145	146	147	148	149	150	151	152
153 T F	154 T F	155 T F	156 T F	157 T F	158 T F	159 T F	160 T F
161	162	163	164	165	166	167	168
169	170	171	172	173	174	175	176
177 T F	178 T F	179 T F	180 T F	181 T F	182 T F	183 T F	184 T F
185	186	187	188	189	190	191	192
193	194	195	196	197	198	199	200

201 T F	202 T F	203 T F	204 T F	205 T F	206 T F	207 T F	208 T F
209	210	211	212	213	214	215	216
217	218	219	220	221	222	223	224
225 T F	226 T F	227 T F	228 T F	229 T F	230 T F	231 T F	232 T F
233	234	235	236	237	238	239	240
241	242	243	244	245	246	247	248
249 T F	250 T F	251 T F	252 T F	253 T F	254 T F	255 T F	256 T F
257	258	259	260	261	262	263	264
265	266	267	268	269	270	271	272
273 T F	274 T F	275 T F	276 T F	277 T F	278 T F	279 T F	280 T F
281	282	283	284	285	286	287	288
289	290	291	292	293	294	295	296
297	298	299	300				

TEAR OUT ALONG THIS LINE AND MARK YOUR ANSWERS AS INSTRUCTED IN THE TEXT

VI. FINAL REVIEW EXAMINATION

Plan on taking this test last, after you have gone through the entire book and after you have done all your testing, probing, and concentrated study on subjects in which, at first, you found yourself weak. It's a real civil service test for the very job you're trying to get. It provides an excellent summary and review of all that you have learned (or should have learned). Your score here will give you an honest statement of where you stand. Certainly, it should be better than your other scores. If you're not satisfied, there's still time. Go back and review your weaker subjects. Then test yourself again. If you show improvement, you may congratulate yourself on having picked up a few more points on the actual exam.

The time allowed for the entire examination is 3 hours. In order to create the climate of the test to come, that's precisely what you should allow yourself . . . no more, no less. Use a watch and keep a record of your time, especially since you may find it convenient to take the test in several sittings.

PREVIOUS TEST QUESTIONS FOR PRACTICE

1. In gardening, the main purpose of establishing good drainage in a planted area is to

   (A) confine the available water to the root area of plants (B) prevent the loss of needed moisture (C) provide additional moisture to growing plants (D) remove excess water from the planted area.

2. A disadvantage of the use of fresh barnyard manure for soil amendment is that such manure

   (A) has little plant food value (B) has many weed seeds (C) makes the soil too acid (D) makes the soil too wet.

3. Peat moss is LEAST valuable to use as a

   (A) plant food (B) rooting medium (C) soil conditioner (D) winter cover on the ground around the base of plants.

4. The addition of organic matter to the soil is often recommended. Of the following, the one which is NOT classed as organic matter is

   (A) leaf mold (B) lime (C) manure (D) peat moss.

5. The effect of lime when added to the soil is to

(A) give the soil a finer texture (B) make the soil more acid (C) make the soil more alkaline (D) provide plant food directly to the plants.

6. Of the following, the most accurate statement about humus is that it

(A) consists of decomposed animal and vegetable matter (B) has no plant food value (C) holds moisture poorly (D) is the mineral part of the soil.

7. "Clay soils should not be cultivated when they are wet." Of the following, the most important reason for this rule is that

(A) clay soils cannot be spaded when wet (B) excessive soil moisture will be lost by evaporation (C) moisture remaining on tools will cause them to rust (D) the soil will dry into a hard solid mass.

8. To "force" plants means to cause them to grow

(A) beyond their normal life cycle (B) earlier and more quickly than normally by providing them with unnaturally stimulating or favorable conditions (C) in a certain form or shape with the aid of physical supports and by pinching off all side growth (D) in an otherwise unfertile soil by limiting the number of plants to be grown in a given area.

9. To say that a seed has "germinated" means that it has

(A) become infected with a harmful plant disease (B) begun to grow into a plant (C) developed abnormally (D) rotted because of too much moisture.

10. The term "hardy" is usually applied to a plant which can

(A) be transplanted easily (B) go without water for a considerable period of time (C) live from year to year (D) withstand cold.

11. In gardening, to "broadcast" seed means to

(A) rake it into the soil (B) scatter it by hand (C) sow it in rows (D) test it for purity.

12. The term "green manure" usually refers to

(A) a crop grown to be plowed under so as to improve the soil (B) a freshly produced animal manure (C) a manure manufactured artificially out of chemicals (D) the material obtained from a compost pile.

13. To "mulch" means to

(A) allow a prepared seed bed to stay idle for several days before planting (B) cover the ground around plants with light litter such as leaves or straw (C) encourage excessive growth of plants by overfeeding (D) remove unwanted growth from plants.

14. A fertilizer that is readily "soluble"

(A) becomes available to plants for food very quickly after application (B) becomes "fixed" and held in the soil when applied (C) is not likely to be washed out of the soil in the drainage water and may be applied in large doses (D) must be dissolved before application.

15. Furnishing plants with an excessive amount of nitrogen results in

(A) abundant flower and fruit production but retarded stem and foliage growth (B) increased foliage, flower and fruit growth (C) increased root growth but reduced stem and foliage growth (D) luxuriant stem and foliage growth at the expense of flower and fruit production.

16. Of the following, a major purpose of the coldframe is to

(A) keep plants cold before transplanting (B) protect growing plants by supplying artificial heat (C) protect plants from burning by excessive sunlight (D) start seedlings in advance of the outdoor season.

17. Of the following hand tools used in the garden, the one which is the largest in overall size is the

(A) dibble (B) spading fork (C) trowel (D) Warren hoe.

18. Annuals are plants which

(A) complete their life cycle in one year and then die (B) flower every year (C) live from year to year (D) produce seed the second year of growth.

19. The dusting of plants to control insects and diseases is

(A) frequently done with materials that are also used as sprays (B) more effective than the spraying of plants for the same purpose (C) not recommended because of injury to the worker from inhalation of the dust (D) recommended only where the underside of the leaves cannot be reached by a spray.

20. The best time to sow lawn grass seed is usually in

(A) early summer (B) mid-summer (C) the fall (D) the spring.

21. If ground which has been newly prepared for a lawn area must remain idle for several days before seed is sown, it is desirable to rake the surface from time to time during this period with a steel garden rake. Of the following, the most important purpose of this raking is usually to

(A) destroy weed seedlings as they start to grow (B) fill in depressions (C) insure even distribution of fertilizer which has been applied (D) level off high spots.

22. In the planting and care of a new lawn it is NOT considered good practice to

(A) give the ground a light rolling after the seed has been sown and top-dressed (B) rake the soil just before the seed is sown (C) sow half the seed while walking back and forth in one direction and the other half while walking back and forth at right angles over the same area (D) water heavily till the seed germinates, then to water lightly.

23. In permanent lawn seed mixtures, the "nurse" grasses which are often included because they come up quickly and offer protection to the slower growing permanent grasses are

(A) fescues and redtop (B) Kentucky blue and fescues (C) Kentucky blue and rye (D) rye and redtop.

24. The kind of clover that is most commonly used in lawn seed mixtures is

(A) alsike clover (B) crimson clover (C) red clover (D) white clover.

25. It is most correct to state that crab grass is usually

(A) considered to be a lawn weed (B) included in lawn seed mixtures because it is quick to grow (C) nitrogen fixing (D) tall growing.

26. It is most correct to state that the dandelion

(A) has short, fine roots (B) is considered a lawn weed in this area (C) is distinguished by its large white flowers (D) will die when its top is cut.

27. A properly shaped formal hedge should be

(A) flat at the top (B) narrower at the bottom than at the top (C) narrower at the top than at the bottom (D) of the same width, top and bottom.

28. When privet hedges are planted, they are often cut back to within a few inches of the ground. The main purpose of this is usually to

(A) insure dense growth from the ground up (B) remove diseased or dead members (C) remove interfering branches (D) speed up root development.

29. Privet hedges are most commonly propagated by

(A) budding (B) dividing the stem of the parent plant (C) grafting (D) rooting cuttings in moist earth.

30. Of the following, the best way to store nursery stock which cannot be planted for a few days is to

(A) keep it in a tub of water (B) lay it flat on the ground in an exposed sunny location where it may receive the benefit of adequate light and air (C) lay the root end in a trench dug in the earth and cover with soil (D) unwrap it and put it in a dark, dry location.

31. Of the following, the LEAST important reason for cultivating the ground around a shrub border is to

(A) aerate the ground (B) break the crust that forms where wet soil dries (C) destroy surface roots (D) kill weeds.

Each of questions 32 to 40 gives the name of a plant which may be classified under one of the headings given in column I. In the correct space on your answer sheet write the capital letter preceding the group under which each plant is most correctly classified.

32. azalea

33. dogwood

34. forsythia

35. ginkgo

36. juniper

37. mountain-laurel

38. rhododendron

39. spiraea

40. spruce

COLUMN I

(A) narrow-leaved evergreen

(B) broad-leaved evergreen

(C) deciduous tree

(D) deciduous shrub

Each of questions 41 to 46 gives the name of a bulb, corm, or tuber. For each one, in the proper space on your answer sheet, write the letter A if it should be planted outdoors in the spring; write the letter B if it should be planted outdoors in the fall.

41. dahlia

42. gladiolus

43. hardy lily

44. hyacinth

45. narcissus

46. tulip

(A) should be planted outdoors in the spring

(B) should be planted outdoors in the fall

47. In the planting and growing of bulbs, a good procedure to follow is to

(A) allow a space about twice the diameter of a bulb between one bulb and the next (B) plant all bulbs at least 4 inches below the surface of the ground, regardless of size (C) plant spring flowering bulbs in November and December so as to prevent root formation in the fall (D) plant summer flowering bulbs the previous fall.

48. In the growing of bulbs and corms it is good practice to

(A) cut all foliage close to the ground shortly after the flowers have formed (B) leave the bulbs or corms in the ground until the foliage has completely matured and withered (C) leave all bulbs or corms undisturbed in the ground from year to year (D) lift the bulbs or corms from the ground as soon as the flowers have withered.

49. Of the following, the country from which most bulbs are imported into the United States is

(A) Denmark (B) France (C) Germany (D) Holland.

50. In the growth and culture of gladiolus corms it is most correct to state that

(A) corms measuring less than 2 inches in diameter will not give good blooms (B) small cormels are formed under the base of the old corm when the new corm fails to mature fully (C) the larger the root plate or basal area from which the roots arise, the younger the corm (D) the planted corm withers up during the growing period and a new one forms on top of it.

PART II

51. The one of the following which is LEAST suitable for use as a ground cover is

(A) English ivy (B) Japanese pachysandra (C) periwinkle (D) zinnia.

52. Pinching off the top of a growing annual will usually

(A) induce a tall, lanky growth (B) kill the plant (C) make the plant branch (D) stop further growth.

53. The one of the following which cannot usually be accomplished by pruning of a plant is

(A) an improvement in its form (B) an increase in its flower production (C) an increase in its structural strength (D) a permanent change in its natural growing habit.

54. The pruning of early spring flowering shrubs is best done

(A) a week or two after the flowers have fallen (B) in late summer (C) just before growth starts in the spring (D) while the shrubs are dormant.

55. The most accurate of the following statements about the Japanese beetle is that

(A) it is a chewing insect and can be controlled by the use of a stomach poison (B) it is injurious in its adult stage but harmless as a grub (C) it will attack the flowers but not the leaves of plants (D) the period of greatest feeding activity of the adult beetle in the New York City area occurs during June and July.

56. Aphids, the garden insects popularly called plant lice,

(A) are beneficial because they eat other harmful insects (B) are best controlled by using a stomach poison (C) eat the leaves of plants (D) feed by sucking the sap from plants.

57. Of the following insects, the one which is NOT generally considered benef[illegible] is the
(A) bee (B) ladybird beetle (C) praying mantis (D) red spider.

58. A 5-10-5 fertilizer contains approximately
(A) 5% nitrogen (B) 10% nitrogen (C) 20% nitrogen (D) 25% nitrogen.

59. Of the following, the most accurate statement about fertilizers is that

(A) an organic fertilizer should be wetted down as soon as it is applied (B) commercial or chemical fertilizers must be applied in heavy concentrations because of their low plant food content (C) some fertilizers consist of a combination of organic and inorganic materials (D) the plant food in an organic fertilizer becomes available to plants more quickly than the plant food in an inorganic fertilizer.

60. A "complete" fertilizer is one which contains

(A) nitrogen, phosphorus and potassium (B) nitrogen, phosphorus and sodium (C) nitrogen, potassium and calcium (D) nitrogen, potassium and iron.

61. Late summer application of nitrogenous fertilizer to woody plants is inadvisable mainly because

(A) frost-sensitive tender new growth is encouraged (B) nitrogenous fertilizer is not the best fertilizer for woody plants (C) the fertilizer will be leached away by spring thaw and rains before it can be used by the plants next summer (D) there is insufficient rainfall at this time.

62. The one of the following which supplies mainly phosphorus to plants is

(A) bonemeal (B) dried blood (C) nitrate of soda (D) wood ashes.

63. In the New York City area the average frost free date in the spring comes during the

(A) first half of March (B) second half of March (C) first half of April (D) second half of April.

64. In the New York City area the average first killing frost in the fall comes during the

(A) first half of October (B) second half of October (C) first half of November (D) second half of November.

65. The Long Island Agricultural and Technical Institute is located at

(A) Farmingdale (B) Garden City (C) Hempstead (D) Mineola.

66. The New York State College of Agriculture is located at

(A) Albany (B) Ithaca (C) Syracuse (D) Utica.

67. The practice of hilling or earthing-up soil around the roots of shrubs and hedges during the growing season is generally

(A) desirable mainly because it prevents sun scorch (B) desirable mainly because it roots the plants more firmly (C) undesirable mainly because it detracts from the appearance of normally attractive looking plants (D) undesirable mainly because it develops a shallow root system readily injured in a period of drought.

68. When propating plants by means of cuttings, the cuttings should

(A) be permanently planted as soon as they are removed from the parent plant
(B) be planted outdoors when they have developed sufficient root growth
(C) have all the leaves removed before they are placed in the rooting medium
(D) have foliage to the base of the stem when inserted in the rooting medium.

69. Conifers are

(A) bulbous plants (B) flower bearing shrubs (C) trees bearing fruit
(D) trees bearing woody cones.

70. The LEAST accurate of the following statements about the plane tree is that it

(A) has a dense maple-like foliage (B) has a tough bark which is difficult to remove (C) is also known as the buttonball tree (D) is frequently used for street planting.

71. In the trunk of a tree, the

(A) cambium is the growing portion of the trunk (B) heartwood is located next to the outer bark (C) sap flows down in the sapwood and up in the heartwood
(D) sap flows up and down in the innermost portion of the trunk.

72 Oak leafmold, when spaded into a neutral soil, will generally tend to

(A) make the soil acid (B) make the soil alkaline (C) make the soil more neutral (D) have no effect on the acidity or alkalinity of the soil.

73. The most accurate of the following statements is that arborvitae is

(A) a broad-leaved evergreen (B) an extremely rapid grower and requires very frequent clipping (C) suitable for use as hedge material (D) the botanical name for the genus commonly called Thuja.

74. A neutral soil is indicated by a pH reading of
(A) 1 (B) 7 (C) 14 (D) 20.

75. An alkaline soil is indicated if upon contact with the soil
(A) blue litmus paper turns purple (B) blue litmus paper turns white
(C) red litmus paper turns blue (D) red litmus paper turns green.

76. The one of the following which is LEAST suitable for use as formal hedge material is
(A) abelia (B) California privet (C) Japanese barberry (D) yew.

77. In gardening, a "herbaceous" plant is any plant which
(A) dies to the ground (B) is perennial (C) produces a flower (D) produces a fruit.

78. When, in pruning, a part of a twig or branch is cut off, the cut should be made
(A) about one quarter of an inch above a bud (B) halfway between two buds
(C) immediately above and as close to a bud as possible (D) just below a bud.

79. It is most correct to state that in the control of insect pests of plants
(A) contact insecticides are most often used against insects with biting and chewing mouth parts (B) copper compounds are most often used as contact insecticides (C) lead arsenate is most often used as a stomach poison
(D) stomach poisons are most often used against insects with piercing and sucking mouth parts.

80. Insecticides and fungicides which are "incompatible"
(A) are useless unless applied as a mixture (B) have a lasting effect (C) must be applied in liquid solution (D) will injure the plant if applied in combination.

81. The one of the following which is recommended for use against broad-leaved weeds in a lawn is
(A) chlordane (B) DDT (C) potassium cyanate (D) 2,4D.

82. Brown patch is a disease of grasses caused by
(A) fungus (B) an insect (C) excessive alkalinity (D) insufficient moisture.

83. Bordeaux mixture is most properly used as
(A) a fertilizer (B) a fungicide (C) an insecticide (D) a soil conditioner.

84. With regard to oil sprays, it is most correct to state that they are
(A) best applied during the summer months when insects are actively feeding
(B) best sprayed on the plant without diluting the oil with water (C) injurious to plant life and should not be used (D) used chiefly for spraying plants in a dormant condition.

85. Materials used to kill fungi which cause plant diseases usually consist of some form of

(A) arsenic (B) lead (C) sulphur (D) zinc.

86. Of the following flowering shrubs, the one which flowers latest is

(A) Almond (B) Althea (Rose-of-Sharon) (C) Lonicera Fragrantissima (Bush Honeysuckle) (D) Spiraea Vanhouttei (Bridal Wreath).

87. Of the following flowering shrubs, the one which flowers earliest is

(A) Buddleia (Butterfly-bush) (B) Common Lilac (C) Hydrangea (D) Weigela.

88. The one of the following which is an annual is

(A) Columbine (B) Cosmos (C) English Daisy (D) Lily-of-the-Valley.

Correct Answers For The Foregoing Questions

(Please try to answer the questions on your own before looking at our answers. You'll do much better on your test if you follow this rule.)

1.D	12.A	23.D	34.D	45.B	56.D	67.D	78.A
2.B	13.B	24.D	35.C	46.B	57.D	68.B	79.C
3.A	14.A	25.A	36.A	47.A	58.A	69.D	80.D
4.B	15.D	26.B	37.B	48.B	59.C	70.B	81.D
5.C	16.D	27.C	38.B	49.D	60.A	71.A	82.A
6.A	17.B,D	28.A	39.D	50.D	61.A	72.A	83.B
7.D	18.A	29.D	40.A	51.D	62.A	73.C	84.D
8.B	19.A	30.C	41.A	52.C	63.C	74.B	85.C
9.B	20.C	31.C	42.A	53.D	64.C	75.C	86.B
10.D	21.A	32.B,D	43.B	54.A	65.A	76.A	87.B
11.B	22.D	33.C,D	44.B	55.A	66.B	77.A	88.B

PART THREE

Basic Information Directly Connected With The Job

TEST____ PART____________________

DATE____________________

RATING

(Slightly reduced from standard size used with many tests)

USE THE SPECIAL PENCIL. MAKE GLOSSY BLACK MARKS.

1 A B C D E	26 A B C D E	51 A B C D E	76 A B C D E	101 A B C D E
2 A B C D E	27 A B C D E	52 A B C D E	77 A B C D E	102 A B C D E
3 A B C D E	28 A B C D E	53 A B C D E	78 A B C D E	103 A B C D E
4 A B C D E	29 A B C D E	54 A B C D E	79 A B C D E	104 A B C D E
5 A B C D E	30 A B C D E	55 A B C D E	80 A B C D E	105 A B C D E
6 A B C D E	31 A B C D E	56 A B C D E	81 A B C D E	106 A B C D E
7 A B C D E	32 A B C D E	57 A B C D E	82 A B C D E	107 A B C D E
8 A B C D E	33 A B C D E	58 A B C D E	83 A B C D E	108 A B C D E
9 A B C D E	34 A B C D E	59 A B C D E	84 A B C D E	109 A B C D E
10 A B C D E	35 A B C D E	60 A B C D E	85 A B C D E	110 A B C D E

Make only ONE mark for each answer. Additional and stray marks may be counted as mistakes. In making corrections, erase errors COMPLETELY.

11 A B C D E	36 A B C D E	61 A B C D E	86 A B C D E	111 A B C D E
12 A B C D E	37 A B C D E	62 A B C D E	87 A B C D E	112 A B C D E
13 A B C D E	38 A B C D E	63 A B C D E	88 A B C D E	113 A B C D E
14 A B C D E	39 A B C D E	64 A B C D E	89 A B C D E	114 A B C D E
15 A B C D E	40 A B C D E	65 A B C D E	90 A B C D E	115 A B C D E
16 A B C D E	41 A B C D E	66 A B C D E	91 A B C D E	116 A B C D E
17 A B C D E	42 A B C D E	67 A B C D E	92 A B C D E	117 A B C D E
18 A B C D E	43 A B C D E	68 A B C D E	93 A B C D E	118 A B C D E
19 A B C D E	44 A B C D E	69 A B C D E	94 A B C D E	119 A B C D E
20 A B C D E	45 A B C D E	70 A B C D E	95 A B C D E	120 A B C D E
21 A B C D E	46 A B C D E	71 A B C D E	96 A B C D E	121 A B C D E
22 A B C D E	47 A B C D E	72 A B C D E	97 A B C D E	122 A B C D E
23 A B C D E	48 A B C D E	73 A B C D E	98 A B C D E	123 A B C D E
24 A B C D E	49 A B C D E	74 A B C D E	99 A B C D E	124 A B C D E
25 A B C D E	50 A B C D E	75 A B C D E	100 A B C D E	125 A B C D E

GARDENER'S HANDBOOK

POINTERS ON MAKING GOOD LAWNS

FOURTEEN steps are necessary in making a good lawn.

1. Before excavation is started for the house, the top 5 or 6 inches of soil should be pushed off to one side until the building and grading operations are completed. Afterward, the topsoil should be spread evenly over the surface of the lawn. Some topsoils may be little better than the subsoil, but in most cases it is worth saving.

2. Building debris—plaster, stones, trash—should be removed, not buried.

3. The subgrade should be sloped away from the house. Terraces should be avoided if possible; slopes should be gradual to the sidewalk. A gentle slope away from the house will carry off water and reduce the risk of a damp basement.

4. If, in grading and leveling, the surface is raised around shade trees, provision should be made to protect the trees. Shallow wells of brick or stonework should be built around the trunks of the trees to allow air to reach the roots. Deep layers of soil around the trunk of a tree may kill it.

5. In establishing the subgrade, special attention should be given to spots that are likely to be poorly drained. Sometimes tile may be necessary. The advice of competent authorities should be sought in putting in tile drains.

6. After the subgrade has been finished, about 75 pounds of lime (if soil tests show the need) and 25 pounds of superphosphate per 1,000 square feet should be harrowed or spaded into the subsoil to a depth of 3 or 4 inches. The lawn begins with the subsoil.

7. The topsoil should then be replaced and graded.

8. Lime, fertilizer, and other amendments, such as organic matter (peat manure, compost, spent mushroom soil and so on) should be incorporated into the topsoil before the finish grade is established. For many lawnmakers, cost and availability may determine the amounts. If one cannot get an analysis of degree of acidity from his county agent, State experiment station, or State department of agriculture, or if he does not test the soil himself with a soil test kit, a rough rule of thumb in the eastern half of the country is to apply 75 pounds of ground limestone on 1,000 square feet. Plenty

of balanced fertilizer is needed—say 25 to 50 pounds of a commercial fertilizer of 5–10–5 analysis.

9. The surface should be smoothed by raking and rolling.

10. Then seeding, sodding, or sprigging may be done, depending upon the type of grass to be used and the rapidity of cover desired. Because of its relatively high cost, sodding is recommended only when there is need for rapid completion of the job.

Hand sowing of seed is usually the most satisfactory method of securing a complete and uniform coverage on a small lawn. The seed may be diluted by mixing it with soil or fertilizer. It should be divided in two lots. One lot should be broadcast while walking lengthwise of the area and the other lot should be sown while walking at right angles to the direction of the first sowing. The seed should be covered lightly by raking.

11. Light rolling will press the seed gently into the soil where it will be encouraged to germinate in the shortest possible time.

12. Spreading a bale of straw or hay to 1,000 square feet on slopes will reduce erosion, conserve moisture, and facilitate establishment. It seldom is necessary to remove the mulch. Special types of netting also may be purchased to protect new seedings.

13. New seedings (or sod or sprigs) may be complete failures unless adequate moisture is available constantly during the period of establishment. Watering need only be light, but it must be frequent enough to avoid drying of the surface soil where the new tender rootlets are gaining a foothold.

14. Mowing should be started as soon as there is enough top growth to cut with the mower set at the proper height for the principal species of grass planted. Delayed mowing, so that the grass blades bend over and become matted, should be avoided.

There are 10 points to observe in keeping a lawn in good condition.

1. The lawn should be fertilized in the proper season—when the grass becomes thin or unthrifty. A commercial fertilizer of 5–10–5 (or similar) analysis is recommended. That means 5 percent nitrogen, 10 percent phosphoric acid, and 5 percent potash. A good standard is 20 pounds per 1,000 square feet. Because in some regions other types of fertilizers may be needed, it is wise to consult local and State authorities. In the cool humid regions, applications should be made in early fall and very early spring. In warm humid regions applications should be made in spring and early summer when the grass is growing actively. Fertilizer may be distributed by some of the fertilizer distributors on the market. Care must be used to prevent skipping and overlapping. Another good way is to broadcast the fertilizer by hand. If that method is used, the fertilizer should be divided into two lots. The first lot should be distributed while walking lengthwise of the area and the second lot should be broadcast while walking crosswise of the area, to insure a thorough and uniform coverage.

2. Soil tests are the basis upon which the need for lime should be determined. Generally speaking, soils in the eastern United States require lime.

Ground limestone is the cheapest form of lime. It is usually considered to be equal in value to other kinds.

Lime can be applied at any season—late fall or early spring are good times.

3. Frequent mowing with a sharp, properly adjusted mower will keep a lawn looking neat. Mowing also promotes tillering and spreading of the grass plants.

Height of mowing depends upon the dominant species of grass in the lawn. Stoloniferous (creeping or spreading) grasses—bent, Bermuda, Zoysia, centipede, St. Augustine—will withstand close mowing if they are kept fertilized. They may be kept mowed at ½ to 1 inch. The fescues, bluegrasses, and other grasses that do not produce stolons should be mowed at 1½ inches or higher.

4. Watering is the maintenance practice that is most often done incor-

rectly. The few rules are simple enough.

Do soak the ground thoroughly at infrequent intervals when the grass begins to suffer from drought. Water just often enough to keep the plants alive.

Do not sprinkle lightly every day "just to cool things off." Light sprinkling encourages shallow root systems and helps crabgrass more than it does the permanent grasses. It does more harm than good.

Many of the grasses of the cool humid region go through a dormant period in midsummer. If they are forced into active growth, the plants may actually be injured.

5. Rolling the lawn in the spring helps to firm the soil that has been loosened by the heaving action of frost. The ground should be moist, but not wet enough to "puddle" from the rolling operation. For the same reason, the roller must not be too heavy, or the soil will be compacted too tightly.

6. To keep weeds out, grow good grass—that is, proper management of the turf is the most important phase in the growing of a weed-free lawn. A good, healthy turf will not allow weeds to encroach. Any weed-control measure must be accompanied by appropriate fertilizer practices, and reseeding where necessary to fill in bare spaces.

Broadleaf weeds generally can be controlled by 2,4–D, which is sold under many trade names and in a number of forms. Manufacturer's directions should be observed strictly to avoid injury to shrubs or trees. Sprayers and other containers should be cleaned thoroughly after they have been used to apply 2,4–D; otherwise, plants sprayed subsequently with the equipment may be injured by the 2,4–D residue. In fact, it is wise to have two sets of spraying equipment; one for 2,4–D and one for other purposes.

Experiments to date have established that 2,4–D is not harmful to persons or animals, a point to be considered by those who have children and pets that play on the lawn.

Experimental work in controlling weeds has been done with a great many other chemicals, arsenicals, chlorates, dinitro compounds, various petroleum fractions, and others. All have some value, but none of them (except lead arsenate) can be recommended without qualification. If they are to be used, workers at an experiment station or other authorities should be consulted. If used improperly the chemicals can be harmful to the grass and to the persons who handle them or come in contact with them.

Lead arsenate is a poisonous compound, but if one is careful he can use it with relative safety to himself, children, pets, and plants. It is effective against chickweed, Poa annua, and crabgrass in the more acid soils. In heavier soils high in lime and phosphorus its effects have been variable and repeated applications may be necessary. Lead arsenate should be applied at the rate of 20 pounds per 1,000 square feet. It may be applied at any time of year—fall is as good a time as any. Lead arsenate also is effective against most insects that live in the soil.

7. Insects most troublesome in lawns are beetle grubs, cutworms, armyworms, sod webworms, ants, chinch bugs, and mole crickets. Ticks and chiggers are not harmful to the lawn but they are a nuisance to the lawn owner and his children.

Most of the turf insects can be controlled by various DDT compounds. Ants, mole crickets, and chinch bugs are not readily controlled by DDT, but can be checked by the Chlordane products. These materials are sold under various trade names and in several forms. The manufacturers' directions should be followed. Advice about them can be had from county agents and State entomologists.

Most species of earthworms may be controlled by the use of lead arsenate at the rate of 20 pounds to 1,000 square feet. Lead arsenate is effective against grubs and other soil insects but it is not so economical as some of the newer insecticides. We mention earthworms because, although they are not insects and may not be pests, they might be numerous enough to make the lawn unsightly with their casts.

8. Disease control measures may be necessary on some specialized lawns. Bent lawns are susceptible to attacks of brownpatch and dollarspot.

Brownpatch may be checked by the use of Tersan. Dollarspot may be controlled by the use of mercury or cadmium compounds. These materials should be used according to the manufacturers' directions.

Most of the diseases attacking turf grasses are not easily controlled. Some new strains of grasses being developed at State and Federal experiment stations are resistant to disease. Your experiment station will be the source of information regarding the development of any new strains or species that may be adapted to your area.

9. Densely shaded areas under trees often present problems in the growing of a good turf. There are several reasons: Competition for nutrients and moisture by tree roots, the shading effect of the foliage, and the smothering of turf by fallen leaves.

There are ways to combat these difficulties. Deep placement of fertilizer around trees and heavy fertilizer applications on the turf may compensate for the scarcity of available plant food. The use of shade-tolerant species (the fescues and trivialis bluegrass in the cool humid regions, and the Zoysia grasses and St. Augustine in the warm humid regions) will overcome the shading effect. The prompt raking or sweeping of fallen leaves prevents any smothering effect which they might have. The grass should be forced into rapid growth during the period when the leaves are off the trees in order that strong turf will be established by the time trees begin growth in spring.

If, despite good fertilization, grass will not grow in your shaded areas, ground covers like vinca, pachysandra, and thyme are sometimes used.

10. The growth of algae is a condition caused by standing water on the surface of the soil. Improving the drainage so that water may be removed from the soil and loosening the soil to provide conditions favorable for grass will eliminate the condition.

Slime molds are organisms that cause gray, unsightly patches in lawns during wet seasons. These primitive fungi are not harmful to the grass and may be brushed off the grass blades when it is dry. The fruiting bodies of the fungi may give off a "smoke" or "dust" of spores when disturbed.

Renovating the Lawn

To renovate a lawn:

Mow the old stand of grass closely.

Apply weed-control materials if necessary.

Rake severely or cultivate with a hand disk or spiker to loosen surface soil.

Apply fertilizer and lime as needed.

Seed, sod, or sprig.

Roll.

If the ground is bare, apply mulch on slopes.

Water.

Mow as soon as there is enough growth.

Renovation becomes necessary when the turf is wholly undesirable and when replanting to the same or to a different grass is contemplated.

It is essential first to determine the reason for the unsatisfactory turf and to plan a program that will correct the previous deficiencies. Unless all the factors for satisfactory plant growth are favorable, the turf will become unsatisfactory again in a year or so. The details of the renovation program will depend largely upon the conditions that must be corrected or modified. It is best to seek expert advice when planning renovation.

Destruction of all unwanted growth usually is the first step. To accomplish this it is best to mow closely and remove the clippings. The use of strong chemicals to kill weeds is justified in a renovation program.

Selectivity is secondary because the area is to be replanted and the loss of some desirable grass is not likely to be serious. Sodium arsenite is favored by many greenkeeping superintendents for the renovation of turf because planting can be accomplished very soon after its use. No general recommendations for any chemical can be made here—it is impossible on a subject like this to give suggestions that will hold good for the whole country. Always seek the advice of your county agent, extension specialist, experiment station, the greenkeeper near you, or the manufacturer or dealer of the product you plan to use.

Preparation of a seedbed is essential to a successful job of replanting the area. Lime (if needed) and fertilizer should be well incorporated by raking or spiking. Other operations follow in logical order and may be the same as for building the lawn.

Grasses for Lawns

In choosing a grass for his lawn, the owner usually has the choice of selecting a grass that will thrive under existing conditions or of selecting the grass that he wants and then modifying the conditions to meet the requirements of that grass.

Grasses suitable for lawns in the cool humid region are: Kentucky bluegrass, red fescue, Alta fescue, bentgrass, redtop, ryegrass, and *Zoysia japonica*.

Grasses suitable for lawns in the warm humid region are: Bermuda, centipede, carpetgrass, St. Augustinegrass, and the *Zoysia* species.

In the dry-land area, buffalograss and the grama grasses are suitable on nonirrigated areas. Crested wheatgrass (Fairway strain) is used in the Northern Great Plains. Where irrigation is practiced, Kentucky bluegrass and bentgrass do well in the cooler areas and Bermuda-grass in the warmer sections.

Generally recommended seeding rates are: Bermuda-grass, carpetgrass, and the bentgrasses, 4 ounces to 1,000 square feet; buffalograss, 12 ounces to 1,000 square feet; the grama grasses, 1 pound to 1,000 square feet; Kentucky bluegrass, red fescues, Alta fescue, redtop, the ryegrasses, and crested wheatgrass (Fairway strain), 2 pounds to 1,000 square feet.

Requirements

Grasses for which no seed is available and which must be planted vegetatively are centipedegrass, St. Augustinegrass, and the Zoysias. Selected strains of Bermuda-grass must also be planted vegetatively because no seed is available.

Grasses that require a well-drained soil are Kentucky bluegrass, red fescue, Bermuda, centipede, grama, buffalo, and crested wheat. Those more tolerant of poorly drained soils are bentgrass, the Zoysias, carpetgrass, and St. Augustinegrass.

Grasses that require a relatively high level of fertility are Kentucky bluegrass, Bermuda, and bent. Those tolerant of lower levels of fertility are red fescues, the Zoysias, carpetgrass centipedegrass, St. Augustinegrass, grama, buffalograss, and crested wheatgrass.

The grasses that do well in shade are red fescue, St. Augustine, and the Zoysias. Grasses that require more sunlight are bent and centipede. Those that have a high sunlight requirement are the Kentucky bluegrass, Bermuda-grass, carpetgrass, grama, the buffalograss, and crested wheatgrass.

Grasses that need a large amount of moisture are Kentucky bluegrass, bent, carpetgrass, and St. Augustinegrass. Drought-tolerant grasses are red fescue, the Zoysias, Bermuda, and centipede. Grasses that are extremely drought-hardy are the gramas, buffalograss, and crested wheatgrass.

Bentgrass should be mowed to one-half inch or less. The Zoysias, Bermuda, carpet, centipede, and St. Augustine should be cut at one-half inch or 1 inch. Kentucky bluegrass, red fescue, grama, buffalo, and crested wheatgrass should be cut 1½ inches or higher.

GROWING ANNUAL FLOWERING PLANTS

PLANT CULTURE

Soil for the growing of annual plants needs to be well supplied with available plant food and should be reasonably retentive of moisture, though well drained. In short, because the plants make a quick growth they must be provided with good growing conditions in order to enable them to make that growth. Among these plants, however, there is a great difference in the requirements.

The best soil for most of these plants is a light, rich loam well supplied with rotted manure. A subsoil taken from the bottom of a cellar in excavating for a house is not suitable material upon which to depend as a satisfactory foundation for a flower bed. Where the soil is not naturally of the desired character, often much may be done to modify small areas to make them ideal for the culture of annuals. If the soil is thin and poor, a bed 2 feet deep can be excavated and filled with soil specially prepared for the plants it is intended to grow. More clay can be used in the soil for plants requiring heavy soil and more sand and leaf mold in the soil for plants requiring lighter soils.

An ideal soil for general purposes can be made from sods of bluegrass from a rather heavy clay loam rotted for a year, then mixed with equal quantities of rotted manure, leaf mold, and sand. The manure and sod can be rotted together for a year, if just as convenient. A specially prepared soil of this kind will probably not be benefited much by another coat of manure the second year, but after that it should have annual dressings. Where good garden soil or other rich soil of suitable texture is available, probably the more common practice is to make the bed of suitable depth and fill it with this soil well enriched with rotted manure. For permanent beds a careful preparation with good soil of proper texture is well worth the effort.

If for any reason such thorough preparation is not considered advisable, as on a place that may not be used for more than a year or two or on rented property where the tenure is regarded as comparatively temporary, the attempt to have annual flowers should not be abandoned, as even with much less preparation results may be obtained that are well worth the effort if the kinds of flowers grown are selected with consideration of the conditions that prevail.

Rotted manure, hen manure, prepared sheep or cow manure (obtainable from dealers in agricultural supplies), cottonseed meal, bone meal, or some similar organic manure, however, is almost essential to success. The value of these fertilizers is about in the order named.

GROWING ANNUAL FLOWERING PLANTS

There should be as much rotted cow manure, or even rotted horse manure, worked into the soil as can be done reasonably. Less hen manure should be used, as it is several times richer than cow or horse manure. The prepared cow and sheep manure can be used at the rate of 1 pound for 3 square feet, and the cottonseed meal and bone meal at the rate of 1 pound for 5 square feet. All these materials should be thoroughly worked into the soil. They will not bring satisfactory results, however, unless the ground is reasonably good to start with, especially as to texture.

When larger areas are used for flowers, as in a special garden that can be handled with a plow, like a large vegetable garden or part of the vegetable garden, soil-improvement crops, like crimson clover and vetch in wincer or cowpeas in summer, may be used to enrich the soil and thus prepare it for another season's crops. It is possible sometimes to adapt some of these soil-improvement crops to the smaller areas of flower beds, although it is seldom advisable, as the limited quantity of fertilizing materials usually needed can ordinarily be provided.

WATER

A proper water supply is essential. The provision of a deep soil of proper texture well enriched with organic manure makes a water-holding reservoir that acts something like a sponge in its ability to supply water for the plants. Such a soil will absorb a large amount of water whenever given an opportunity and will give it up readily to the plants as it is needed. On the other hand, provision must be made so that when such a soil has absorbed all that it is capable of properly holding, the surplus will drain away. If the surplus water does not naturally pass away freely, then artificial drainage must be provided. In poorly drained soils, beds specially prepared, as already described, should be excavated 3 feet deep instead of 2 feet, and in the bottom a layer of stone should be placed, covered by inverted sods, which in turn should be covered by 2 feet of soil. (Fig. 3.) This layer of drainage should be given some suitable outlet to carry off any water that might otherwise collect in it. This would preferably be by a drainpipe taken to a sewer or to some suitable outlet. A stone drain may be used, but it is likely to become clogged.

FIGURE 3.—A bed specially prepared for plant growth where the normal drainage is inadequate

Throughout much of the United States the natural rainfall on a bed well prepared, as already described, would be sufficient in most seasons. Beds close to a house, so that much of the rain is kept off by the building, need to have the natural rainfall supplemented by occasional waterings. Irrigation is necessary in dry climates and also in moist climates in unusually dry seasons, also on sandy or other unusually dry soils. The amount and frequency of watering will depend upon the dryness both of the atmosphere and of the soil.

A well-prepared retentive soil 2 feet deep would probably not require watering oftener than once a week, except possibly in the driest parts of the country, where the evaporation is excessive. Gravelly or sandy soils, especially if not well provided with organic matter, may require a thorough watering every other day. The watering should be done as infrequently as the soil and the climatic conditions will permit. Only experience can teach the best method. Too frequent watering is as bad as too long an interval between waterings. If watered too often the surface soil is kept moist and the root growth is encouraged near the surface. A day's neglect or unusual drying conditions will dry the feeding ground of the roots and kill them. But if the roots are required to go deeper by permitting the surface to become dry for 2 or 3 inches between waterings, there will be less danger of unfortunate results from unusual conditions or a slight deviation from the regular schedule of watering.

STARTING THE PLANTS

Ornamental annual plants can be started readily from seed in the spring and will give bloom or satisfactory foliage effects the same season. Nearly all of these can be started in the open ground over at least a large part of the United States, and will give the desired results before they are cut off by frost. In order to get a longer season of effect from the plants many of them are usually started under glass, or early plantings are started that way. In the more northern sections of the country some kinds must be started in this way in order to have a season long enough to mature; others so that they may become established before the coming of dry or hot weather, which would be injurious to the young plants but would not affect established ones.

Seed sowing and germination.—All of the plants mentioned in this bulletin can be propagated from seed. In some cases, however, the seeds require special care in order to insure a good stand of plants, and it is for that reason that the particular methods necessary for that purpose are described.

A few of these plants must be sown where they are to mature, as they will not stand being moved. Many may be sown where they are to grow, though most of them are helped by one or two transplantings. Because better plants are obtained by transplanting, most annuals are sown in seed beds and moved to their permanent places. Such seed beds should be in well-prepared mellow soil, preferably somewhat protected from drying winds. If the soil is not mellow, the seedlings, especially from the smaller seeds, will have trouble breaking through any crust that may form, especially if moisture conditions are not exactly right. Protection from winds also helps to maintain uniform moisture conditions. The timely use of a watering can is often a great help in promoting germination, but care should be taken not to use it too much. Seed beds require frequent light waterings rather than the infrequent drenchings best suited to more mature plants.

Seeds may be sown either broadcast or in rows. The inexperienced gardener should plant seeds in rows, especially slow-germinating seeds, as quick-starting weeds may be more readily recognized and removed with less danger of disturbing the germinating seeds.

Weeds starting near the seed row may be removed at once with great care or may be left until the seedlings are well sprouted. The dates of sowing the different kinds of seeds will be mentioned under the respective headings in connection with the discussion of other special cultural requirements.

The germination of seeds depends upon a proper degree of heat, moisture, and oxygen from the air. Some seeds germinate best under a high temperature (80° to 90° F.), while others do best at a low temperature (40° to 60° F.). For most seeds, however, a soil temperature of 65° to 70° F. with an air temperature of 60° F. will prove very satisfactory for germination. Strange as it may seem, nature maintains conditions during the early part of the growing season approximating those above specified. But naturally the high temperatures are much later in the season than the low ones. In order to obtain the higher temperatures early in the season a greenhouse, hotbed, coldframe, or a sunny kitchen window must be used.

Seeds in most cases grow best when the moisture in the soil is slight rather than excessive. A good test for moisture is to take a handful of soil and compact it gently in the palm of the hand by closing the fingers. If when released the soil remains solid and retains the impressions of the hand, it is too wet; but if when released it springs back and slowly crumbles or parts, it is in ideal condition for seed sowing. Such soil is well aerated, while the soil containing an excess of moisture has the air largely replaced by water.

The seed bed should be carefully guarded against extremes of moisture. It should not be allowed to get too wet and remain in that condition for any length of time; neither should it be allowed to get too dry. In the open these conditions are not likely to occur during a normal season. However, there are frequent exceptions. If the seed bed is too wet, little can be done to overcome the bad results, but if drought occurs irrigation will remedy the evil. Under artificial conditions, such as are obtained in a greenhouse, hotbed, or coldframe, the moisture content of the soil of the seed bed can be very carefully controlled. The confined atmosphere of such a structure prevents rapid or excessive evaporation, while any loss of moisture from the soil can be made good by watering. On a small scale the same results can be approached by placing a pane of glass over the receptacle in which the seeds are sown.

Slight variations in the temperature of the soil in which seeds are sown are usually a benefit rather than a hindrance to germination. With the grasses and clovers and probably with practically all other plants, germination is more rapid and more complete in seeds subjected to alternations of temperature than in those kept under constant temperatures. Under normal conditions the warming of the soil during the day and the cooling at night furnish sufficiently wide variations. While these variations are less easily controlled than the variations in moisture, yet in structures such as hotbeds and coldframes the change from day to night temperature will be perceptible.

Seeds in order to germinate promptly must be placed under conditions that will enable them to take up moisture readily, and at the same time they must have a temperature that will be congenial to the young plant when it appears. The soil is the medium by which heat and moisture, under normal conditions, are transferred to the seed. In order to insure a quick exchange of moisture from the soil to the seed, the soil should be carefully firmed or compacted about the seed. By compacting the soil about the seed the capillary power of the soil is increased and the soil moisture is more quickly brought to the seed. In outdoor operations large seeds may have the soil compacted about them by tramping the row with the feet, while fine seeds may be treated by resting a board over the row and walking upon it from end to end. In hotbeds, greenhouses, and coldframes the compacting of the soil is usually accomplished by the use of a float, which consists of a piece of board about 6 inches wide and 9 or 10 inches long, with a handle attached, as shown in Figure 4.

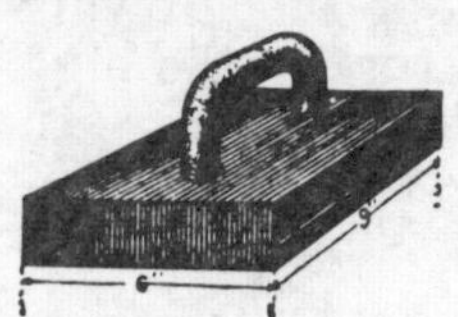

FIGURE 4.—A float for firming the soil

For all conditions save in the open, seeds may be sown in seed pans or in flats, as shown in Figure 5. These boxes can be very conveniently and cheaply made from the pine boxes largely used for packing canned goods, soap, or other merchandise, usually 9 or 10 inches deep, which is sufficient to permit cutting them with a ripsaw into three sections, each about 3 inches high. The top and bottom of the box will each make a complete flat, while the middle section will be a frame which can be provided with a bottom by the destruction of a box for three sections; i. e., four boxes will furnish nine complete flats or by using other lumber for the bottom of the middle section each box will make three flats. Seeds may also be planted directly in the soil of the hotbed, coldframe, or in that upon the greenhouse bench as well as in the garden. Here, too, they may be sown broadcast, but it is preferable to sow in rows.

In covering seeds the rule under artificial conditions is to bury the seed to the depth of its greatest diameter, while outdoors they are usually covered about three to five times their diameter. With seeds the size of a grain of wheat it is safe generally to plant them 1 inch deep, and for those the size of beans, 2 inches deep. Small seeds, the size of those of petunia or tobacco, should be scattered over the surface and the soil compacted with a float.

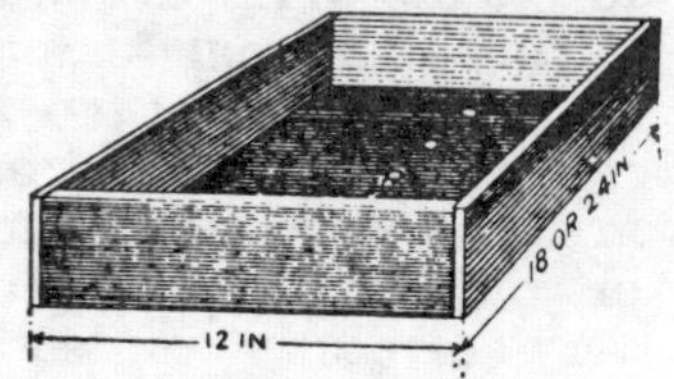

FIGURE 5.—A flat

Transplanting.—The young seedling plants should be transplanted as soon as the first true leaves are formed, so that they will stand at some distance from one another. Preliminary to transplanting, the seed bed should be wetted thoroughly an hour or so before digging the plants, so that they can be removed from the soil without breaking the roots. The beds, flats, or pots into which the transplanting is to be done are previously prepared with soil that is moist but not wet; that is, it must spring apart again promptly if squeezed in the hand. Holes for the plants are satisfactorily made with a short stick three-eighths or a half inch in diameter and sharpened at one end. A flat stick sharpened at one end, as for example, a 6-inch pot label, makes an excellent implement for digging the seedlings. The seedlings should be carefully loosened in the soil so that they may be lifted out with any soil that may possibly adhere to the roots, then be placed in the prepared holes at about the depth they were before, and then the earth should be pressed about the roots firmly but gently. A frequent practice is to dig the plant with the right hand, lift with the left one, and press the soil about the roots with the right one. Sometimes the pot label is used to open the holes as the planting is being done, one motion of the label opening the hole and another motion pressing the soil about the roots after the plant is placed in position.

The plants should be thoroughly but carefully watered at once and then should be kept somewhat shaded until root contact has become reestablished. Longer shading is required in hot, dry weather than in cool, partially cloudy weather. In dark, cloudy weather shading may often be omitted. Watering must receive especial attention until growth starts.

For small, rather slow growing plants, such as pansies, 1 inch apart each way will afford ample room; with most plants 2 inches each way will be best; but with robust growing plants, like the castor-bean, 4 inches will not be too much. With such vigorous growing plants, however, it is best to place the seeds directly in pots or cans in order to prevent disturbing the roots of the young seedlings as well as to afford them ample space. If ordinary pots are not available, paper pots may be obtained cheaply, or old strawberry boxes may be used. Transplanting has a tendency to make the plants stocky and provides opportunity for the development of an extensive root system.

HOTBEDS AND COLDFRAMES

The pleasure derived from floral decorations depends not only upon the perfection of the flowers but upon having a continuous display throughout the season. With most of the garden annuals early bloom can not be secured if seed sowing in the open must be relied upon exclusively. Fortunately, gardeners have devised cheap and efficient means of lengthening the growing season several weeks by the use of coldframes and hotbeds. In the latitude of Washington, D. C., the time of sowing seed requiring the higher temperatures for germination can be advanced from May 1, the normal date of sowing in the open, to March 1, a gain of two months. Seed sown in a gentle hotbed at this date will give plants which, if properly handled, will forward the season of bloom two weeks or more.

HOTBEDS

Hotbeds are usually constructed in one or the other of the following ways:

Temporary hotbeds.—A temporary hotbed may be made by using fermenting stable manure from grain-fed horses, preferably that with a small quantity of straw or litter in it. The manure should be placed in a broad, flat heap and thoroughly compacted by tramping. A heap 8 or 9 feet wide and any multiple of 3 feet in length, with the manure 14 to 16 inches deep, will give sufficient heat for the latitude of New York City and of Kansas City, Mo. Farther north, the heap should be made deeper and broader. Upon the surface of the manure heap a frame made like that shown in Figure 6 will afford ample space for the development of the plants within. The backboard of this frame is usually 12 inches wide and the front 8 inches, and the two are connected by a tapered board 12 inches wide at one end, 8 inches wide at the other, and 6 feet in length. The back and front of the frame are made in multiples of 3 feet in length, with an inch added for each division space between sash, which is provided for by the use of a T-shaped piece let into the frame to stiffen

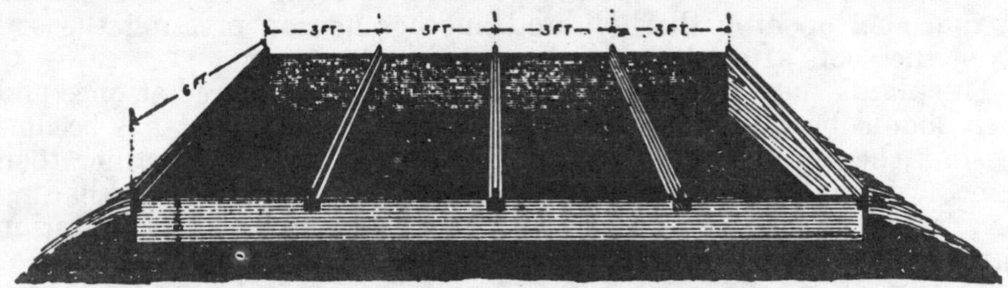

FIGURE 6.—A frame to carry the sash of a hotbed or coldframe

it and serve as a guide for the sash. The manner of making the guide as well as its appearance when in place is shown in Figure 6. A cross section is illustrated by Figure 7. If severe weather is likely to occur during the time the hotbed is in use, the frame should be banked with manure to give additional heat and protection. After placing the frame upon the manure heap, about 3 inches of good garden loam should be scattered uniformly over the area inclosed by the frame. Place the sash in position immediately and allow the bed to heat up. Do not plant any seed in the bed until the temperature begins to subside, which will be in about three days after the sash are put in place.

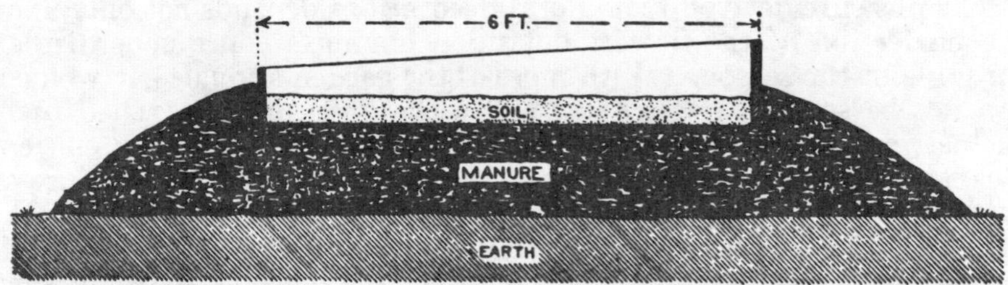

FIGURE 7.—Cross section of a temporary hotbed

When the temperature has fallen to 85° or 90° F. planting may be safely begun.

Permanent hotbeds.—A permanent hotbed may be so constructed as to be heated with fermenting manure or by radiating pipes from the dwelling or greenhouse heating plant. For a permanent bed, in which manure is to supply the heat, a pit 2 to 2½ feet in depth, according to the latitude in which the work is to be done, should be provided. The sides and ends may be supported by a lining of planks held in place by posts 4 feet apart, or, better still, a brick wall 9 inches thick, as shown in Figure 8, may be used. In either case the pit lining should come flush with or above the surface of the soil.

GROWING ANNUAL FLOWERING PLANTS

The site for the pit should be on naturally well-drained land, and a tile drain from the bottom of the excavation should be provided to prevent water from accumulating in the pit and stopping the fermentation of the manure during the period the hotbed is in use.

Standard hotbed sash are 3 by 6 feet in size, and the interior crosspieces for holding the sash are 1 inch wide. The pit, therefore, should be some multiple of 3 feet 1 inch in length less 1 inch, and the width should be the same as the length of the sash—6 feet. The plank frame or brickwork of the pit may be extended above the surface of the ground sufficiently to allow for placing the sash immediately upon these permanent structures, or a frame such as is described in connection with the construction of a temporary hotbed (fig. 6) may be used. In the fall the pit should be filled with leaves or straw and covered with loose boards or shutters to prevent it from becoming filled with snow and ice in the North, so that it may be ready for use early in March there, or in January or February farther south.

Sash.—Hotbed sash should be constructed of white pine, cypress, or redwood, and the sash bars should run in one direction only and that lengthwise of the sash. The bars may be braced through the middle by a transverse bar placed through the long bars below the plane occupied by the glass. The two ends of the sash should be made of sound timber 3 inches wide at the top and 4 inches wide at the bottom end, mortised to receive the ends of the sash bars and with a tenon at the ends to pass through the side pieces, which should be 2½ inches wide.

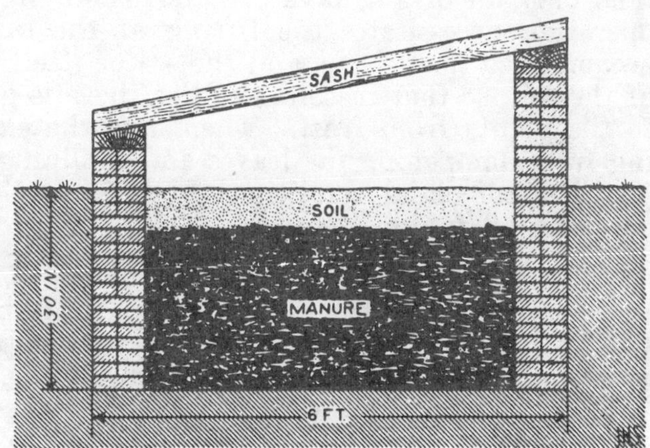

FIGURE 8.—Cross section of a permanent hotbed or pit

Glazing.—Placing the glass in the sash is one of the most important operations in the construction of a hotbed and is also a factor that largely determines the success or failure of the bed. The glass should be bedded in putty, i. e., the rabbet in the sash bar that is made to carry the glass should be filled with soft putty, and the glass, crowning side up, pressed firmly into the bed of putty and securely fastened with shoe nails or wire brads. Glazing points are not sufficiently secure. The first glass to be placed in any frame is a bottom light, i. e., the pane nearest to the front or lowest side of the hotbed when the sash is in place. The next light should be bedded in the same manner as the first and so placed as to lap about three-sixteenths of an inch over the top edge of the one first placed, like shingles on a roof. Brads should be driven below the lower corners of the second pane in order to prevent it from slipping down over the under one. The same method of procedure should be continued until the frame is filled with glass.

While a frame with two courses of glass will admit a little more light than one with three, the breakage is somewhat less with small glass and the cost of repairing correspondingly less, and for these reasons the 3-course frame is more desirable. Nowadays many hotbed sash are made with a groove or slot into which the glass may be slipped and fastened at the bottom by brads to prevent it from slipping out. Grooved sash have the commendable feature of being cheaply and quickly glazed, but as the glass can not be lapped and as no putty is used, the sash are not water tight and do not furnish as good protection from the wind as those in which the glass is bedded in putty.

Care of a hotbed.—In the North, besides the glazed sash, board shutters, straw mats, or mats of burlap or carpet will be needed as an additional protection during cold nights. On bright days, even when the temperature outside is near the freezing point, it will be necessary to lift the sash a little at the high side of the frame to allow the hot air to escape and prevent injury to the young plants.

Watering.—Hotbeds should be watered in the morning only, and then only on bright days. Watering at night is dangerous, as the operation necessitates the lifting of the sash and the loss of the accumulated heated air, and the water itself lowers the temperature of the soil, so that in cold weather there is greatly increased danger to the plants from frost. Then, too, the excessive moisture resulting from dampening the leaves and confining them during the night provides congenial conditions for the development of mildew and damping-off fungi.

COLDFRAMES

Coldframes are devices intended to protect plants from cold, without forcing them into growth. They differ from hotbeds in that no artificial means of heating are employed. The coldframe in its simplest form consists of a frame constructed like the one described in the section on hotbeds and illustrated in Figure 6. When complete, the frame is placed upon a sheltered, well-drained piece of ground convenient to some main line of traffic between the house and some other important and frequently visited portion of the grounds. The frame, as above stated, is made to carry hotbed sash. The glass allows the sun during bright days to temper the air of the frames, so that by properly covering them at night with shutters, straw, or jute mats the heat can be retained and the plants within safely carried through severe weather. The frames may be banked with earth as an added precaution against cold.

The chief winter use of a coldframe is to retain plants in a healthy condition without adding to their growth, while in spring it is to protect from occasional cold weather before time for planting out. It is therefore important that the temperature of the frame be at all times such that it will not induce rapid growth, the chief factor in successful management being proper ventilation.

During bright, sunny weather the sash should be lifted sufficiently to admit outside air in order to preserve a low temperature about the leaves of the plants. In some cases it will be found that during bright days even in midwinter the sash will have to be removed from the frame for a few hours at midday in order to preserve a sufficiently low temperature. On the other hand, care should be exercised in ventilation and watering so as not to reduce the temperature of the frame late in the afternoon, as such treatment is liable to lead to frost injury.

It stands to reason that only the hardiest plants can safely be carried over winter in a coldframe. Many of the plants that are grown as annuals will, with protection, become perennials, or can be made to give a much longer period of bloom if sown in the fall and carried over winter in a coldframe. Among plants that will be greatly benefited by such treatment are pansies, dianthus, and chrysanthemums.

PITS

The pit is a more elaborate and efficient coldframe which, as its name indicates, consists of an excavation. This excavation may be from 2 to 4 feet in depth, with sides protected by plank or brick walls, as shown in Figure 8, upon which a frame similar to the one described for the coldframe is placed and covered with sash. The pit has some advantages over the coldframe, as for instance, for storing some of the hardier flowering plants that require more protection than that afforded by an ordinary coldframe. Plants in a pit are protected by the warmth of the soil. In latitudes where the soil does not freeze to a depth of more than 10 to 15 inches the pit will be found of greatest use. Seedling plants may be held over winter in trays or flats in pits as safely as in frames.

The same precautions in regard to ventilation, covering, and watering must be observed in the care of a pit as in the case of a coldframe.

PLANTS FOR SPECIAL SOILS OR CONDITIONS

Some plants that are desirable for special conditions are specified in the following lists:

For bright sunshine with plenty of fertility and moisture: Over 4 feet high, castor-bean, cosmos, sunflower, sorghum, feterita, milo, and Indian corn; over 3 feet, Josephs-coat, love-lies-bleeding, feather cockscomb, orange sunflower, princesfeather, spiderflower, and summer-cypress; 30 inches, cornflower, larkspur, scabiosa, scarlet sage, strawflower, and zinnia; 24 inches, balsam, calliopsis, China-aster, summer chrysanthemum, cockscomb, coneflower, four-o'clock, gaillardia, Aztec marigold, platycodon, poppy, salpiglossis, snapdragon, and snow-on-the-mountain; 18 inches, Jobs-tears, mignonette, and stock; 12 inches, calendula, California-poppy, calliopsis, candytuft, French marigold, petunia, Drummond phlox, pink, and Iceland poppy; under 12 inches, ageratum, cockscomb, lobelia, portulaca, sweet alyssum, and verbena.

Of easiest culture under ordinary garden conditions: Over 4 feet, sunflower; about 3 feet, Josephs-coat, love-lies-bleeding, heliopsis, and princesfeather; about 30 inches, cornflower, strawflower, and zinnia; about 24 inches, calliopsis, summer chrysanthemum, coneflower, gaillardia, marigold, poppy, and snow-on-the-mountain; about 18 inches, mignonette; about 12 inches, Cape-marigold, calendula, California-poppy, balsam, candytuft, petunia, Drummond phlox, pink, dwarf nasturtium, portulaca, and sweet alyssum.

On light fertile soil: Gaillardia, marigold, Drummond phlox, and portulaca.

On light soil, not too rich: Cockscomb and feather cockscomb.

On poor soil: Love-lies-bleeding, princesfeather, Josephs-coat, Cape-marigold, godetia, dwarf nasturtium, portulaca, grass-pink, sweet alyssum, garden balsam, and calliopsis.

On lands near the seacoast: Plants from the three foregoing lists, depending on the fertility of the soil, together with the castor-bean, sunflower, heliopsis, spiderflower, cornflower, strawflower, zinnia, calliopsis, snow-on-the-mountain, four-o'clock, stock, calendula, California-poppy, petunia, and sweet alyssum.

In partial shade: Basketflower, sweet-sultan, clarkia, platycodon, godetia, Drummond phlox, pansy, sweet alyssum, lupine, and forget-me-not.

Especially responding to rich soil: Castor-bean, scarlet sage, balsam, and China-aster.

To cut for everlastings: Rose everlasting, feathered cockscomb, globe-amaranth, and strawflower.

Not adapted to the South except for late and early spring: Salpiglossis, pansy, and forget-me-not.

Plants that can be started to advantage in hotbeds and coldframes for early flowering, whether they are to be used for bedding purposes or for cut flowers: Ageratum, China-aster, calliopsis, castor-bean, calendula, cosmos, cockscomb, chrysanthemum, godetia, lobelia, marigold, petunia, grass-pink, scarlet sage, spiderflower, and verbena.

Some plants that may be sown in beds in the open ground and later transplanted to their permanent locations are ageratum, calendula, calliopsis, China-aster, clarkia, cockscomb, dahlia, gaillardia, godetia, lobelia, mignonette, pansy, pink, snapdragon, spiderflower, stock, and zinnia. Most of these may be sown earlier in a hotbed or coldframe and thus be made to bloom earlier.

Some should be sown in the open ground where the plants are to grow.

Among those that should be sown early in that way are alyssum, California-poppy, candytuft, cornflower, forget-me-not, mignonette, nemophila, Drummond phlox, sunflower, poppy, and sweet alyssum.

Among those that should be sown late in this manner after the ground is warm are the castor-bean, sorghum, milo, feterita, Indian corn, garden balsam, portulaca, and four-o'clock.

For August and September sowing: Forget-me-not, pansy, cornflower, pink, and snapdragon.

Seeds that may be sown on well-prepared ground just before winter for early spring germination or on fall-prepared ground very early in the spring while the soil still freezes at night are the poppy, cornflower, cosmos, summer-cypress, larkspur, snapdragon, snow-on-the-mountain, and sweet alyssum.

Flowers that are white or with pure white varieties: 4 feet, cosmos; 3 feet, dahlia and sweet-sultan; 2½ feet, clarkia, cornflower, larkspur, and scabiosa;

2 feet, babysbreath, China-aster, summer chrysanthemum, lupine, balloonflower, snapdragon, garden balsam, and poppy; 1½ feet, godetia, four-o'clock, rose everlasting, and stock; 1 foot, candytuft, Iceland poppy, petunia, ageratum, lobelia, portulaca, sweet alyssum, and verbena.

Flowers having varieties mixed with white: 3 feet, dahlia; 2½ feet, salpiglossis; 1 foot, nemophila, pansy, petunia, and pink.

Flowers yellow or with yellow varieties: 4 feet, sunflower, feather cockscomb, and dahlia; 2½ feet, strawflower, sunflower, and zinnia; 2 feet, calliopsis, summer chrysanthemum, Aztec marigold, snapdragon, and four-o'clock; 1 foot, calendula, Cape-marigold, French marigold, Iceland poppy; California-poppy, dwarf marigold, and portulaca.

Flowers having varieties mixed with yellow: 4 feet, dahlia; 2 feet, calliopsis, rudbeckia, salpiglossis, and summer chrysanthemum; 1½ feet, four-o'clock; 1 foot, dwarf nasturtium and pansy.

Flowers of orange color or with orange varieties: 3 feet, heliopsis; 2½ feet, zinnia; 2 feet, Aztec marigold; 1 foot, calendula, Cape-marigold, French marigold, and California-poppy.

Flowers having varieties mixed with orange: 2 feet, gaillardia; 1 foot, dwarf nasturtium and French marigold.

Flowers lavender or with lavender varieties: 3 feet, basketflower and sweet-sultan; 2½ feet, larkspur; 2 feet, China-aster; 1½ feet, candytuft; 1 foot, Drummond phlox, nemophila, and pansy.

Flowers having varieties mixed with lavender: 2½ feet, salpiglossis; 1 foot, pansy.

Flowers blue or with blue varieties: 2½ feet, cornflower and larkspur; 2 feet, lupine and balloonflower; 1 foot, nemophila, ageratum, lobelia, verbena, and forget-me-not.

Flowers purple or with purple varieties: 3 feet, sweet-sultan; 2½ feet, clarkia and scabiosa; 2 feet, China-aster, 1½ feet, stock; 1 foot, verbena.

Flowers having varieties mixed with purple: 2½ feet, salpiglossis; 1 foot, pansy.

Flowers pink or with pink varieties: 4 feet, cosmos; 3 feet, dahlia; 2½ feet, larkspur and zinnia; 2 feet, China-aster, garden balsam, and poppy; 1½ feet, rose everlasting; 1 foot, Drummond phlox, pinks (including carnations), portulaca, and verbena.

Flowers having varieties mixed with pink: 3 feet, dahlia; 1 foot, pinks (including carnations).

Flowers salmon or with salmon varieties: 3 feet, dahlia; 2½ feet, clarkia; 2 feet, snapdragon and poppy; 1 foot, Drummond phlox.

Flowers having varieties mixed with salmon pink: 3 feet, dahlia; 1 foot, Drummond phlox.

Flowers scarlet or with scarlet varieties: 3 feet, dahlia; 2½ feet, scarlet sage and zinnia; 2 feet, snapdragon, poppy, and four-o'clock; 1 foot, Drummond phlox, pinks (including carnations), dwarf nasturtium, portulaca, and verbena.

Flowers having varieties mixed with scarlet: 3 feet, dahlia; 2 feet, snapdragon and poppy; 1 foot, Drummond phlox, pinks (including carnations), and dwarf nasturtium.

Flowers rose or crimson or with rose or crimson varieties: 4 feet, cosmos; 3 feet, princesfeather, feather cockscomb, sweet-sultan, and spiderflower, 2½ feet, clarkia, cornflower, scabiosa, and zinnia; 2 feet, garden balsam, China-aster, cockscomb, and lupine; 1½ feet, godetia, four-o clock, globe-amaranth, stock, and candytuft; 1 foot, Drummond phlox, petunia, and portulaca.

Flowers having varieties mixed with rose or crimson: 1 foot, Drummond phlox and petunia.

Plants used for their foliage or chiefly for it, the foliage being green unless otherwise noted: 4 feet, castor-bean (bronze and green separate), sorghum, feterita, milo, broomcorn, and Indian corn; 3 feet, Josephs-coat (red, yellow, and green mixed), love-lies-bleeding (red), summer-cypress (pea green turning crimson in late summer); 2½ feet, annual poinsettia (scarlet leaves in late summer) and snow-on-the-mountain (white-edged leaves); 1½ feet, Jobs-tears; 1 foot, mignonette (a greenish flower grown for its sweet odor, but in its garden decorative value comparable to a plant grown for its foliage).

PRINCIPAL CHARACTERISTICS OF ANNUAL FLOWERING PLANTS

The following list presents in easily accessible form the principal characteristics of some annual flowering plants.

Some annual flowering plants, showing their hardiness, height of growth, color of flowers, etc.; also the page in this bulletin where a description of each plant and directions for its culture will be found

Common name	Height of plant (feet)	Grown for flowers or foliage	Color of flowers or foliage	Preference for sun or shade	Hardiness to cold
Acroclinium. See Rose everlasting.					
African golden daisy. See Cape-marigold.					
African marigold. See Marigold, Aztec.					
Ageratum	1	Flowers	Blue, white, rose.	Sun	Tender
Alyssum, sweet	1	do	White	do	Very hardy
Amaranth, globe. See Globe-amaranth.	1½	do	Crimson or rose.	do	Hardy
Amaranthus caudatus. See Love-lies-bleeding.					
Amaranthus cruentus. See Princesfeather.					
Amaranthus tricolor. See Josephs-coat.					
Antirrhinum. See Snapdragon.					
Aster, China. See China-aster	2	do	Purple, rose, white.	do	Half hardy
Aztec marigold. See Marigold, Aztec.					
Babysbreath	2	do	White	do	Hardy
Bachelor button. See Cornflower.					
Balloonflower	2	do	Blue, white	Sun, partial shade.	do
Balsam	2	do	Rose, pink, white.	Sun	Tender
Basketflower	3	do	Rose, lavender	Sun, slight shade.	Hardy
Bean, castor. See Castor-bean.					
Bellflower, Chinese. See Balloonflower.					
Bellflower, Japanese. See Balloonflower.					
Belvedere	3	Foliage	Pea green	Sun	Very hardy
Black-eyed-susan. See Rudbeckia.					
Blanketflower. See Gaillardia.					
Bluebottle. See Cornflower.					
Bluet. See Cornflower.					
Broomcorn	4+	do	Green	do	Tender
Calendula	1	Flowers	Yellow, orange	do	Half hardy
California-poppy	1	do	do	do	Very hardy
Calliopsis	2	do	Yellow, brown	do	Tender
Candytuft	1	do	Crimson, lavender, white.	do	Hardy
Cape-marigold	1	do	Orange, yellow	do	do
Carnation, Marguerite. See Pink.					
Carpet of Snow alyssum. See Alyssum, sweet.					
Castor-bean	4	Foliage	Green, bronze	Full sun	Tender
Castor-oil plant. See Castor-bean.					
Celosia plumosa. See Cockscomb, feather.					
Centaurea americana. See Basketflower.					
Centaurea cyanus. See Cornflower.					
Centaurea imperialis. See Sweet-sultan.					
China-aster	2	Flowers	Purple, rose, white.	Sun	Half hardy
Chinese bellflower. See Balloonflower.					
Chinese pink. See Pink.					

***Some annual flowering plants, showing their hardiness, height of growth, color of flowers, etc.*—Continued**

Common name	Height of plant (feet)	Grown for flowers or foliage	Color of flowers or foliage	Preference for sun or shade	Hardiness to cold
Chrysanthemum, summer	2	Flowers	Yellow, white	Sun	Tender
Clarkia	2½	do	Salmon, white	Sun, partial shade.	Hardy
Cleome spinosa. See Spider-flower.					
Cockscomb	2	do	Crimson	Sun	Tender
Cockscomb, feather	3	do	Crimson, yellow.	do	do
Cockscomb, plumed. See Cockscomb, feather.					
Coneflower. See Rudbeckia.					
Coreopsis. See Calliopsis.					
Corn, broom. See Broomcorn.					
Corn, Indian	4+	Foliage	Green	do	do
Cornflower	2½	Flowers	Blue, rose, white.	Sun, shade	Very hardy.
Cosmos	4+	do	Rose, pink, white.	Full sun	Hardy
Cypress, summer. See Summer-cypress.					
Dahlia	3	do	Red, yellow, white.	Sun	Tender
Daisy, African golden. See Cape-marigold.					
Delphinium. See Larkspur.					
Dianthus. See Pink.					
Dimorphotheca. See Cape marigold.					
Drummond phlox. See Phlox, Drummond.					
Dwarf marigold. See Marigold, dwarf.					
Dwarf nasturtium. See Nasturtium, dwarf.					
Euphorbia. See Snow-on-the-mountain and Poinsettia.					
Everlasting, rose. See Rose everlasting.					
Farewell-to-spring. See Godetia.					
Feather cockscomb. See Cockscomb, feather.					
Feterita	4+	Foliage	Green	Full sun	do
Fire plant, Mexican. See Poinsettia.					
Flame plant, Mexican. See Summer-cypress.					
Flossflower. See Ageratum.					
Forget-me-not	1	Flowers	Blue	Partial shade.	Hardy
Four-o'clock	1½	do	Crimson, yellow, white.	Sun	Tender
French marigold. See Marigold, French.					
Gaillardia	2	do	Orange, crimson.	do	Hardy
Globe-amaranth	1½	do	Crimson or rose.	do	do
Glow, golden. See Rudbeckia.					
Godetia	1½	do	Rose, light purple, white.	Sun, half shade	do
Goldenglow. See Rudbeckia.					
Gomphrena. See Globe-amaranth.					
Grass-pink. See Pink.					
Gypsophila. See Babysbreath.					
Heartsease. See Pansy.					
Helichrysum. See Strawflower.					
Heliopsis	3	do	Orange	Sun	do
Iceland poppy. See Poppy, Iceland.					
Impatiens. See Balsam.					
Indian corn. See Corn, Indian.					
Japanese bellflower. See Balloonflower.					
Japanese pink. See Pink.					
Jobs-tears	1½	Foliage and fruit.	Green	do	Half hardy
Josephs-coat	3	Foliage	Red, yellow, green	Full sun	Tender

GROWING ANNUAL FLOWERING PLANTS

***Some annual flowering plants, showing their hardiness, height of growth, color of flowers, etc.*—Continued**

Common name	Height of plant (feet)	Grown for flowers or foliage	Color of flowers or foliage	Preference for sun or shade	Hardiness to cold
Kaiserblume. See Cornflower.					
Kochia scoparia. See Summer-cypress.					
Ladyslipper. See Balsam.					
Larkspur	2½	Flowers	Blue, pink, white.	Full sun	Very hardy
Lobelia	1	do	Blue, white	Sun	Hardy
Love-lies-bleeding	3	Foliage	Red	Full sun	Tender
Lupine	2	Flowers	Blue, rose, white.	Sun	Hardy
Marguerite carnation. See Pink.					
Marigold, African. See Marigold, Aztec.					
Marigold, Aztec	2	do	Yellow, orange	do	do
Marigold, Cape. See Cape-marigold.					
Marigold, dwarf	1	do	Golden yellow.	do	Tender
Marigold, French	1	do	Yellow, orange, brown.	do	Half hardy
Marigold, pot. See Calendula.					
Marvel-of-Peru. See Four-o'clock.					
Matthiola. See Stock.					
Mexican fire plant. See Poinsettia.					
Mexican flame plant. See Summer-cypress.					
Mignonette	1½	do	Greenish (sweet scented).	do	do
Milo	4+	Foliage	Green	Full sun	Tender
Mourning bride. See Scabiosa.					
Nasturtium, dwarf	1	Flowers	Scarlet, orange, yellow.	Sun	do
Nemophila	1	do	Blue, lilac, white.	Shade	Hardy
Niggerhead. See Rudbeckia.					
Orange sunflower. See Heliopsis.					
Painted leaf. See Poinsettia.					
Painted tongue. See Salpiglossis.					
Pansy	1	do	Purple, yellow, blue.	Shade, sun	do
Petunia	1	do	Rose, purple, white.	Sun	Tender
Phlox, Drummond	1	Flowers	Red, lilac, buff, white.	do	Hardy
Phlox drummondii. See Phlox, Drummond.					
Pincushion flower. See Scabiosa.					
Pink	1	do	Scarlet, pink, white.	do	do
Pink, Chinese. See Pink.					
Pink, grass. See Pink.					
Pink, Japanese. See Pink.					
Pink, Scotch. See Pink.					
Platycodon. See Balloonflower.					
Plumed cockscomb. See Cockscomb, feather.					
Poinsettia	2½	Foliage	Green, turning to scarlet.	do	Tender
Poppy	2	Flowers	Scarlet, pink, white.	do	Very hardy
Poppy, California. See California-poppy.					
Poppy, Iceland	1	do	Yellow, orange, white.	do	Hardy
Poppy, Shirley. See Poppy.					
Portulaca	1	do	Reds and yellows.	do	Tender
Pot marigold. See Calendula.					
Princesfeather	3	do	Red	do	do
Ragged-robin. See Cornflower.					
Ragged sailor. See Cornflower.					
Ricinus. See Castor-bean.					
Robin, ragged. See Cornflower.					

Some annual flowering plants, showing their hardiness, height of growth, color of flowers, etc.—Continued

Common name	Height of plant (feet)	Grown for flowers or foliage	Color of flowers or foliage	Preference for sun or shade	Hardiness to cold
Rose everlasting	1½	Flowers	Pink and white.	Sun	Half hardy
Rudbeckia	2	do	Yellow, crimson.	Sun, partial shade.	Hardy
Sage, scarlet	2½	do	Brilliant scarlet.	Sun	Tender
Sailor, ragged. See Cornflower.					
Salpiglossis	2	do	Purple, crimson, white.	do	do
Salvia. See Sage, scarlet.					
Salvia, scarlet. See Sage, scarlet.					
Scabiosa	2½	do	Crimson, rose, blue, white.	do	do
Scabious, sweet. See Scabiosa.					
Scarlet sage. See Sage, scarlet.					
Scarlet salvia. See Sage, scarlet.					
Scotch pink. See Pink.					
Shirley poppy. See Poppy.					
Snapdragon	2	do	Scarlet, yellow, white.	do	Very hardy
Snow-on-the-mountain	2	Foliage	Green leaves with white edge.	do	do
Sorghum	4+	do	Green	Full sun	Tender
Spiderflower	3	Flowers	Rose	Sun	do
Standing-cypress. See Cypress, summer.					
Stock	1½	do	Crimson, purple, white.	do	Hardy
Strawflower	2½	do	Lemon, yellow	do	do
Sultan, sweet. See Sweet-sultan.					
Summer chrysanthemum. See Chrysanthemum, summer.					
Summer-cypress	3	Foliage	Pea green	do	Very hardy
Sunflower	4+	Flowers	Yellow	Full sun	Hardy
Sunflower, orange. See Heliopsis.					
Sun plant. See Portulaca.					
Sweet alyssum. See Alyssum, sweet.					
Sweet scabious. See Scabiosa.					
Sweet-sultan	3	do	Red, purple, lavender, white.	Sun	Half hardy
Sweet-william. See Pink.					
Tagetes. See Marigold, dwarf.					
Tasselflower. See Ageratum.					
Tom Thumb nasturtium. See Nasturtium, dwarf.					
Verbena	1	do	Scarlet, blue, purple, white.	do	Tender
Youth-and-old-age. See Zinnia.					
Zinnia	2½	do	Rose, scarlet, yellow, orange.	do	Hardy

HERBACEOUS PERENNIALS

ADAPTABILITY OF DIFFERENT KINDS OF PLANTS

Table 1 summarizes the principal features relating to the adaptability of different herbaceous perennials, arranged in alphabetic order, showing their suitability in regard to season of blooming, height of growth, and climatic requirements, for use in the various regions of the United States.

Column 1 gives the scientific name of the plant. The common name will be found in the index of common names. Column 2 gives the initial page where the plant is described.

Columns 3 to 7 show by means of the symbol x the time of year when the flowers may be expected. The date will vary according to latitude and altitude and to a small extent according to longitude. Thus, if the symbol appears in column 3, marked E, the blooms may be expected early in the flowering season; if in column 5, under M, about midsummer; and if in column 7, under L, just before frost. Columns 4 and 6 denote intermediate seasons.

Columns 8 to 13 show by means of the symbol x the approximate height of the plant under ordinary conditions. There will be much variation from this in many locations, depending upon the adaptability of the plants to the particular location.

HERBACEOUS PERENNIALS

Columns marked R. 1 to R. 32, under "Regions," indicate the different locations, as shown on the map. (Fig. 66.) In these regional columns the symbol I indicates that the plant requires irrigation during the dry season; N indicates that the plant is native to the region; P indicates that special winter protection is required; X indicates that in the region thus designated the plant may be expected to thrive under average care with respect to water, shade, and other cultural conditions, including special treatment that would be required for the particular plant anywhere.

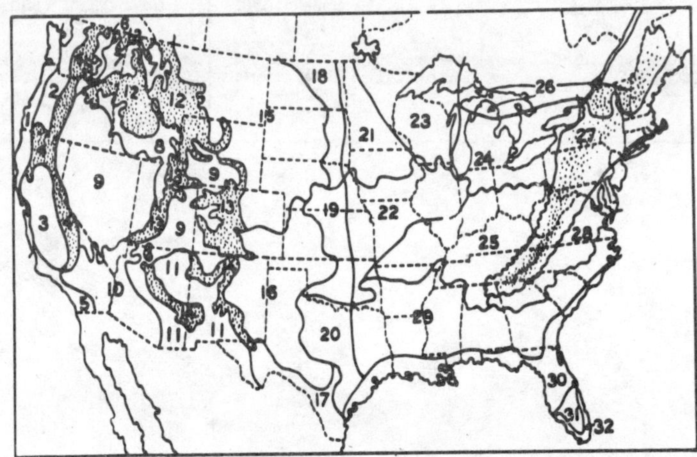

FIGURE 66.—Map of the United States, showing by numbers within heavy border lines the regions having approximately similar growing conditions. The stippled areas are mountain regions

TABLE 1.—*Some herbaceous perennials suitable for use in the different sections of the United States*

Scientific name of plant	Reference page	Season E	—	M	—	L	Height (feet) 0	1	2	3	4	5	Regions [Reference is made to the map (fig. 66)] R. 1.	R. 2.	R. 3.	R. 4.	R. 5.	R. 6.	R. 7.	R. 8.	R. 9.	R. 10.	R. 11.	R. 12.	R. 13.	R. 14.	R. 15.	R. 16.	R. 17.	R. 18.	R. 19.	R. 20.	R. 21.	R. 22.	R. 23.	R. 24.	R. 25.	R. 26.	R. 27.	R. 28.	R. 29.	R. 30.	R. 31.	R. 32.
1	2	3	4	5	6	7	8	9	10	11	12	13																																
Adiantum—																																												
capillus-veneris	68												I	I	I	I	I															X					X			N	N	N		
pedatum	68							x					I	I		I																		N	X	N	N	N	N	X	X			
Althaea—																																												
ficifolia	60		x	x						x	x	x	I	I	I	I																				X	X	X	X	X	X	X	X	X
rosea	57		x								x	x	I	I	I	I	I	I	I	I	I	I	I	X	X	X	X	X		X	X		N	N	N	N	N	N	N	N	N	X		
Anemone—																																												
canadensis	62		x	x	x			x											I	I											X			N	X	N	N	X	N	X	X			
coronaria	62	x	x				x						I	I	I	I																			X	X		X	X					
japonica	62				x	x			x	x		[illegible]	I	I	I	I	I					I	I					I			I	I		X	X	X	X	X	X	X	X	X		
Aquilegia—																																												
canadensis	28	x	x					x					X	X	X	X	X	X	I	I	I		I	X	X	X	N	N	N	N	N	X	N	N	N	N	N	N	N	N	N	X		
chrysantha	28		x	x						x			X	X	X	X	X	X	X	X	X	X	N	X	X	N		X			X	X	X	X	X	X	X	X	X	X	X	X		
caerulea	28		x	x				x					X	X	X	X		X	X	X	X	X	X	N	N	N		X			X	X	X	X	X	X	X	X	X	X	X			
vulgaris	28		x	x				x					X	X		X		X	X	X	X			X	X	X		X			X	X	X	X	X	X	X	X	X	X				
Arundo donax	65											x	X	X	X	X	I					I	I						X			X					X		X	X	X	X		
Asplenium spp	68							x	x				I	I										I	I	I										X	X	X	X	X	X	X	X	
Bambusa	65												X		X		X					I																			X	X	X	X
Bergerocactus emoryi	54								x								N					X							X															X
Campanula—																																												
carpatica	31			x	x			x	x				I	I	I	I		I	I		I			X	X		X						X	X	X	X	X	X	X					
glomerata	31			x	x			x	x				I		I	I		I	I		I			X	X								X	X	X	X	X	N	N					
latiloba	31			x									I	I		I		I	I		I			X	X								P			P	X	X	X					
medium	32		x	x					x	x			I	I	I	I	I	I	I		I	I	I	X	X		X			X			X		X	X	X	X	X	X	X	X		
medium calycanthema	32			x	x				x				I	I		I		I	I		I			X	X								X		X	X	X	X	X					
persicifolia	31		x	x					x				I	I		I		I	I		I			X	X								X			X	X	X	X	X	X	X		
pyramidalis	32		x	x	x				x	x			I	I	I	I		I	I		I			X	X								X	X	X	X	X		X	X				
rotundifolia	31		x	x	x		x	x					I	I	I	N		I	I		I			N	N	N				N			N	N	N	N	X	N	N	X				
Camptosorus rhizophyllus	67						x																										N	N	N	N	N	N	N	N	N			
Chrysanthemum—																																												
coccineum	27		x	x				x																										X			X	X	X					
hortorum	27					x				x	x		X	X	X			X					I					I				X					X			X	X	X	X	X
indicum	27					x		x	x				X	X	X		X				X	X	X					I			X	X		X			X							
maximum	27		x	x	x			x	x				X	X	X	X	X	X	X	X	X	X							I			X	X	X	X	X	X	X	X	X	X	X		
morifolium	27					x				x	x		X	X	X			X										I				X					X	X	X	X	X	X		
uliginosum	27									x	x					X		X	X	X	X							I			X	X		X	X	X		X	X	X				
Convallaria majalis	63	x					x						X	X		X		I	I	I	I			X	X	X	I	I		I	I		X	X	X	X	X	X	N	X				

HERBACEOUS PERENNIALS

Cortaderia argentea	65	--	--	--	--	--	--	--	--	--	--	x	X	--	X	--	X	--	--	--	--	I	I	--	--	--	--	--	I	--	--	X	--	--	--	--	X	--	--	X	X	X	X	X
Delphinium—																																												
cardinale	41	--	--	x	--	--	--	--	x	x	--	--	X	--	X	--	N	--	--	--	--	I	X	--	--	--	--	--	X	--	--	X	--	--	--	--	--	--	--	--	X	X	--	--
cultorum	41	--	x	x	x	--	--	--	--	x	x	x	I	I	I	I	--	I	I	I	I	--	--	X	X	X	X	--	--	X	--	--	--	--	--	X	X	--	X	X	--	--	--	--
elatum	40	--	x	x	x	--	--	--	--	x	--	--	I	I	I	I	--	I	I	I	I	--	--	X	X	X	X	--	--	X	--	--	X	--	X	X	--	X	X	--	X	X	--	--
exaltatum	40	--	--	x	--	--	--	--	--	x	--	--	I	I	I	I	--	--	--	--	--	--	--	--	--	--	--	--	--	--	--	--	--	X	--	--	X	--	--	X	--	--	--	--
fissum	40	--	x	x	x	--	--	--	--	--	x	--	I	I	I	I	--	I	I	I	I	--	--	X	X	X	X	--	--	X	--	--	X	X	X	X	X	X	X	X	X	X	--	--
formosum	40	--	x	x	--	--	--	--	x	--	--	--	I	I	I	I	--	I	I	I	I	--	--	X	X	X	X	--	--	X	--	--	X	X	X	X	X	X	X	X	X	X	--	--
grandiflorum	40	--	x	x	x	--	--	x	x	--	--	--	I	I	I	I	I	I	I	I	I	I	--	X	X	X	X	--	--	X	--	--	X	X	X	X	X	X	X	X	X	X	--	--
Dennstaedtia punctiloba	67	--	--	--	--	--	--	x	--	--	--	--	I	I	--	I	--	--	--	--	--	--	--	--	--	--	--	--	--	--	--	X	N	N	N	N	N	N	N	N	X	--	--	--
Dianthus—																																												
barbatus	33	--	x	--	--	--	--	x	--	--	--	--	I	I	I	--	--	I	--	--	--	--	I	--	--	--	--	I	--	--	--	X	X	X	X	X	X	X	X	X	X	X	--	--
caryophyllus	34	--	x	x	x	--	--	x	--	--	--	--	I	I	I	I	I	I	--	--	I	I	X	X	X	X	--	--	X	--	--	X	X	X	X	X	X	X	X	--	--	--	--	--
deltoides	34	--	x	--	--	--	x	--	--	--	--	--	I	I	--	I	--	I	--	--	--	--	I	--	--	--	--	X	--	--	X	--	X	X	X	X	X	X	X	X	--	--	--	--
plumarius	33	--	x	--	--	--	x	--	--	--	--	--	I	I	I	I	--	I	I	I	I	--	I	X	X	X	P	X	I	X	X	I	X	X	X	X	X	X	X	X	X	--	--	--
plumarius semperflorens	34	--	x	x	x	--	x	--	--	--	--	--	I	I	--	I	--	I	--	--	--	--	--	--	--	--	--	--	--	--	--	--	X	X	X	X	X	X	X	X	--	--	--	--
Dicentra sp.		--	x	--	--	--	--	--	--	--	--	--	I	I	I	I	I	I	N	I	I	--	--	P	P	P	--	P	--	P	X	X	X	N	N	N	N	N	N	N	X	--	--	--
Dryopteris—																																												
cristata	68	--	--	--	--	--	--	x	--	--	--	--	I	I	--	I	--	I	I	N	--	--	--	X	X	X	--	--	--	X	X	X	N	N	N	N	N	N	N	X	X	--	--	--
filixmas	67	--	--	--	--	--	--	x	x	--	--	--	I	I	--	N	--	I	I	I	--	--	--	N	N	N	X	X	--	N	X	--	N	X	N	N	X	N	X	X	X	--	--	--
novaboracense	67	--	--	--	--	--	--	x	--	--	--	--	I	I	--	I	--	I	I	I	--	--	--	X	X	X	--	--	--	X	X	X	N	N	N	N	N	N	N	N	X	--	--	--
spinulosa intermedia	67	--	--	--	--	--	--	x	--	--	--	--	--	--	--	I	--	I	I	I	--	--	--	N	X	X	N	--	--	N	--	--	N	N	N	N	N	N	N	N	X	--	--	--
Echinocactus—																																												
polycephalus	51	--	--	--	--	--	--	x	--	--	--	--	X	X	N	--	N	--	--	--	N	N	X	--	--	--	--	--	X	--	--	--	--	--	--	--	--	--	--	--	X	X	--	--
viridescens	51	--	--	--	--	--	x	--	--	--	--	--	X	--	X	--	N	--	--	--	--	N	X	--	--	--	--	--	X	--	--	--	--	--	--	--	--	--	--	X	X	--	--	--
Echinocereus rigidissimus	53	--	--	--	--	--	--	--	--	--	--	--	X	--	X	--	N	--	--	--	--	N	X	--	--	--	--	--	X	--	--	--	--	--	--	--	--	--	--	--	X	X	--	--
viridiflorus	53	--	--	--	--	--	--	--	--	--	--	--	--	X	X	X	X	X	X	X	N	X	N	--	X	X	--	N	N	--	N	X	--	--	--	--	--	--	--	--	--	--	--	--
Erythronium sp.	69	--	--	--	--	--	--	--	--	--	--	--	N	N	--	N	--	--	--	--	--	--	--	N	N	N	--	--	--	--	--	--	N	N	N	N	N	N	N	N	N	N	--	--
Funkia. See Niobe.																																												
Gentiana sp.	69	--	--	x	--	--	x	x	--	--	--	--	--	--	--	N	--	--	--	--	--	--	--	N	N	N	--	--	--	--	--	--	N	--	N	N	N	N	N	N	N	--	--	--
Gormania oreganum	45	--	--	--	--	--	x	--	--	--	--	--	N	N	--	N	--	N	N	X	X	--	--	X	X	X	--	--	--	--	--	--	--	--	X	X	--	X	X	--	--	--	--	--
Helenium—																																												
autumnale	56	--	--	--	x	x	--	--	x	x	--	--	X	X	X	X	X	X	X	X	X	X	I	X	X	X	N	X	X	N	N	X	N	N	N	N	N	N	N	N	N	X	--	--
hoopesi	56	--	x	x	x	--	--	x	x	--	--	--	--	--	--	X	--	X	X	X	X	--	--	N	N	N	P	--	--	--	--	--	--	--	--	X	--	X	X	X	--	--	--	--
Helianthus—																																												
decapetalus	55	--	--	x	x	--	--	--	--	x	x	--	X	X	X	--	X	--	--	--	--	X	X	--	--	--	--	X	X	--	--	X	X	X	X	N	N	N	N	N	X	X	--	--
rigidus	55	--	--	--	x	x	--	x	x	--	--	--	X	X	X	--	X	--	--	--	--	--	--	--	--	--	--	N	--	--	--	N	N	N	N	N	N	X	X	X	N	X	--	--
Hemerocallis	41																																											
aurantiaca		--	--	x	--	--	--	--	x	--	--	--	X	X	X	X	X	X	X	X	X	X	--	X	X	X	--	X	X	--	X	X	X	X	X	X	X	X	X	X	X	X	X	X
dumortieri		--	x	--	--	--	--	x	x	--	--	--	X	X	X	X	I	X	X	X	X	I	--	--	--	--	X	X	X	X	X	X	X	X	X	X	X	X	X	X	X	X	X	X
lilio-asphodelus		--	x	x	--	--	--	x	--	--	--	--	X	X	X	X	I	X	X	X	X	I	--	--	--	--	X	X	X	X	X	X	X	X	X	X	X	X	X	X	X	X	X	X
fulva		--	x	x	x	--	--	x	x	--	--	--	X	--	X	X	I	X	X	X	X	I	--	--	--	--	X	X	X	X	X	X	X	X	X	X	X	X	X	X	X	X	X	X
thunbergi		--	--	x	x	--	--	--	--	x	--	--	X	X	X	--	X	--	--	--	--	X	I	--	--	--	--	I	I	--	X	X	--	X	X	X	X	X	X	X	X	X	X	X
Hibiscus—																																												
coccineus	61	--	--	x	x	--	--	--	--	x	x	--	--	--	I	--	I	X	--	--	--	--	--	--	--	--	--	--	X	--	--	X	--	--	--	--	--	--	--	--	N	N	X	X
lasiocarpus	61	--	--	--	x	--	--	--	--	--	x	x	--	--	--	--	--	X	--	--	--	--	X	--	--	--	--	X	X	--	--	N	--	--	--	--	N	--	--	X	N	N	--	--
militaris	61	--	--	--	x	--	--	--	--	x	--	--	X	X	X	--	X	X	--	--	--	X	X	--	--	--	--	X	X	X	X	X	N	N	N	N	N	X	N	N	N	N	X	X
moscheutos	61	--	--	--	x	--	--	--	--	--	x	x	X	X	X	--	--	X	--	--	--	X	X	--	--	--	--	X	X	--	X	X	X	X	X	N	N	X	N	N	N	N	X	X
Homalocephala texensis	51	--	--	--	--	--	x	--	--	--	--	--	--	--	--	--	X	--	--	--	--	X	--	--	--	--	--	--	N	--	--	--	--	--	--	--	--	--	--	--	--	--	--	X

TABLE 1.—*Some herbaceous perennials suitable for use in the different sections of the United States*—Continued

Scientific name of plant	Season					Height (feet)						Regions [Reference is made to the map (fig. 66)]																															
	E	—	M	—	L	0	1	2	3	4	5																																
1	3	4	5	6	7	8	9	10	11	12	13	R. 1.	R. 2.	R. 3.	R. 4.	R. 5.	R. 6.	R. 7.	R. 8.	R. 9.	R. 10.	R. 11.	R. 12.	R. 13.	R. 14.	R. 15.	R. 16.	R. 17.	R. 18.	R. 19.	R. 20.	R. 21.	R. 22.	R. 23.	R. 24.	R. 25.	R. 26.	R. 27.	R. 28.	R. 29.	R. 30.	R. 31.	R. 32.
Iris																																											
albicans	x							x				X	X	X	X	X	X	X	X	X	X	X	X	X	X	X	X	X	X	X	X	X	X	X	X	X	X	X	X	X	X		
aphylla	x							x				X	X	X	X	X	X	X	X	X	X	X	X	X	X	X	X	X	X	X	X	X	X	X	X	X	X	X	X	X			
biflora	x					x						X	X	X	X	X	X	X	X	X	X	X	X	X	X	X	X	X	X	X	X	X	X	X	X	X	X	X	X	X			
cristata	x					x						X	X	X	X	X	X	X	X	X	X	X	X	X	X	X	X	X	X	X	X	X	X	X	X	N	X	N	X	X			
flavescens	x							x				X	X	X	X	X	X	X	X	X	X	X	X	X	X	X	X	X	X	X	X	X	X	X	X	X	X	X	X	X			
florentina	x						x					X	X	X	X	X	X	X	X	X	X	X	X	X	X	X	X	X	X	X	X	X	X	X	X	X	X	X	X	X			
germanica	x							x				X	X	X	X	X	X	X	X	X	X	X	X	X	X	X	X	X	X	X	X	X	X	X	X	X	X	X	X	X	X		
kaempferi		x							x			X	X	X	X		X	X	X	I		I				I	X		X	X		X	X	X	X	X	X	X	X				
laevigata		x							x			X	X	X	X		X	X	X	I		I				I	X		X	X		X	X	X	X	X	X	X	X				
missouriensis	x					x						X	X		X		X	X	X	N		N	N	N	N	N	N		N	X	X	X	X	X	X	X	X	X	X	X			
neglecta	x							x				X	X	X	X	X	X	X	X	X	X	X	X	X	X	X	X	X	X	X	X	X	X	X	X	X	X	X	X	X	X		
pallida	x							x				X	X	X	X	X	X	X	X	X	X	X	X	X	X	X	X	X	X	X	X	X	X	X	X	X	X	X	X	X	X		
pallida dalmatica	x								x			X	X	X	X	X	X	X	X	X	X	X	X	X	X	X	X	X	X	X	X	X	X	X	X	X	X	X	X	X	X		
plicata	x							x				X	X	X	X	X	X	X	X	X	X	X	X	X	X	X	X	X	X	X	X	X	X	X	X	X	X	X	X	X	X		
pseudacorus		x						x				X	X	X	X	X	X	X	X	X	X	X	X	X	X	I	X	X	X	X	X	X	X	X	X	X	X	X	X	X			
pumila	x					x						X	X	X	X	X	X	X	X	X	X	X	X	X	X	X	X	X	X	X	X	X	X	X	X	X	X	X	X	X	X		
sambucina	x							x				X	X	X	X	X	X	X	X	X	X	X	X	X	X	X	X	X	X	X	X	X	X	X	X	X	X	X	X	X	X		
siberica		x						x	x			X	X		X		X	X	X	X			X	X	X	X	X		X	X	X	X	X	X	X	X	X	X	X	X			
squalens	x							x				X	X	X	X	X	X	X	X	X	X	X	X	X	X	X	X	X	X	X	X	X	X	X	X	X	X	X	X	X			
variegata	x							x				X	X	X	X	X	X	X	X	X	X	X	X	X	X	X	X	X	X	X	X	X	X	X	X	X	X	X	X	X			
versicolor	x	x					x	x				X	X	X	X	X	X	X	X	X	X	X	X	X	X	N	X	X	N	X	X	N	N	N	N	N	N	N	N	N	N		
xiphioides	x						x					X	X	X	X	X	X	X	X	X	X	X													X								
xiphium	x							x				X	X	X	X	X	X	X	X	X	X	X											X			X							
Lilium sp		x	x	x	x		x	x	x	x		I	I	I	I	I	I	I	I	I	I	I	X	X	X		X				X	X	X	X	X	X	X	X	X	X	X	X	X
Mammillaria—																																											
grahami						x						X	X	X	X	N	X	X	X	X	N	N	X	X	X	X	X	N	X	X	X												
missouriensis						x							X		X	X	X	X	X	X	X	X	X	X	X	N	N	X	N	N	X									X	X		
Miscanthus sinensis					x					x	x	X	X	X	X	X	X	X	X	X	I	I					I	I		X	X		X	X	X	X	X	X	X	X	X	X	X	X
Niobe—																																											
caerulea			x				x																									X	X	X	X	X	X	X	X	X	X		
fortunei			x				x					X	X	I			X																X		X	X	X	X	X	X	X		
lancifolia			x	x			x					X	X	I			X																X		X	X	X	X	X	X	X		
sieboldiana		x					x					X	X	X			X																X			X	X	X	X	X	X		
subcordata				x			x					X	X	I			X																X			X	X	X	X	X	X		
Opuntia—																																											
arenaria	x					x								X		X					X	X						N			N									N	N		
humifusa						x								X	X	X	X	X	X	X	X	X	X	X	X		X	X	N		N	N	N	N	N	N							
phaecantha							x							X	X	N	X	X	X	X	N	N	X	X	X		X	N		X	X		X			X							
polyacantha						x						X	X	X	X	X	X	X	X	X	X	X	X	X	X	N	N	X	N	N	X	N	N	N	X	X	X	X	X	X	X		

HERBACEOUS PERENNIALS

Osmunda—																																											
cinnamomea	--	--	--	--	--	--	--	X	X	X	--	I	I	--	I	--	I	I	I	--	--	N	X	N	X	--	--	--	X	X	X	X	N	N	N	N	N	N	N	N	--	--	--
claytoniana	--	--	--	--	--	--	--	X	X	X	--	I	I	--	I	--	I	I	I	--	--	--	X	X	X	--	--	--	X	X	X	N	N	N	N	N	N	N	X	X	--	--	--
regalis	--	--	--	--	--	--	--	--	X	X	X	I	I	--	I	--	I	I	I	--	--	--	X	X	X	--	--	--	X	N	X	N	N	N	N	N	N	N	N	N	N	--	--
Paeonia officinalis	X	--	--	--	--	--	--	X	--	--	--	X	X	X	X	--	X	X	X	X	--	X	X	X	X	X	X	--	X	X	X	X	X	X	X	X	X	X	X	X	--	--	--
Pediocactus simpsoni	--	--	--	--	--	X	--	--	--	--	--	X	X	X	X	X	X	X	X	N	X	X	N	N	X	--	X	X	--	X	X	--	--	--	--	--	--	--	--	--	--	--	--
Pennisetum—																																											
japonicum	--	--	--	--	--	--	--	X	--	X	--	--	--	--	--	I	--	--	--	--	X	--	--	--	--	--	--	--	--	--	--	--	--	--	--	X	--	--	X	X	X	X	X
longistylum	--	--	--	--	--	--	X	--	--	--	--	--	--	I	--	I	--	--	--	--	--	--	--	--	--	--	--	--	--	--	--	--	--	--	--	--	--	--	--	--	X	X	--
ruppeli	--	--	--	--	--	--	--	X	--	--	--	--	--	I	--	I	--	--	--	--	--	--	--	--	--	--	--	--	--	--	--	--	--	--	--	--	--	--	--	--	X	X	--
Phegopteris polypodioides	--	--	--	--	--	X	--	--	--	--	--	--	--	--	N	--	N	N	--	--	--	--	N	--	--	N	--	--	N	--	--	N	--	N	N	--	N	N	--	--	--	--	--
Phlox—																																											
divaricata	X	X	--	--	--	X	--	--	--	--	--	I	I	--	I	--	I	I	I	--	--	--	X	X	X	X	X	--	X	X	X	X	N	N	N	N	N	N	N	N	N	--	--
maculata	--	X	X	--	--	X	X	X	--	--	--	I	I	--	I	--	I	I	I	--	--	--	X	X	X	X	X	--	X	X	X	X	N	N	N	N	X	N	N	N	N	--	--
ovata	--	--	--	--	--	--	X	X	--	--	--	I	I	I	I	--	I	I	I	--	--	--	X	X	X	X	X	--	X	X	X	X	X	X	X	X	--	N	N	N	X	--	--
paniculata	--	--	--	--	--	--	--	X	X	--	--	I	I	I	I	--	I	I	I	--	--	--	X	X	X	X	X	--	X	X	X	X	N	X	X	N	X	N	N	N	N	--	--
subulata	X	--	--	--	--	X	--	--	--	--	--	I	I	I	I	--	I	I	I	--	--	--	X	X	X	X	X	--	X	X	X	X	X	X	N	N	X	N	N	N	N	--	--
Platycodon grandiflorum	--	--	X	--	--	--	X	X	--	--	--	I	I	--	I	--	I	I	I	--	--	--	X	X	X	--	X	X	X	X	X	X	X	X	X	X	X	X	X	X	--	--	--
Polystichum acrostichoides	--	--	--	--	--	--	X	--	--	--	--	--	--	--	--	--	--	--	--	--	--	--	--	--	--	--	--	--	--	--	N	--	N	N	N	N	N	N	N	N	--	--	--
Rudbeckia—																																											
hirta	--	--	--	X	--	--	X	X	--	--	--	X	X	X	X	X	X	X	X	X	X	X	X	X	X	N	N	X	N	N	N	N	N	N	N	N	N	N	N	N	N	--	--
laciniata	--	--	X	X	--	--	--	--	X	X	X	X	X	X	X	X	X	X	X	X	X	N	N	N	N	N	N	N	N	N	N	N	N	N	N	N	N	N	N	N	N	--	--
nitida	--	--	--	X	--	--	--	X	X	--	--	X	X	X	X	X	X	--	--	--	X	X	--	--	--	--	X	--	--	X	N	--	X	--	--	X	--	--	X	N	N	--	--
Sedum—																																											
acre	--	X	--	--	--	X	--	--	--	--	--	X	X	X	X	X	X	--	--	--	X	X	--	X	X	--	X	X	--	X	X	X	X	X	X	X	X	N	X	X	X	X	X
aizoon	--	--	--	X	--	X	--	--	--	--	--	X	X	X	X	X	X	--	--	--	X	X	--	X	X	--	X	X	--	X	X	X	X	X	X	X	X	X	X	X	X	X	X
album	--	--	X	X	--	X	--	--	--	--	--	X	X	X	X	X	--	--	--	--	X	X	X	X	X	--	X	X	--	X	X	X	X	X	X	X	X	X	X	X	X	--	--
fabaria	--	--	--	--	--	X	X	--	--	--	--	X	X	X	X	X	--	--	--	--	X	X	--	--	--	--	X	X	--	X	X	--	X	X	X	X	X	X	X	X	X	--	--
hybridum	--	--	X	--	--	X	--	--	--	--	--	X	X	X	X	X	X	X	X	X	X	X	X	X	X	X	X	X	X	X	X	X	X	X	X	X	X	X	X	X	X	--	--
kamtschaticum	--	--	X	X	--	X	--	--	--	--	--	X	X	X	X	X	X	X	X	X	X	X	X	X	X	X	X	X	X	X	X	X	X	X	X	X	X	X	X	--	--	--	--
maximowiczi	--	--	--	X	--	X	--	--	--	--	--	X	X	X	X	X	X	--	--	--	X	X	--	X	X	--	X	X	--	X	X	X	X	X	X	X	X	X	X	X	X	X	X
maximum	--	--	--	--	--	--	X	--	--	--	--	X	X	X	X	X	X	X	--	--	X	X	--	--	--	--	X	X	--	X	X	--	X	X	X	X	X	X	X	X	--	--	--
reflexum	--	--	--	--	--	X	--	--	--	--	--	X	X	X	X	X	X	X	--	X	X	X	--	--	--	--	X	X	--	X	X	--	X	--	X	X	X	N	X	X	X	--	--
roseum	--	--	X	X	--	X	--	--	--	--	--	X	X	X	X	X	X	--	--	--	X	X	--	--	--	--	X	X	--	X	X	--	X	--	X	X	N	X	X	X	X	--	--
rupestre	--	--	--	--	--	X	--	--	--	--	--	X	X	X	X	X	X	--	--	--	X	X	--	--	--	--	X	X	--	X	X	--	X	--	X	X	X	X	X	X	X	--	--
sexangulare	--	X	--	--	--	X	--	--	--	--	--	X	X	X	X	X	X	X	X	X	X	X	X	X	X	X	X	X	X	X	X	X	X	X	X	X	X	X	X	X	X	X	X
sieboldi	--	--	--	X	--	X	--	--	--	--	--	X	X	X	X	X	X	--	--	--	X	X	--	--	--	--	X	X	--	X	X	--	X	X	X	X	X	X	X	X	X	X	X
spectabile	--	--	--	X	--	--	X	--	--	--	--	X	X	X	X	X	X	--	--	--	X	X	--	--	--	--	X	X	--	X	X	X	X	X	X	X	X	X	X	X	X	X	X
stoloniferum	--	--	--	--	--	X	--	--	--	--	--	X	X	X	X	X	--	--	--	--	X	X	--	--	--	--	X	X	--	X	X	X	X	X	X	X	N	X	X	X	X	X	X
telephium	--	X	X	X	--	--	X	--	--	--	--	X	X	X	X	X	X	X	X	X	X	X	X	X	X	--	X	X	--	X	X	--	X	X	X	X	X	X	X	X	X	X	X
Syndesmon thalictroides	X	X	--	--	--	X	--	--	--	--	--	I	I	--	I	--	I	I	I	--	--	--	X	X	X	X	X	--	N	N	N	N	N	N	N	N	X	N	N	N	X	--	--
Trillium grandiflorum	X	--	--	--	--	X	--	--	--	--	--	--	--	--	--	--	--	--	--	--	--	--	--	--	--	--	--	--	--	--	--	--	N	N	N	N	N	N	N	--	--	--	--
Woodsia obtusa	--	--	--	--	--	--	--	--	--	--	--	--	--	--	--	--	--	--	--	--	--	N	--	--	--	--	N	--	--	N	N	--	N	N	N	N	N	N	N	N	--	--	--
Yucca—																																											
baccata	--	--	--	--	--	--	--	--	--	--	--	X	X	X	X	N	X	X	X	N	N	N	X	X	X	X	N	X	X	X	X	X	X	X	X	X	X	X	X	X	X	X	X
filamentosa	--	--	X	--	--	--	--	--	X	--	--	X	X	X	X	X	X	X	X	X	X	X	--	X	X	--	X	X	--	X	X	--	X	--	X	X	X	X	N	N	N	--	--
flaccida	--	--	X	--	--	--	--	--	X	--	--	X	X	X	X	X	X	X	X	X	X	X	--	X	X	--	X	X	--	X	X	--	X	--	X	X	X	X	N	N	X	--	--
glauca	--	--	X	--	--	--	--	X	X	--	--	X	X	X	X	X	X	--	--	--	N	N	--	--	--	--	N	N	N	N	N	N	N	X	X	X	X	X	X	X	X	--	--
harrimaniae	--	--	--	--	--	X	--	--	--	--	--	X	X	X	X	X	X	X	X	N	X	N	X	X	N	X	X	X	--	X	X	--	X	X	X	X	X	X	X	X	X	--	--

INDEX OF COMMON NAMES

Common name	Scientific name
Adams Needle	Yucca flaccida
Adams-needle-and-thread.	Yucca filamentosa
Alyssum, sweet	Lobularia maritima
Amaryllis	
American shield fern.	Dryopteris spinulosa intermedia.
Anemone:	
Japanese	Anemone japonica
poppy	Anemone coronaria
rue	Syndesmon thalictroides.
Aquilegia	
Arbutus, trailing	
Asplenium	
Aster	
August lily	Niobe plantaginea
Autumn glory	Rudbeckia nitida
Autumn sun	do
Balloonflower	Platycodon grandiflorum.
Bamboo	Bambusa
Beargrass. See Soapweed yucca.	
Bearded iris	Many species
Bee larkspur	Delphinium elatum
Beech fern	Phegopteris
Begonia	
Bell:	
Canterbury	Campanula medium
cup-and-saucer Canterbury.	Campanula medium calycanthema.
peach	Campanula persicifolia.
white peach	Campanula persicifolia alba grandiflora.
Bellflower	Campanula
Canterbury	Campanula medium
chimney	Campanula pyramidalis.
Chinese	Platycodon grandiflorum.
clustered	Campanula glomerata
cup-and-saucer	Campanula medium calycanthema.
great	Campanula latiloba
Japanese	Platycodon grandiflorum.
peach	Campanula persicifolia.
peachleaf	do
Black-eyed-susan	Rudbeckia hirta
Bluebell	Campanula rotundifolia.
Carpathian	Campanula carpatica
Bluet	
Blue flag	Iris
Blue phlox, wild	Phlox divaricata
Blue plantainlily	Niobe caerulea
Bulbs	
Cactus	
cob	
dwarf	Mammillaria
plains	Pediocactus simpsoni
rainbow	Echinocereus viridiflorus.
snowball	Pediocactus simpsoni
star	Mammillaria missouriensis.
strawberry	
Campanula	
Canna	
Canterbury-bells	Campanula medium
Carnation	Dianthus
Castor-bean	Ricinus communis
Chimney bellflower	Campanula pyramidalis.
Chinese bellflower	Platycodon grandiflorum.
Christmas fern	Polystichum acrostichoides.
Chrysanthemum	
florists	Chrysanthemum hortorum.
hardy	do
Cinnamon fern	Osmunda cinnamomea.
Clayton fern	Osmunda claytoniana
Clove pink	Dianthus caryophyllus.
Coleus	
Columbine:	
American	Aquilegia canadensis
Colorado	Aquilegia caerulea
common European.	Aquilegia vulgaris
golden spurred	Aquilegia chrysantha
Common yellow iris.	Iris pseudacorus
Creeping jenny	Sedum reflexum
Crimson-eye rosemallow.	Hibiscus oculiroseus
Crinum	
Crocus	
Cup-and-saucer Canterbury-bells.	Campanula medium calycanthema.
Cup-and-saucer bellflower.	do
Cushion plantainlily.	Niobe sieboldiana
Dahlia	
Daisy:	
Alaska	
giant	Chrysanthemum uliginosum.
painted	Chrysanthemum coccineum.
Shasta	Chrysanthemum maximum.
yellow	Rudbeckia hirta
Daylily	Hemerocallis and Niobe.
dwarf orange	Hemerocallis dumortieri.
early	do
Japanese	Hemerocallis thunbergi.
lemon	Hemerocallis lilioasphodelus.
old-fashioned	Hemerocallis fulva
orange	Hemerocallis aurantiaca.
tawny	Hemerocallis fulva
yellow	Hemerocallis
Delphinium	
Dianthus	
Dogtooth violet	Erythronium
Dutchmans-breeches	Dicentra cucullaria
Dwarf iris	Iris aphylla, cristata
Dwarf orange daylily.	Hemerocallis dumortierii.
Early daylily	do
English iris	Iris xiphioides
Eulalia	Miscanthus sinensis
Japanese	do
striped	Miscanthus sinensis variegatus.
Fern	
American shield	Dryopteris spinulosa intermedia.
beech	Dryopteris phegopteris
Christmas	Polystichum
cinnamon	Osmunda cinnamomea.
Clayton	Osmunda claytoniana
maidenhair	Adiantum pedatum
male	Dryopteris filixmas

HERBACEOUS PERENNIALS

Index of common names—Continued

Common name	Scientific name
Fern—Continued.	
New York	Dryopteris noveboracensis.
royal	Osmunda regalis
walking	Camptosorus
Feverfew	Chrysanthemum parthenium.
Figleaf hollyhock	Althaea ficifolia
Flag	
Flag, blue. See Bearded iris.	
Fleur-de-lis. See Bearded iris.	
Florists chrysanthemum.	Chrysanthemum hortorum.
Fortune plantainlily.	Niobe fortunei
Fountain grass, hardy.	Pennisetum japonicum.
purple	Pennisetum rupelli
white	Pennisetum longistylum.
Foxglove	
Funkia. See Plantainlily.	
Gaillardia	
Gentian	
Geranium	
German iris. See Bearded iris.	
Giant daisy	Chrysanthemum uliginosum.
Giant-flowered rosemallow.	Hibiscus hybrids
Giant reed	Arundo donax
Glory-of-the-snow	
Goldenglow	Rudbeckia laciniata
Goldenrod	
Goldmoss	Sedum acre
Grass	
bear	Yucca glauca
fountain	Pennisetum
pampas	Cortaderia argentea
Grass pink	Dianthus plumarius
Great bellflower	Campanula latiloba
Great stonecrop	Sedum maximum
Green-flowered petaya.	Echinocereus viridiflorus.
Ground pink	Phlox subulata
Harebell	Campanula rotundifolia.
Carpathian	Campanula carpatica.
Hardy chrysanthemum.	Chrysanthemum hortorum.
garden pink	Dianthus plumarius
Helenium	
Heliotrope	
Hexagon stonecrop	Sedum sexangulare
Holland bulbs	
Hollyhock	Althaea rosea
figleaf	Althaea ficifolia
Homestead pink	Dianthus plumarius semperflorens.
Iris	
bearded	Iris hybrida, germanica, neglecta, etc.
common yellow	Iris pseudacorus
dwarf	Iris aphylla and others
English	Iris xiphioides
German. See Bearded iris.	
Japanese	Iris kaempferi
Siberian	Iris siberica
Spanish	Iris xiphium
wild native	Iris versicolor
yellow water	Iris pseudacorus
Japanese anemone	Anemone japonica
bellflower	Platycodon grandiflorum.
daylily	Hemerocallis thunbergi.
eulalia	Miscanthus sinensis
iris	Iris kaempferi

Common name	Scientific name
Ladyslipper	Cypripedium
Lanceleaf plantainlily.	Niobe japonica
Lantana	
Larkspur, bee	Delphinium elatum
perennial	Delphinium
Lemon daylily	Hemerocallis lilio-asphodelus.
Lily	
Lily, August. See Plantainlily.	
day. See Daylily and Plantainlily.	
homestead	Hemerocallis fulva
of-the-valley	Convallaria majalis
old-fashioned	Hemerocallis fulva
plantain. See Plantainlily.	
Liveforever	Sedum telephium
Love-entangle	Sedum acre
Maiden grass	Miscanthus sinensis gracillima.
Maidenhair fern	Adiantum pedatum
Maiden pink	Dianthus deltoides
Male fern	Dryopteris filixmas
Mallow, Meehan's Marvel.	Hibiscus hybrids
Marshmallow. See Rosemallow.	
Mellish, Miss. See Miss Mellish.	
Mesembryanthemum.	
Miss Mellish	Helianthus rigidus
Missouri pricklypear.	Opuntia polyacantha
Moss pink	Phlox subulata
Mossy stonecrop	Sedum acre
Mountain pink	Phlox ovata
Narcissus	
Needle, Adams	Yucca flaccida
Needle-and-thread, Adams.	Yucca filamentosa
New York fern	Dryopteris noveboracensis.
Niggerhead	Rudbeckia hirta
Old-fashioned daylily.	Hemerocallis fulva
Opuntia	
Orange daylily	Hemerocallis aurantiaca.
Orange stonecrop	Sedum kamtschaticum
Oregon stonecrop	Gormania oregana
Painted daisy	Chrysanthemum coccineum.
Pansy	
Peony	
Pepper, wall. See Wall pepper.	
Perennial larkspur	Delphinium
Perpetual pink	Dianthus plumarius semperflorens.
Petaya, green-flowered.	Echinocereus viridiflorus.
Petunia	
Pheasanteye pink	Dianthus plumarius
Phlox	
garden	Phlox paniculata
moss	Phlox subulata
wild blue	Phlox divaricata
Picotee	Dianthus caryophyllus
Piney	Paeonia officinalis
Pink	Dianthus spp
clove	Dianthus caryophyllus
garden	Dianthus plumarius
grass	Dianthus plumarius
ground	Phlox subulata
hardy garden	Dianthus plumarius
homestead	Dianthus plumarius semperflorens
maiden	Dianthus deltoides
moss	Phlox subulata

Index of common names—Continued

Common name	Scientific name
Pink—Continued.	
mountain	Phlox ovata.
perpetual	Dianthus plumarius semperflorens.
pheasanteye	Dianthus plumarius.
Scotch	Dianthus plumarius.
Plains cactus	Pediocactus simpsoni.
Plantain lily	Niobe.
blue	Niobe caerulea.
cushion	Niobe sieboldiana.
Fortune	Niobe fortunei.
lanceleaf	Niobe japonica.
white	Niobe plantaginea.
Platycodon	
Poppy anemone	Anemone coronaria.
Pricklypear	Opuntia.
Missouri	Opuntia polyacantha.
Pyrethrum	Chrysanthemum coccineum.
Rainbow cactus	Echinocereus rigidissimus.
Reed, giant	Arundo donax.
Riverton Beauty	Helenium.
Riverton Gem	do.
Rosemallow	Hibiscus moscheutos.
crimson-eye	Hibiscus oculiroseus.
giant-flowered	Hibiscus hybrids.
Roseroot stonecrop	Sedum roseum.
Royal fern	Osmunda regalis.
Rudbeckia	
Rue anemone	Syndesmon thalictroides.
Running stonecrop	Sedum stoloniferum.
Sage, scarlet	
Scarlet running stonecrop.	Sedum stoloniferum coccineum.
Scilla	
Scotch pink	Dianthus plumarius.
Sedum	
Shasta daisy	Chrysanthemum maximum.
Shield fern, American.	Dryopteris spinulosa intermedia.
Showy stonecrop	Sedum spectabile.
Siberian iris	Iris siberica.
Siebold stonecrop	Sedum sieboldi.
Sneezeweed	Helenium.
Riverton Beauty.	do.
Riverton Gem	do.
Snapdragon	
Snowball cactus	Pediocactus simpsoni.
Snowdrop	
Soapweed	Yucca glauca or Yucca angustifolia.
Soapweed yucca	Yucca glauca.
Soleil d'Or	Helianthus decapetalus.
Spanish iris	Iris xiphium.
Squirrelcorn	Dicentra (canadensis).
Star cactus	Mammillaria missouriensis.
Stonecrop	
great	Sedum maximum.
hexagon	Sedum sexangulare.
hybrid	Sedum hybridum.
mossy	Sedum acre.
orange	Sedum kamtschaticum.
Oregon	Gormania oregana.
roseroot	Sedum roseum.
running	Sedum stoloniferum.
scarlet running	Sedum stoloniferum coccineum.
showy	Sedum spectabile.
Siebold	Sedum sieboldi.
Striped eulalia	Miscanthus sinensis variegatus.
Sunflower	
Miss Mellish	Helianthus rigidus.
Soleil d'Or	Helianthus decapetalus.
Susan, black-eyed	Rudbecia hirta.
Sweet-william	Dianthus barbatus.
wild	Phlox divaricata.
Tawny daylily	Hemerocallis fulva.
Thread, Adam's-needle-and.	Yucca filamentosa.
Trailing arbutus	Epigaea repens.
Trillium	
Troutlily	Erythronium.
Violet	
Violet, dogtooth	Erythronium.
Wakerobin	Trillium.
Wall pepper	Sedum acre.
Walking fern	Camptosorus.
Water iris, yellow	Iris pseudacorus.
White plantainlily	Niobe plantaginea.
stonecrop	Sedum album.
Wild blue phlox	Phlox divaricata.
native iris	Iris versicolor.
sweet-william	Phlox divaricata.
Windflower	
Yellow daisy	Rudbeckia hirta.
daylily	Hemerocallis.
iris, common	Iris pseudacorus.
water iris	do.
Yucca	
soapweed	Yucca glauca.
Zebra grass	Miscanthus sinensis zebrina.
Zinnia	

CARE OF TREES

—*Selecting, Planting, and Caring for Trees*

ANALYSIS

Operation	Standard or accepted practice
1. Mark location and arrangement of tree plantings.	Review available literature,[1] pictures, and diagrams of ornamental planting to see how trees may be used to best advantage. Study your map and landscaping plan to determine the most desirable location for trees A helpful procedure for deciding the location of trees is to study kodak pictures of the place taken from different angles and try to visualize where the addition of trees would make the view more attractive. Avoid straight line arrangement except along roads. Indicate final tree locations on your map. Allow plenty of room for trees to develop.
2. Select suitable types and varieties of trees.	Make a trip or two in the locality to determine availability of native plantings. Use, as far as possible, types and varieties that are native to and representative of your locality which are suitable for your particular situation. Give consideration to the following points in choosing trees: *a.* Maximum height and spread when mature. Tall spreading trees are desirable for background or screening effects. Low compact growths may be more suitable for other purposes. *b.* Ease of starting, especially when transplanted from wild state. Trees vary in their ability to withstand transplanting. *c.* Rapidity of growth. For quick effect, rapid-growing trees may be used, although such trees are apt to be rather short lived. Such trees as the poplars, box-elder, cottonwood, and other soft woods are relatively early maturing. *d.* Permanence. The hardwoods, such as maples, elms, oaks, hickory, and other nut-bearing trees are relatively long lived. *e.* Susceptibility to insects or disease. Some varieties are especially susceptible to damage or serve as a host plant for insects and diseases which makes them undesirable as ornamental plantings.

Selecting, Planting, and Caring for Trees—Continued

Operation	Standard or accepted practice
2. Select suitable types and varieties of trees—Con.	Give consideration to the following points in choosing trees—Continued. *f.* Flower or foliage habits. Permanence of foliage throughout the summer season should be considered in selecting deciduous varieties. Some trees necessitate undue work in preventing an unsightly litter on the lawn due to their habits of shedding flowers, seeds, or leaves. Indicate on your map the type and kind of trees to be used.
3. Secure planting stock	Locate and mark available native young trees suitable for transplanting. Inspect closely and select only good, vigorous, healthy specimens with well-shaped top, free from insect or disease damage. Young trees are usually transplanted with greater success than older ones. Larger ones require greater precaution and care in transplanting. Trees growing in outer edges of woods or in open spaces are more desirable than those growing in thickets or deep woods. Plan to transplant native stock selected at the proper season. Order stock from reputable nurseries or from dealers located permanently in your region whose stocks are of high quality and likely to be adapted to local climatic conditions. If possible, inspect stock before purchasing. Keep roots of planting stock well dampened and protected from wind and sun until ready to set out. Keep stock in a cool damp place or "heel in" if the planting must be delayed for a few days.
4. Prepare holes	Dig holes large enough to receive all the roots when spread in their natural position, without bending or doubling them back. Dig the holes deep enough to set the tree at the same depth as before transplanting. Place 3 or 4 inches of rich top soil, which has been thoroughly pulverized, in the bottom of the hole. A small amount of well-rotted manure may be used if it is so thoroughly mixed with the soil that it does not come in contact with the roots.
5. Prepare the stock for planting.	Nursery stock will usually come properly prepared for planting. Locally transplanted stock may need some root pruning as well as top pruning. Trim off all broken or bruised root ends, taking care to preserve as much of the general root mass undisturbed as possible. Preserve all small and fine roots. Remove dead roots. Tops should be pruned back *after trees are set.*

***—Selecting, Planting, and Caring for Trees*—Continued**

Operation	Standard or accepted practice
6. Plant tree	Set the tree in the hole at about the same depth at which it originally grew, filling under the roots with good soil to bring it to the proper height. Spread the roots as necessary to get them in natural position. Work very fine top soil well around the roots packing it firmly so that no open spaces are left under or around the roots. Tamp the soil well as you fill the hole. When the hole is about two-thirds full slowly add as much water as will be absorbed readily. Finish filling the hole with top soil without additional compacting. Tops should be pruned back after the trees are set somewhat in proportion to the loss of roots. Severe top pruning to the extent of one-half of the original top is usually recommended for deciduous trees. Remove whole limbs or branches and cut back the ends of remaining branches without changing general natural shape. Cut branches close and smoothly without leaving stubs. Broad leaf evergreens are pruned similar to deciduous plants. Other evergreens require little or no pruning if a good ball of earth has been removed with the roots.
7. Protect newly planted trees	Tie young trees securely to a heavy stake or to a framework to prevent loosening by the wind or damage from animals. Large trees should be held firmly in place by guy wires attached to "dead men" on at least three sides. Provide wire screening if there is likelihood of gnawing by rabbits or other pests. Soak the newly planted trees thoroughly at frequent intervals during dry weather. Keep the soil cultivated around the trees and cover with a mulch of manure worked into the surface soil.

INTERPRETIVE SCIENCE AND RELATED INFORMATION

Woody plants, including trees, may be divided into two main groups—deciduous and evergreen. Deciduous plants shed their leaves at the close of the growing season. This group constitutes the principal tree growth in most parts of the country and in most localities. Evergreens hold their leaves during the winter, shedding them gradually as new leaves are formed so that a continuous green foliage is maintained throughout the year.

Evergreens are divided into two groups—coniferous and broad leaf. The cone-bearing or coniferous evergreens, such as pines, firs, and cedars, have leaves in the form of slender needles or close scales. Broad leaf evergreens, such as the magnolia, rhododendron, and mountain laurel, have leaves with relatively broad blades. Coniferous varieties are common in the northeastern States, the upper Great Lakes region, the Rocky Mountain area, the Puget Sound region, and the mountainous regions of the South. The broad leaf varieties are found chiefly in the Southeastern States and the humid areas of the Pacific coast, although a few varieties are adapted to the hot dry climate of the southwestern interior. Comparatively few evergreens are suited to the drier parts of the United States unless they are given ample protection from the drying winds to prevent excessive evaporation. Among these is the Western yellow pine.

The use of native trees in landscaping is important for two reasons: (1) Such trees are accustomed to the soil and climate of the locality, and (2) the expense of plantings is kept to a minimum. Transplanting trees provides new growth where it is desired or replaces growth which has been destroyed.

The moving of selected plants from one location to plant them in another is called "transplanting". Successful transplanting depends upon the types and varieties selected, care in moving, soil moisture, and climatic conditions.

Trees are usually transplanted more successfully while very young due to the fact that this results in less root disturbance, but they will not develop fully for several years after transplanting. If proper care is exercised in digging and handling, trees up to 3 or 4 inches in diameter may be transplanted with reasonable success. Evergreens should be removed carefully with a good ball of earth to preserve the original root mass and during their removal the roots should be protected with wet burlap against the hot sun and drying winds which wither the tiny root hairs and dry up the root sap. Therefore, cool cloudy days with little or no wind are best for transplanting.

Trees that grow close to the edge of a wood or grove, when transplanted, are usually less affected by changes in shade and moisture conditions. Ample holes should be dug for transplanted trees so that roots will not be crowded and soft soil will settle around them. Too much coarse organic matter in the hole hinders the movement of capillary water in dry weather.

Severe top pruning is usually necessary in order to cut down the loss of moisture from the leaf surface until the root system again develops sufficiently to take care of the moisture supply needed. Cultivating the soil around the trees conserves the moisture supply by reducing evaporation, and also supplies plant food.

The right time for transplanting varies with the type of tree and the weather conditions. Deciduous trees should be moved during their dormant period—from the time season growth ends in the fall until just before root growth starts in the spring. With extra care they may be moved at other times. The best time to move them is usually in the spring or fall when the ground is not too wet. Because their foliage demands a continuous and abundant supply of moisture, evergreens, as a rule, require more care in transplanting than deciduous trees.

In selecting trees, attention must always be given to those native to or commonly found in the locality. Following is a suggested list of shade and ornamental trees:

SHADE AND ORNAMENTAL TREES SUITABLE FOR GROUNDS

I. Large Trees Used Chiefly for Shade, Wind Protection, Screening, or Background Effects

A. Deciduous

- **Ailanthus (Tree of Heaven)**
- **Ash—**
  - **Arizona**
  - **Black**
  - **Blue**
  - **European**
  - **Green**
  - **Oregon**
  - **White**
- **Basswood**
- **Beech**
- **Birch**
- **Box-elder**
- **Catalpa**
- **Chestnut**
- **Cottonwood**
- **Elm—**
  - **American**
  - **Chinese**
  - **English**
- **Gum—**
  - **Sour**
  - **Sweet**
- **Hackberry**
- **Hickory**
- **Linden, European**
- **Locust—**
  - **Black**
  - **Honey**
  - **Thornless Honey**
- **Maple—**
  - **Ash Leaved (Box-elder)**
  - **Norway**
  - **Oregon**
  - **Red**
  - **Sugar**
- **Mulberry**
- **Oak—**
  - **Live**
  - **Mossycup**
  - **Pin**
  - **Red**
  - **Spanish**
  - **Texas**
  - **White**
  - **Willow**
- **Pecan**
- **Planetree, London**
- **Poplar—**
  - **Carolina**
  - **Lombardy**
  - **Norway**
  - **Silver**
- **Sycamore—**
  - **California**
  - **Common**
- **Walnut—**
  - **Black**
  - **California Black**
- **Willow**

B. Evergreens

- **Arborvitae**
- **Camphor**
- **Cedar—**
  - **Himalayan**
- **Cypress—**
  - **Arizona**
  - **Guadalupe**
  - **Monterey**
- **Eucalyptus**
- **Fir**
- **Hemlock**
- **Holly**
- **Magnolia**
- **Palm—**
  - **Canary Island Date**
  - **Washington**
- **Palmetto—**
  - **Carolina**
  - **Texas**
- **Pine—**
  - **Austrian**
  - **Norway**
  - **Scotch**

Pine—
- Western Yellow
- White

Red Cedar
Redwood

Spruce—
- Black Hills
- Blue
- Norway
- White

II. Small Trees or Large Shrubs Having Distinctive Shape, Foliage, or Flowers Used Chiefly for Ornamental Purposes

A. Deciduous

Birch—
- Cutleaf Weeping
- White

Catalpa, Dwarf
Cherry—
- Black
- Choke
- Japanese Flowering
- Pin

Cockspur Thorn
Crab, Flowering
- Bechtel
- Double Flowering
- Parkman

Crabapple, Wild
Dogwood
Hawthorne
Hoptree, Common
Japanese Lilac
Mock Orange, Sweet
Mountain Ash—
- American
- European
- Showy

Nannyberry
Ninebark, Common
Redbud
Russian Olive
Shadblow—
- Downy
- Thicket

Siberian Pea Tree
Sumac—
- Shining
- Shredded
- Staghorn

Wahoo
Weeping Willow

B. Evergreens

Arborvitae
Holly
Juniper—
- Chinese
- Colorado
- Common

Magnolia
Spruce
Yew, Japanese

CARE OF DAMAGED SHADE TREES

Wounds, to which the woody parts of trees are constantly subject, are a primary cause of many tree troubles. In vigorously growing trees, most small wounds heal promptly without leading to any important damage. However, in each open wound lies potential disfigurement, impaired health, or untimely death. In many cases the ultimate harmful results that may follow such injuries can be rendered less threatening by prompt treatment after wounding occurs.

CAUSES OF WOUNDS AND HOW THEY MAY BE AVOIDED

Wounds involving the bark and woody parts of ornamental trees generally result from unfavorable meteorological or biological growing conditions. Most of these causes are so obvious and so well known as to warrant only brief summarizing here. Several of the more important of these causes are described in the following paragraphs, with suggestions for avoiding as far as is possible all unnecessary injuries to woody parts.

INJURIES DUE TO THE WEATHER

Unfavorable weather is one of the chief causes of shade-tree wounds. High winds at any season may break the tops and branches. In winter, deposits of glaze, sleet, and wet snow may so burden the trees by their weight as to cause failure of limbs, tops, and crotches, and leave in the wake of the storm countless jagged wounds. During the growing season hailstorms may bruise and tear the soft bark of less mature parts, causing myriads of small wounds. Electrical storms record their passing in shattered trunks and ragged streaks, which trace the paths of some of the lightning strokes. Frost cracks and dead areas of inner bark and cambium are common types of wounds resulting from low winter temperatures and early or late frosts and freezes. Sunscald may produce bark wounds regardless of the season. Prolonged drought may kill numerous branches and leave slow-healing branch stubs.

Although it is impossible to prevent adverse weather, much can be done to avert damage caused by it. Judicious pruning to eliminate closely crowded branches and to shorten abnormally long branches, or better still to prevent their formation, does much to avoid breakage by wind and sleet. Bolting and cabling of weak crotches are important. The installation of lightning rods in unusually valuable or priceless historic trees protects them from lightning. Vigorous, well-nourished trees are less subject to winter injury than are weak, starved trees. Marked differences in hardiness occur among various species and varieties of shade trees. Well-planned planting avoids the use of tender southern forms where they will suffer from rigorous winters, or conversely, the planting of northern forms where they will be exposed to very high summer temperatures. If the danger of sunscald is foreseen, the damage may often be averted by wrapping, or even by temporarily shading, the trunks with boards when conditions are particularly trying. Be especially solicitous of trees that are not only subjected to direct sun but are also exposed to its radiated and reflected heat from adjacent walls, sidewalks, and concrete roads. Remember that this type of injury is not restricted to summer. During the winter similar burning is common, especially in the case of evergreens. This usually occurs during periods when the air temperature is fairly high, the sun brilliant, and the ground frozen. Ice and snow often aid in causing the damage by reflecting the light.

Trees suddenly exposed to a marked increase in sunlight are liable to sunscald. If landscaping demands the thinning of natural forest, the work should be extended over a period of years rather than performed in a single release cutting. If a specimen tree requires heavy pruning, it is best to perform the work by degrees rather than as a single operation.

MAN-MADE WOUNDS

Man's lack of understanding of fundamental principles of tree welfare, his indifference in applying what knowledge he has, or the necessity for haste in war emergency construction results in much avoidable injury to trees.

Imprudent use of fire wounds many trees. There is little excuse for the careless burning over of land on which ornamentals are planted, for the burning of slash, brush, and litter too close to the tree, or for the too numerous cases where the path of a steam roller through a street is traceable by a wake of scorched limbs and foliage.

Automobiles wound many street trees. Carelessly used lawn mowers bark many trees growing on lawns. The average small boy armed with a knife or a hand ax causes damage to ornamental trees that grow in more secluded places. Some contractors work havoc with steam shovels, grading tools, and blasting materials, producing untold wounds of trunk, branch, and root. The installation of curbing and of sewer, water, and gas lines is frequently very damaging to street trees.

Ironical though it may seem, many of the injuries that man inflicts on trees are brought about by his misguided efforts in their behalf. Careless pruning provides many such examples. Lopping off enormous limbs unnecessarily often spoils the symmetry of a tree and leaves large exposed wounds. Badly filled cavities furnish another such menace. Careless application of routine tasks of guying and cabling without an understanding of the basic principles involved may cause choking or girdling. Tree bands not applied according to the recommendations of the entomologists are also a frequent cause of severe wounds. The application of cup grease directly to the bark in the hope of protecting the tree from insects is especially to be avoided. The burning out of caterpillar nests is another practice in which the control obtained is frequently not warranted when weighed against the injury done by scorching the bark.

ANIMAL-CAUSED WOUNDS

Animals also cause tree wounds. The gnawing of bark by hungry or impatient horses hitched within reach of trees was in the past one of the chief sources of damage to street trees. Tree guards generally furnish a simple and effective means of protection against such injury. Mice and rabbits frequently injure shade trees. Sapsuckers and other woodpeckers occasionally do damage. Information on the injuries caused by birds and rodents can be obtained from the Fish and Wildlife Service of the United States Department of the Interior, Washington, D. C.

INJURIES INFLICTED BY INSECTS

Insects cause untold damage to trees by direct attack on healthy tissue, by attack following openings or weaknesses induced by some other insects or other causes, or by acting as carriers for disease-producing agencies. Along with a multiplicity of widely varied injuries they produce and enlarge wounds. The Bureau of Entomology and Plant Quarantine of the United States Department of Agriculture and the State entomologist should be consulted in regard to all information relating to damage caused by insects.

INJURIES CAUSED BY PLANTS

Plants as well as animals may cause injury to trees. Among such plants are some of the flowering plants. Parasites such as the mistletoes, common on the shade trees of the South and far West, furnish a classic example of such injury. The American mistletoe can generally be held in check by occasionally breaking it off with a pole. Sometimes climbing vines become so tightly wound about the growing trunks and branches that they strangle them. Either the vines or the strangled parts are as a rule easily removed by judicious pruning. Some tree wounds are self-inflicted or are caused by adjacent trees. Abrasion of branches that rub together when blown by the wind is a common cause of such wounds. Natural pruning produces numerous wounds. Another type of self-inflicted wound results from girdling roots.

Many kinds of plants that do not produce true flowers or true seeds also occur upon trees. Most of these do not cause wounds. For example, where the air is free from smoke pollution, lichens are found to occur almost universally on trees. Their beautifully varied and fantastic growth is in no wise harmful. Should it be considered objectionable rather than a thing of beauty, control is generally easy to accomplish by an occasional spraying with bordeaux mixture. A similar superficial relationship exists in the case of many forms of fungi that live upon dead parts.

Bordeaux mixture may cause gastronomic disturbances if taken internally, and all unused portions should be disposed of or covered, in order to be inaccessible to children and animals. It is also somewhat irritative to the eyes and skin.

Other forms of fungi and bacteria obtain their nutriment not from the dead parts but from the living parts of the tree. These cause varying degrees of injury that range from scarcely perceptible detriment to injury so marked as to quickly kill large trees. Even among the most parasitic of these fungi, few have the ability to pass through the mature, unbroken, healthy bark and attack the living parts beneath. For the most part the fungi are largely dependent upon entry through breaks in the protective covering such as are afforded by open wounds. Others are able to gain entrance through thinner or less mature protective coverings and working internally kill tissue in such a way as to leave open wounds. The present discussion is not particularly focused upon fungi as a cause of wounds, but rather on the role that they play in interfering with the normal healing of existing wounds, for the fungi probably more than any other single factor cause complications that are generally much more dangerous than are the wounds themselves.

WOUND HEALING

HOW WOUNDS HEAL

Normal healing of wounds is closely related to the growth of woody parts. Increases in the diameter of these parts is brought about, except in the case of such trees as the palm, by growth that takes place directly under the bark. If the growth is not equal for all seasons of the year it is possible to observe how it has taken place by cutting off and examining a small branch Increases in length are indicated by the spacing between the ringlike scars left by the terminal buds during successive years of growth. Increases in diameter are shown at the cut end of a twig by a series of layers of wood that encircle the pith in concentric rings. Each growth ring usually indicates a year of growth, and is therefore called an annual ring. This is particularly true of northern trees. Commonly in the South and occasionally in the North in certain trees, the resumption of growth following its retardation by severe drought or defoliation may sometimes result in the formation of more than one ring of growth during a given year, but such cases are to be considered as the exception and not the rule.

If, instead of a cross section of a twig, a cross section of a large tree trunk is examined, essentially the same structure as in the twig will

CARE OF DAMAGED SHADE TREES

be found (fig. 1). The outer rings of wood are living and are light in color. They comprise the sapwood. Within this circle the wood is generally darker in color and is dead save for the rays that can be seen, especially in oak, to extend as radial lines, part way or entirely, from the pith to the bark. The darkened area comprises the heartwood. It has ceased to function in the growth processes and acts largely to provide mechanical support.

Bark surrounds the wood. It is differentiated into two layers. The outer layer of bark forms a more or less inert, dry, corky protective covering. Within it lies an active, moist layer of inner bark. Between the inner bark and the wood is a very thin and generally

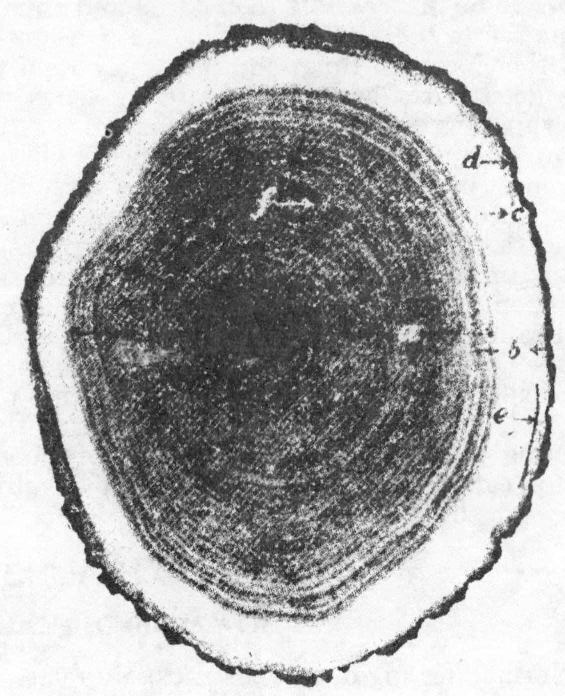

FIGURE 1.—Cross section of a trunk showing: *a*, Heartwood; *b*, sapwood; *c*, inner bark; *d*, outer bark; and *e*, cambium. The concentric growth rings (*f*) are called annual rings. The radial lines are called rays.

inconspicuous layer of cells that comprise the cambium. These cells divide when growth is taking place so as to form bark elements toward the outside and wood elements toward the inside of the layer.

For building material with which to grow in size and number, the living cells are dependent upon a solution of elaborated food that bathes them during the growing season. This food solution moves for the most part downward through the inner bark after being elaborated in the leaves and other green-colored parts of the trees. In order to form this food in the presence of air and light, the leaves require enormous quantities of soil water containing dilute solutions of raw, food-building ingredients. The soil water is mostly transferred upward from the roots to the leaves through the sapwood. Ordinarily growth is most rapid in the spring, slows up as the season progresses, and ceases when the tree is dormant.

Essentially the same growth processes that enable the tree to increase the length or the diameter of its woody parts also function in healing its wounds. If the end of a branch is broken off, the branch does not necessarily cease to grow in length because it has lost its terminal bud. A shoot from a lateral bud may shortly outgrow its companions and form a new terminal so that the branch continues to grow in length. In like manner growth processes may heal a wound on the trunk or branch. Living cells about the margin of such a wound may form a roll of callus that closes in a little each growing season until the wound is completely covered and healed over (fig. 2)

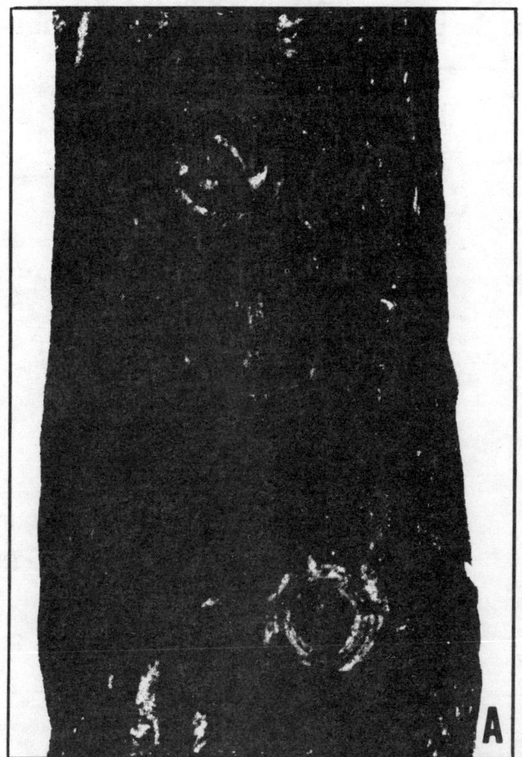

FIGURE 2.—Healing wounds. *A*, Two wounds that resulted from natural pruning under forest conditions. These wounds have been partially covered by callus. *B*, Three scars left by sawing off branches in the pruning of a shade tree. These wounds have been entirely covered by callus.

Accompanying this healing there are generally internal protective changes that close the vessels in the wood with tiny bladderlike sacs and by the deposition of wound gums.

INCREASING TREE VIGOR AS AN AID TO HEALING

The ability of a tree to callus over wounds is closely correlated with its vigor. Ordinarily a weak or sickly tree will not make marked increases in height and girth, and the owner should not be disappointed with the rate at which wounds heal on such trees. The building-up of the natural vigor of the tree is a very important part of wound treatment, especially if the wounds are large. To a marked degree the success of commercial tree experts in treating wounds, especially cavity wounds, is due to the care and skill with which they look to the maintenance of vigor in the trees treated. Too often the home deficient. Sometimes these are blown into the soil with compressed air or applied in solution. More usually they are applied in crowbar or auger holes distributed about the base of the tree (fig. 3). The ground in the immediate vicinity of the trunk is left untreated in order to avoid injury. For large trees, these holes should be kept 6 or 8 feet away from the base of the tree; in treating small trees, the holes should be somewhat closer to the trunk. The perforations are usually made to extend out somewhat beyond the drip of the branches. The holes are spaced about 2 feet apart within the area bounded by these two circles. The more numerous the holes, the more even the distribu-

FIGURE 4.—Pruning cuts made on the same day. The bottom cut was made correctly. The branch stub was left too long on one side of the top cut and has interfered with healing.

tion of the fertilizer. A commonly recommended depth for these holes is 18 inches. If the holes are filled with a material likely to injure sod, it should be poured into the holes through a funnel to within a few inches of the top, and the remaining opening plugged by stamping with the heel or by filling it with loam or compost.

Authorities differ widely as to the fertilizer dosages and formulas best suited for shade-tree use. For the most part, they are agreed on the advisability of using high-grade complete fertilizers varying in formulas from 6 to 10 percent nitrogen; 3 to 8 percent phosphorus; and 3 to 6 percent potash The most commonly used rules for deowner ignores this essential feature and fails to take proper steps to counteract the effect of one of the most common causes of unsatisfactory vigor; viz, soils that do not supply adequate water, air, and food-building materials for normal growth.

Probably the unnatural conditions under which many shade trees are grown are chiefly responsible for unfavorable soil conditions. Too frequently sidewalks, roads, and buildings restrict normal root development, and taste in lawns dictates the maintenance of closely

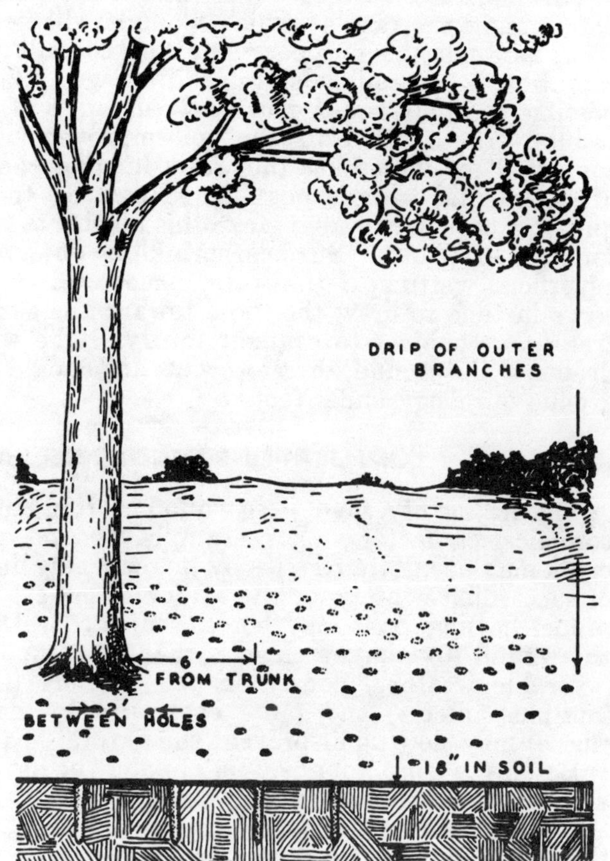

FIGURE 3.—Method of fertilizing a tree by the punch-hole system.

clipped heavy turf from which all leaf litter is raked clean. The natural accumulation of loose duff, similar to that found on the forest floor, is discouraged. The ground becomes abnormally hard and compact. Mineral elements and humus ordinarily supplied by the decomposing leaves are no longer returned to the soil nor are the normal beneficial bacteria and other soil flora and fauna maintained. The air and water-holding properties of the soil are impaired and its nutrient content impoverished. If it is suspected that such conditions prevail and are the cause of unsatisfactory vigor it is often possible to remedy them.

Manure, compost, and peat are substances much used to improve the physical structure of compacted soils so as to make possible normal movement of air and water to the roots. Mechanical loosening is also helpful. Various fertilizing ingredients may be supplied if termining the quantity to be applied for any given tree call for from 1 to 3 pounds of fertilizer for each inch that the trunk measures in circumference at breast height. The dosage varies with the kind of fertilizer used and with the need of the tree for increased soil fertility. Less fertilizer is generally applied for evergreen than for deciduous trees. Used in these quantities, it is felt by most workers to be safe to fertilize the trees at any season of the year. Spring and fall are considered especially advantageous seasons for fertilizing.

The moisture content of the soil is also an important factor in determining the rate at which wounds will heal. When excess soil water is responsible for poor vigor it is generally possible to remedy the condition by installing suitable drainage. Conversely, where it is possible to apply water generously in times of drought great benefit results. In addition to the soil-improvement treatments already suggested for increasing the water-holding capacity, some watering of ornamental trees is possible. However, the enormous water requirements of large trees make this much less practical for trees than for smaller plants. Surface sprinkling does not suffice. Frequent superficial wetting, if the water penetrates the sod at all, will only serve in time to draw the roots toward the surface and so make the trees more subject to drought injury. The water must soak down deep into the ground, therefore watering should be continued until the ground is spongy under foot.[2]

COMPLICATIONS THAT HINDER HEALING

The healing of a shade-tree wound is often hindered or prevented by complicating factors. For example, the normal healing of a frost crack may be interfered with by its reopening during low temperatures of succeeding winters, or the attack of insects may interfere with its proper healing, or it may become infected with a fungus that causes the wound to enlarge. In this manner complications caused by unfavorable weather, poorly shaped wounds (fig. 4), lack of vigor, injurious insects, and more especially by disease-producing fungi (fig. 5) may slow up or prevent the natural healing processes.

Besides causing wounds, fungi hinder the healing of wounds. They are largely dependent on food developed by other organisms. Fungi that obtain their food from living tissues are called parasites, whereas those that obtain their food from dead organic matter are called saprophytes. In the vegetative stage, fungi are comprised of fine threads called hyphae that grow through the wood or other food medium. Such a mass of vegetative threads is termed a mycelium. The fungi also have a reproductive stage. This has to do with the dissemination and perpetuation of the organism and with carrying it through unfavorable growing conditions. The essential product of reproduction is spores. These are produced in enormous numbers. They are microscopic in size and variable in appearance. They may branch off very simply from the mycelium or be produced in complex-fruiting structures formed by the mycelium. It is these fruiting structures that are generally the most conspicuous and characteristic evidence of the presence of the particular fungi that produce them. They are referred to as mushrooms, toadstools, conks, puffballs, etc.

Spores are distributed by such agents as wind, rain, insects, birds, and other animals. If they reach suitable locations and meet with favorable conditions, particularly an abundance of moisture, the spores may start new colonies of mycelial growth. In this manner many disease-producing fungi are capable of causing widespread infection of trees. Among these fungi are numerous forms that infect open wounds of woody parts. Once established in these wounds, the fungus mycelium may interfere with healing or bring about the decay of the wood. If unchecked by natural causes or by treatment, infection may extend to produce large cankers or extensive areas of decay which ultimately lead to the death or disfigurement of the parts attacked.

When practicable, the removal of fruiting bodies is advised. This will lessen the amount of inoculum released and theoretically, at least, slow the spread of the spores to other trees. This procedure is to be considered as a precautionary step rather than a treatment of the condition. Since the mycelium permeates the tissue, the removal of the fruiting bodies will not destroy the fungus. To control this type of infection, it is necessary to remove the fungus entirely, to kill it, or to render conditions unfavorable to its further development.

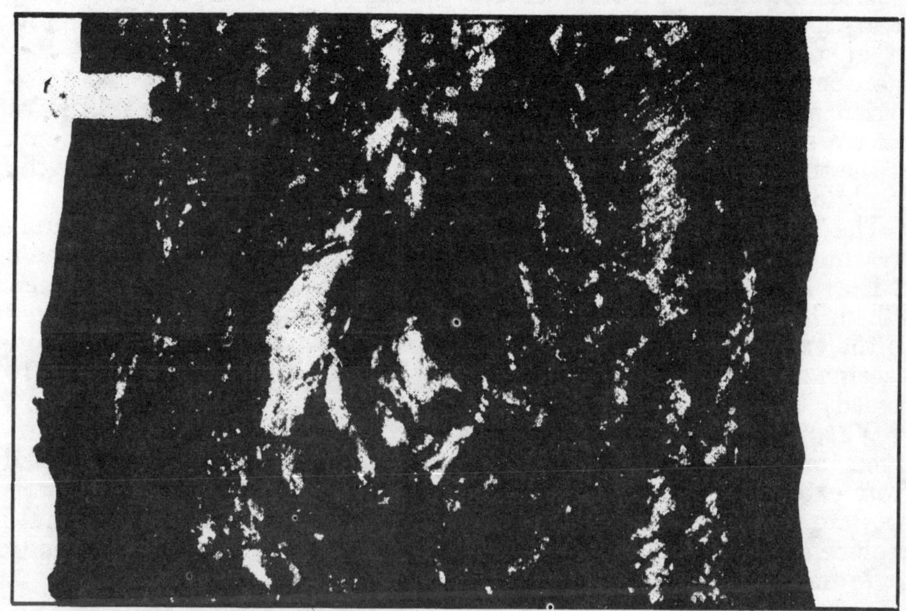

FIGURE 5.—The stub of this pruning wound was correctly cut, but the wound dressing with which it was painted was not antiseptic. Fungi have infected the wound and are causing it to increase in size. Antiseptic wound dressings do not always prevent fungus infections of this nature.

WOUND TREATMENT

PROCEDURE

Excepting seasonal effects, which must sometimes be considered, promptness of treatment is of the utmost importance. All splintered or diseased wood or bark should be removed by clean cuts that conform to the natural lines of sap flow. The tools used for this work

CARE OF DAMAGED SHADE TREES

should be sterilized. Unless an antiseptic wound dressing is to be used, the cuts should also be sterilized. All exposed surfaces should be coated with a wound dressing. The completed work should be periodically inspected and any defects repaired.

IMPORTANCE OF PROMPT TREATMENT

Shade trees that perish or are disfigured through neglect not only represent the loss of valuable property, but they are hard to replace. It takes many years to produce sizable specimens of some of the more desirable slow-growing species. The promptness and thoroughness with which treatment is given injured trees have much to do with the results obtained. If wounds are left untreated, or are carelessly treated, disease and decay may become so extensively established as to make repair difficult or impossible. Not only is prevention better than cure; it is usually the only practicable treatment for the inexperienced worker. Most large cavities and decayed limbs could have been prevented by relatively simple shaping and dressing treatments at the time the wounds occurred. It is best to treat wounds before the condition becomes aggravated or complicated.

The average owner can render valuable aid to his trees by simple treatments promptly applied. He may also be able to care for them if delay has allowed the extension of infection to a few sizable branches. When, however, neglect has permitted the infection to go unchecked to the extent that numerous large limbs have died or the trunks have become seriously pocketed with rot, it may be too late to attempt to remedy the condition.

When a tree is very badly decayed, especially if it is of a short-lived, rapid-growing type, or of a species that does not recover well from extensive repairs, it is generally best to consider it a case that is too late for treatment. It is often better to provide for the ultimate replacement of such a tree by planting a vigorous young understudy or to immediately replace it by moving in a sizable tree.

SEASON

Tree repair can be undertaken at almost any time of year when weather conditions permit. In most cases it is best, however, to avoid periods of very active sap flow. These may occur at any time of year, but the most troublesome bleeding is in the spring. The exact time varies for the different tree species. In general it coincides roughly with the time at which the buds expand. Later in the season, when the trees are making rapid growth in diameter, there is a period in which the wood and bark tend to separate. In making repairs at that time, extreme care should be exercised to avoid loosening the bark.

In many cases it is advantageous to make small cuts at a period just prior to sap flow. Such wounds tend to plug and callus quickly after dormancy has broken and thus are not open to possible infection over a prolonged period. Midsummer is an excellent time for pruning out any weak or diseased branches that may have been overlooked in the spring pruning, as such branches are more readily detected by the novice when the trees are in full leaf.

Cavity work and the pruning of large deadwood is probably less favored by the selection of any particular season. Such cuts are too large to callus over in 1 year, and the wood exposed is usually too mature to produce much natural plugging.

TOOLS AND HARDWARE NEEDED

Much of the wound treatment described in this bulletin can be undertaken with the tools ordinarily found about the average house. Some of the treatments, however, either require special tools or can be performed better and more easily with such equipment.

Unless work is to be done near the ground, ladders and ropes add to the safety of operation. Ordinary ladders are suitable for this purpose. Never use spurs or climbing irons. They injure the trees and spread diseases. If ropes are to be used for climbing or for lowering branches, safety demands that they be reasonably strong. The best grade of long-strand manila rope is well suited to the work. For ordinary purposes a ½-inch rope is used as a hand line and a ¾-inch rope for a lowering line. The usual length for these ropes is 150 feet.

When numerous saw cuts are to be made, the purchase of a pruning saw is usually justifiable because the work can be done more efficiently than with ordinary crosscut saws or ripsaws. A pruning saw about 26 inches long with 5 teeth to the inch is useful for most purposes. Do not use double-edged saws. A pole saw is helpful for pruning limbs that would be difficult to reach without it. Pruning shears, pole pruners, and a large pruning knife are essential pruning equipment. Paint brushes will be needed for dressing the wounds.

The tools thus far described will enable the beginner to perform the work described in this section. For the advanced amateur who wishes to try some of the work described in the sections entitled "Cases Requiring Special Handling" (p. 19) and "Supplementary Preventatives and Repairs" (p. 25), other tools and hardware are listed and described in the following paragraphs.

For shaping wounds and cleaning out cavities, several assorted chisels and gouges are desirable. These should be socket-handled and stout enough to withstand rough use in hardwood. The gouges should be outside ground. One-half inch, ¾ inch, and 1¼ inches are desirable sizes for either chisels or gouges. A 2-pound composition mallet is suitable for work with these tools. An oilstone will be required to keep them in condition. Over and above the ordinary sharpness needed for efficiency in cutting, it is essential that these instruments be kept keen-edged to prevent damage to the inner bark and cambium. To maintain this keenness of edge, and even more to protect the worker and the tree, chisels and gouges must be carried in a special tool bag. This consists of a cylinder of heavy leather about a foot long and about 4 inches in diameter, fitted at one end with a wood bottom and at the other with a carrying strap. Under no condition should the worker climb trees or move about in the branches with chisels or gouges carried unprotected in the pockets of his clothing.

For use in bolting, an auger handle and assorted ship augers will be needed. Three of the most used sizes of augers are 9/16, 11/16, and 13/16 inch. A hacksaw, an 18-inch Stillson wrench, and socket wrenches will also be required for bolting operations.

If cabling is to be performed a block and tackle, a pair of pliers with a cutting edge, and a wire stretcher, or come-along, will be useful tools.

CARE OF DAMAGED SHADE TREES

In addition to the tools mentioned, certain hardware will be needed for bolting and cabling. Some of this is procurable at ordinary hardware stores, but other supplies must be obtained from marine hardware stores and from dealers who specialize in tree-surgery equipment. When purchasing hardware for tree repair make certain that it has been cadmium-plated, galvanized, copper-covered, or otherwise protected against weathering. The more necessary items will include the following supplies:

Lag-threaded screw rod in 5/8-, 3/4-, and 7/8-inch sizes.
Assorted hexagonal nuts and round and diamond-shaped washers to fit the sizes of screw rods listed above.
Lag hooks, right- and left-handed in 3/8-, 1/2-, and 5/8-inch sizes.
Eyebolts with assorted nuts and washers to fit, in 3/8-, 1/2-, and 5/8-inch sizes.
Thimbles in 3/16-, 1/4-, 5/16-, 1/2-, and 5/8-inch sizes.
Screw eyes, assorted sizes.
Steel wire No. 10 gage.
Steel cable, 7-wire galvanized or copper-covered strand, in 3/16-, 1/4-, and 5/16-inch sizes.

SHAPING THE WOUNDS

The shape of the wound has a marked effect on the rate at which it is possible for healing to take place. Other things being equal, smooth, regular wounds heal more quickly than do rough, irregular wounds. Movement of the elaborated food necessary for the development of the callus is largely downward through the inner bark. Movement in a sidewise direction is restricted. Hence areas cut off from the natural lines of sap flow heal more slowly, or not at all, depending largely on the completeness of their isolation. Jagged extensions of bark at the margin of the wound or protruding branch stubs are often cut off from the food supply. Even if the food substances were available, the callus would not cover such projections as quickly and efficiently as it would cover similar areas of smooth surface.

Wounds should be so shaped, both in outline and in surface, as to conform to natural lines of sap flow. This means that on all sizable cuts it is advisable that the faces be smoothed and the margins of the areas outlining the wounds be streamlined (fig. 6).

REMOVING BRANCHES AND ROOTS

The treatment here described presupposes that the wood where the final cut is made will be sound. If the wood is infected or decayed, the final treatment given should be that described in the section entitled "Cavities" (p. 19).

Final cuts made in the removal of all branches and stubs should leave only smooth-surfaced, streamlined wounds that conform to those described in the preceding section. Prior to making such flush cuts it is frequently necessary to take certain preliminary steps to prevent stripping the bark below the saw cut (fig. 7). This is especially true if the removal of limbs over 5 inches through is involved.

One of the most common ways of avoiding this bark stripping is to remove the limb by two preliminary cuts so as to leave only a short stub for the final cut (fig. 8). The first of these preliminary cuts is made about 10 inches beyond the point where the final cut is to be made. This is done by sawing upward from the lower side of the branch until the saw begins to pinch or until the limb has been sawed about one-third through. The second preliminary cut is then started from above and about 6 inches beyond the first cut and the sawing continued until the branch splits off. By supporting the weight of small branches with one hand while sawing with the other, it is frequently possible to avoid the necessity for making preliminary saw cuts.

Having made preliminary cuts as described or provided suitable support to prevent the weight of the branch or limb from tearing the bark, proceed with the final cut. This is made by sawing flush with the trunk or limb from which it is pruned (fig. 9). There should be no definite protruding stub left by a correctly made saw cut. On the other hand the worker should avoid carrying the idea of flatness to an

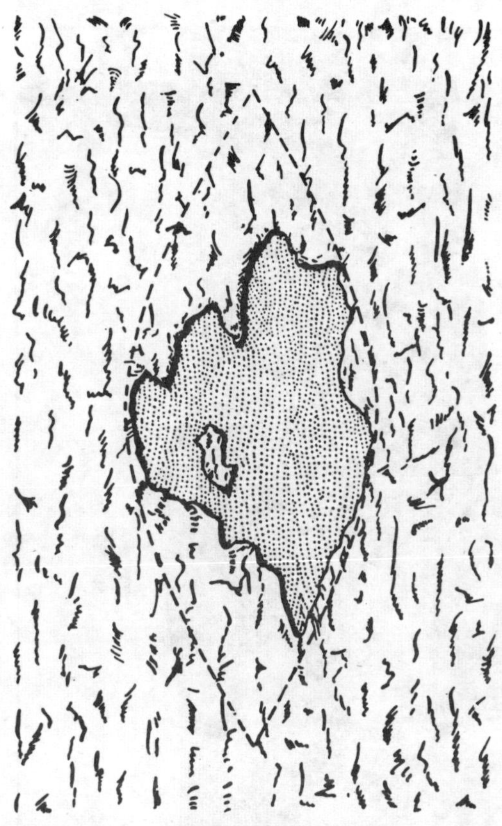

FIGURE 6.—The dotted line indicates the proper shaping for an irregular wound. The bark within the dotted line should be removed.

extreme. To do this increases the size of the resulting wound unnecessarily. With some stubs it is necessary to exercise considerable judgment in order to know just where the final cut should be made in order to assure the most rapid healing. Generally the inexperienced worker errs on the side of leaving too much rather than too little shoulder on the final saw cut. In removing dead branch stubs the wound will heal more quickly if the operator will cut somewhat into the collar of the callus rather than merely sawing off the dead stub.

At times it is not possible to cut to the trunk or a larger branch. This is frequently true in shortening branches and in repairing broken tops. In such cases the cut should be made to a smaller branch or to a vigorous bud. The developing bud and small branch in such cases favor growth to that point and thus aid in healing the wound. If the wood removed is more than an inch or two in diameter it is frequently advantageous to slant these cuts so that the projecting end of the stub points toward the part selected to act as the sap lifter. It is especially desirable that slanting cuts be used when removing parts that grow upright. Not only does this expedite callus formation, but the resulting wound when surrounded by its ring of callus has less tendency to form a pocket in which water will collect.

Small and inaccessible limbs are often removed with pole saws, the same technique being used as has been described for the final cut with the hand saw. Small branches and twigs are generally removed with pole pruners or hand pruners. If the pruners are of a type that bruise

FIGURE 7.—Bark stripping as a result of the improper removal of a large branch by a single cut.

the bark to one side of the cut, care should be exercised to make certain that the bruise is inflicted on the part removed. On very small wood that is within reach an upward cut with a sharp knife gives the best results.

Injured roots sometimes require pruning. In these instances cutting flush to another part is probably less essential than in the cases that have just been considered. The removal of all jagged and irregular exposed wood by clean, sharp cuts and treatment with wound dressing, however, seems just as vital in minimizing infection as it is in the treatment of parts that grow above ground.

KEEPING THE CUTS STERILE

A 1 to 1,000 solution of bichloride of mercury, or a copper sulfate solution made by dissolving 4 ounces of copper sulfate in 1 gallon of water, are helpful antiseptic washes for sterilizing the surface of wounds prior to the application of dressings. **If bichloride of mercury is used it must be handled with extreme caution. It is deadly poison to man and animals if taken internally and is corrosive to the skin and to metals.** It is best mixed from tablets obtainable at drug stores, each tablet making a pint of solution. Blue or amber glass bottles should be used as containers. These should be clearly labeled as to their content and its poisonous properties. Some workers prefer to dissolve the bichloride in alcohol rather than in water. The alcoholic solution gives improved penetration and quicker drying. If the wound dressing selected for use is not an antiseptic, the use of a sterilizing wash is strongly recommended when diseased wood is cut into. This precaution should be taken to prevent the contamination

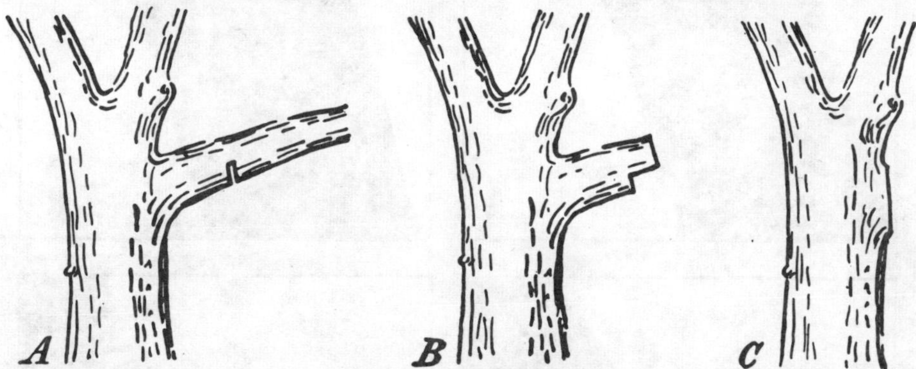

FIGURE 8.—The right way to remove a heavy limb: *A*, First preliminary cut; *B*, second preliminary cut; and *C*, final cut.

of dressings and subsequent spread of the disease. The antiseptic should be permitted to dry before the wound dressing is applied.

The sterilization of tools as well as of wounds is highly important. If due precaution is not observed, pruning and surgery may spread disease rather than retard it. For tool sterilization the writer uses a mixture consisting of 1 part by volume of a 37-percent formaldehyde solution to 9 parts of denatured alcohol. **Since formaldehyde fumes are poisonous due caution should be observed in the mixing and use of the sterilizing solution.** The tools to be sterilized may be swabbed, dipped, or thoroughly sprayed with this solution.

DRESSING THE WOUNDS

It is safest to treat with a wound dressing all shade-tree wounds that expose the wood. Such treatment is less important in the case of small wounds that will heal in one or two growing seasons than for large wounds. It is probably also less important for some conifers that coat their wounds with a resinous exudate than for other trees. A wide variety of materials are used for this purpose. They are applied in the hope of favoring callus growth and of protecting wood that would otherwise be exposed to the ravages of weather and pests during the time required for the new growth to completely close over the wound.

CARE OF DAMAGED SHADE TREES

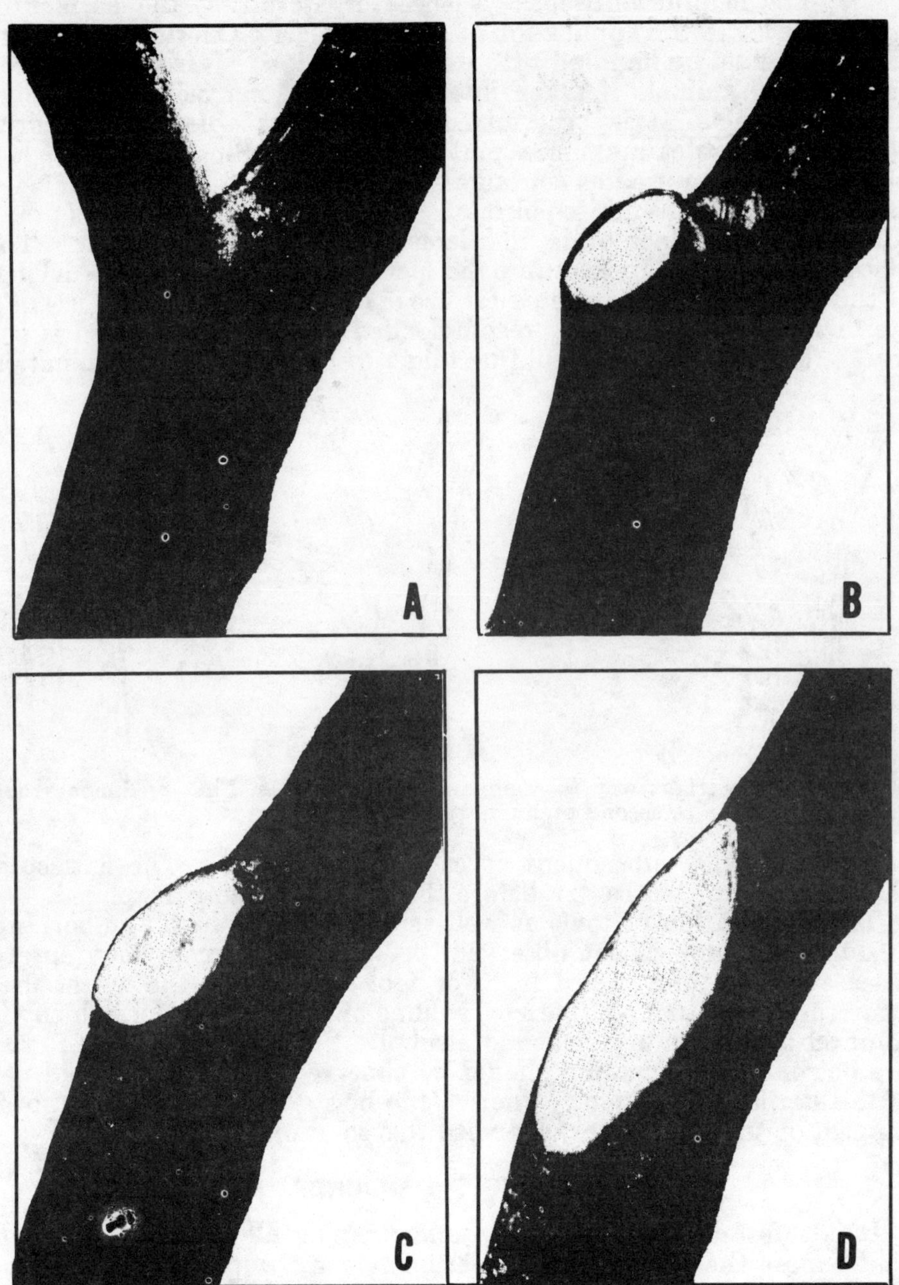

FIGURE 9.—Pruning cuts: *A*, The branch to be removed; *B*, the stub is obviously too long; *C*, the maximum stub length that is satisfactory; *D*, the maximum cut that is satisfactory. Ideal cuts should be a compromise between *C* and *D*.

None of the materials now in use appear to be capable of accomplishing both of these objectives under the various conditions imposed. The ideal wound dressing is yet to be discovered. Climatic conditions, the size of the wound, the species of tree treated, its relative vigor, the particular insects or fungi that it is desired to exclude, as well as many other factors all tend to add to the complexity of the problem and explain why no one wound dressing now in use seems to serve every need. For that reason, it seems advisable to mention several types of dressings.

Creosote and coal tar combinations have long been used and are still popular for dressing tree wounds. The mixtures used are variable. Nor is there uniformity in the unmixed products themselves as sold by various manufacturers. A combination of about one-fourth creosote and three-fourths tar by weight is frequently used. Such mixtures adhere well on freshly made cuts. They are inexpensive. Against these good qualities must be weighed the fact that they frequently become blistered, that they sometimes injure the living parts, and that in many cases they are of questionable antiseptic value. If this type of dressing is used, it is well to be sure that the ingredients selected have been refined by a reliable manufacturer for use in wound dressings. Another safeguard is to avoid contact with the living margin of the wound. This is easily accomplished by leaving the margin untreated when painting the wound with this dressing or by protecting the margin with a coating of shellac before the wound is dressed.

A similar type of dressing that is widely used consists of combinations of creosote and asphalt that are mixed in about the same proportions given for creosote and tar. Asphalt dressings without the addition of creosote are even more popular. Both water emulsions and asphalt cut with various solvents are used. For the most part, the material containing a solvent is mostly used for general work, while the water-emulsion type is valuable for application to wet wood. Generally speaking, the asphalt type of dressing to which no creosote has been added allows the cuts to produce excellent callus. On the other hand, used either alone or mixed with creosote, asphalt applied to wounds that have not been sterilized before they are dressed often fails to prevent infection. Applied in very thick coatings, asphalt not only frequently causes blistering but appears in many cases to stimulate decay rather than to retard it.

Bordeaux paint as developed by S. M. Zeller, of the Oregon Agricultural Experiment Station, is outstanding in its ability to guard wounds from infection and decay, although it will not penetrate bark or wood and destroy fungus mycelium that is already established. The dressing is somewhat pervious and for that reason does not blister or interfere with the natural deposition of wound gums or with tyloses. Bordeaux paint has on the other hand marked disadvantages. It is more expensive than most other dressings. It will not adhere to wet wood. Callus growth under this material is slightly less than that obtained with some of the less pervious dressings. Several investigators have reported an enlargement of wounds following the use of this material. The paint must be freshly mixed. It has an objectionable blue or green color.

Bordeaux paint is made by stirring together raw linseed oil and commercial bordeaux powder to form a thick paint. The bordeaux powder should be fresh and the paint when mixed used promptly. In mixing the materials, a heavy rather than thin mixture is desirable. When first stirred together, the mixture should be very stiff. After standing a short time, it should be stirred again, and this stirring should produce a heavy, creamlike mixture. If the paint becomes thin on being stirred the second time, thicken it by adding more bordeaux powder. The excess oil in thinly mixed bordeaux paint is harmful to the development of healthy callus growth. Bordeaux paint should be applied heavily to the cut surface, with a swab or a short-bristled brush. **This wound dressing is poisonous if taken internally, and consequently neither the material nor the uncleaned brushes or containers used should be placed within easy reach of children or domestic animals. The vessels containing this and other poisonous preparations should be cleaned immediately after using and any remaining poison disposed of.**

Spar varnish is sometimes used for dressing wounds. It has the advantage of being fairly lasting and of not seriously interfering with callus formation, especially if applied over a coat of shellac. It is not an antiseptic.

Shellac, rubber latex, melted beeswax, and numerous forms of grafting waxes are valuable for treating small wounds. They are also useful for ringing large wounds which are to be treated with a sterilizing agent or a wound dressing that would otherwise be injurious to the cambium.

Antiseptic washes and wound dressings should be applied as promptly as possible. Even a brief delay in their use may permit the entrance of infection. Regardless of the type of dressing used, wounds 2 inches or more in diameter should be examined within 6 to 12 months after the work is completed in order to detect defects and make necessary repairs. Reexaminations are often necessary to protect wounds. Under certain conditions the dressings tend to open with the checking of the wood, or they may blister, peel, or weather away. If they are found to be defective, repair the dressings at once after scraping off any loose or blistered material.

CASES REQUIRING SPECIAL HANDLING

CAVITIES

Thus far discussion has been restricted to the treatment of wounds in which the flush cuts have been made in sound wood. In cases where this final cut exposes diseased rather than sound tissue or where parts have not been removed but decay extends into the trunk or branches, it is usually advisable to remove the infected or decayed tissue before applying dressings or other treatments. The removal of this infected or decayed wood and the subsequent treatment of the resulting wound is referred to as cavity treatment. The dissection of trees shows that a large number of wood decays either do not continue to spread or that they die out naturally when the wound is healed over without any of the decayed material having been removed.

The elementary character of this bulletin makes undesirable the inclusion of any extended discussion of cavity work. The reason for this is obvious. This type of treatment generally constitutes a second line of defense against wood-destroying organisms. The necessity for resorting to it generally results either from failure to apply first aid promptly or from the ineffectiveness of such treatment.

Before undertaking any repair whatever where cavity work is involved, the novice should be reasonably sure that the work which he proposes to do will be of benefit to the tree. He must realize that unnecessary work or work improperly done may endanger the life or beauty of the tree rather than prove beneficial to it. None but skilled workers should attempt any major cavity treatment. The novice should confine his cavity work to attempts to prevent the extension of minor pockets of decay. To accomplish this, promptness and thoroughness of treatment are vital.

Regardless of where the decayed or diseased area is located, the essential treatment consists in the removal of the apparently infected wood and the sterilization and dressing of the resulting wound. Theoretically, excavation should be continued until the exposed wood

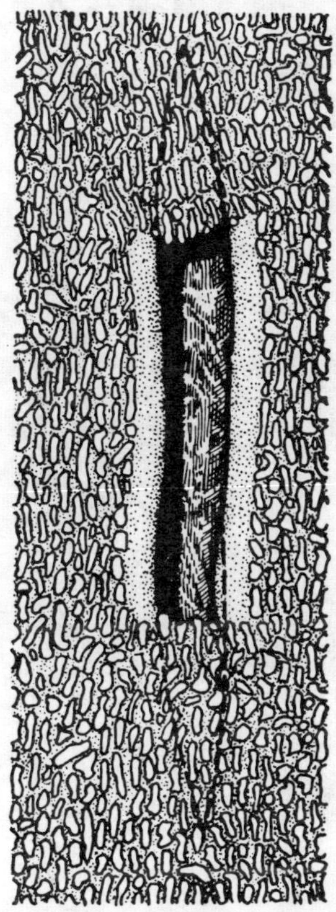

Figure 10.—The dotted lines indicate how cavities that have developed lipped rolls of callus should be streamlined.

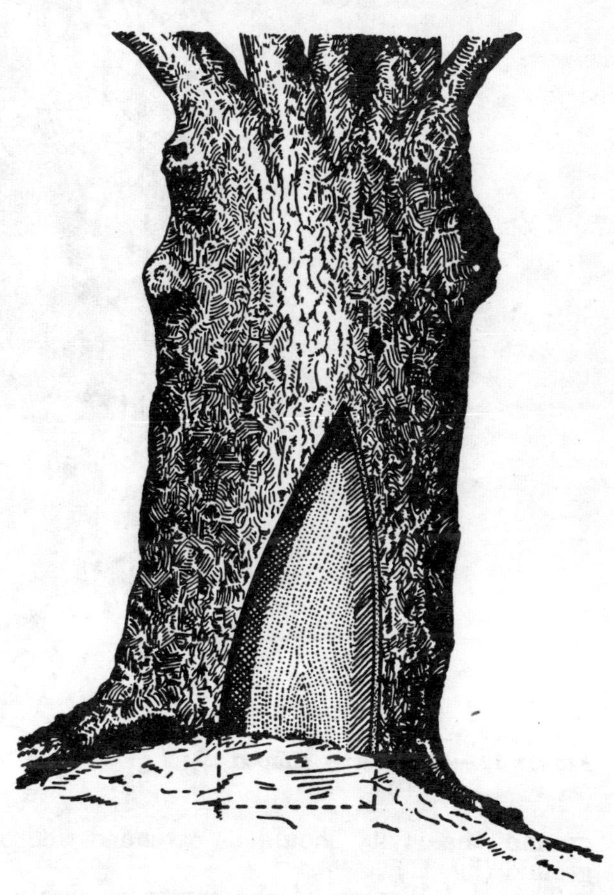

Figure 11.—A good type of basal cavity extending well below the ground line.

is sound and entirely free from infection. In actual practice, it is difficult or impossible to determine how far the mycelia of the rot-producing fungi extend into apparently sound tissue. Some fungi extend lengthwise a foot or more beyond visible decay. For this reason, it is generally advisable to remove a certain amount of the undiscolored wood, if this can be done without structurally weakening the part involved or unduly subjecting it to drying by the removal of all but a shell of sound sapwood. It is often impracticable to remove all of the infected wood.

In excavating, it is desirable that the cavity be kept as narrow as is consistent with suitable cleaning, for increased width much more than increased length retards healing. It is also essential to avoid bruising, springing, or otherwise injuring the bark that surrounds the opening. If the cavity is lipped by rolls of callus, do not cut these unnecessarily for they provide both structural reenforcement and strong lines of sap flow (fig. 10). If the base of the cavity is near the

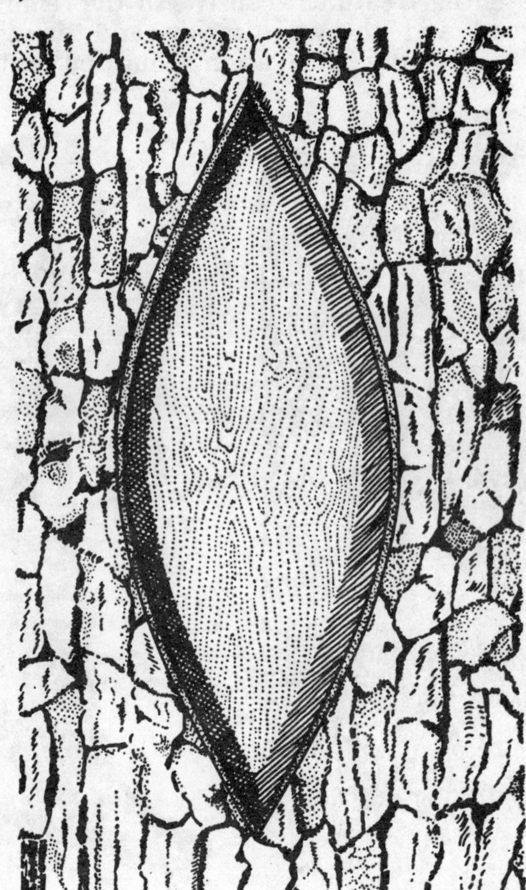

FIGURE 12.—A correctly shaped cavity.

ground, the cavity should be extended well below the surface of the ground (fig. 11).

The final shaping of the cavity is highly important. This must provide for drainage so that water will not be pocketed. It should assure that the outline of the finished cavity be streamlined and have tapering ends (fig. 12). If so shaped, it will best conform to natural lines of sap flow and thus favor rapid marginal healing. The tapering ends should, wherever possible, be carried into areas of strong growth such as are indicated by raised development of the trunk or branch. Depressed bark areas should be avoided, as they are generally areas of slow growth. All margins should be cut back to live, healthy bark tissues. Places where no live bark comes in contact with the margin should be taken out. The interior of the cavity should be made smooth and free from splintered surfaces. The margins should be cut very carefully with a keen-edged chisel or knife, thin clean cuts being made that will not spring the bark or bruise the living tissue. As soon as these final cuts along the edge of the cavity are made, the margin should be protected from drying out and from the sterilizing agent that will eventually be used. Shellac is excellent for this purpose. It should be applied generously to the narrow strip of exposed cambium and the immediately adjoining bark and sapwood that border it. It is safer to protect a few inches of margin following each final cut, rather than to complete all of the final cutting and then apply the shellac.

When the cavity has been excavated and the margins protected, all exposed wood should be sterilized. An alcoholic solution of mercuric chloride is excellent for this work, but any of the sterilizing agents already suggested may be used. **All mercuric chloride solutions are corrosive to the skin and are deadly poisonous if taken internally. The precautions given regarding the use of ordinary solutions of mercuric chloride apply equally to the mixing and application of alcoholic solutions.** Following sterilization, the wound should be dressed as has already been described for pruning cuts. Here, too, frequent inspection and the renewal of defective dressings are of prime importance.

In commercial practice, it is customary to cross-brace many cavities. No directions for this type of reenforcement are here included because it is the opinion of the writer that ordinarily cavities that involve the removal of sufficient wood to require bracing are better handled by tree experts. Such cases are generally not within the realm of what the average untrained worker is able to do well enough to prove of real benefit to his trees.

Equally questionable in the mind of the writer are the results that the average untrained man will be able to obtain from filling the cavities. The type of treatment just described is known as the open cavity. In the commercial field many cavities are treated as filled cavities. Numerous materials including cement, magnesite, rubber, and wood are used for fillings. The proper application of any of these materials improves the appearance of the tree and supplies a surface over which the new growth can spread. However, in the hands of the uninitiated, cavity filling is often injurious rather than beneficial. For this reason, it is not described in this bulletin.

CANKERS

Although cankers are sometimes confused with mechanical wounds, their treatment is essentially different. It more closely resembles that just described for the open cavity. Even though the exposed wood in the center of the canker seems sound and the roll of callus surrounding it appears superficially healthy, merely painting over the canker will seldom bring about healing. The callus tissue surrounding the dead area at the center of the canker usually harbors the living organism that produced the lesion. Such organisms must ordinarily be killed or removed before the wound will heal normally. Although certain chemicals either applied superficially or injected are sometimes helpful in arresting the growth of some of the less virulent of these organisms, it is generally quicker and safer for the amateur to cut away the infected tissue. A possible exception to this statement is the small bleeding canker that is said not to be benefited by cutting. The bark at the margin of the canker should then be cut back to clean, live tissue and the wound shaped as for cavity work except that in most cases canker treatment will not involve the removal of more than a few rings of annual wood. When the wound is cleaned out thoroughly and properly streamlined, it should be sterilized and dressed as previously described. The precautions given regarding the sterilization of tools should also be observed.

SUPERFICIAL BARK WOUNDS

Departure from the more routine method of wound treatment is occasionally justifiable in the case of superficial bark wounds that can be treated immediately following injury. A glancing blow from an automobile or lawn mower may tear off a piece of bark in such a way that some of the cambium tissue remains attached to uninjured wood. If this cambium tissue is immediately protected from drying, it will in many cases form a new layer of bark.

In treating such a wound any ragged margins should be traced back smoothly with a sharp knife. Beeswax heated slightly above the melting point is then applied generously to the exposed surface by means of a paint brush. Grafting wax is another excellent dressing for this type of treatment. A thick layer of moist sphagnum moss held in place with burlap has proved beneficial.

Results from this type of treatment are uncertain. Frequently they are very gratifying. Generally the cambium tissue shows remarkable ability to develop rapidly when thus protected from drying. The nature of the injury and the promptness with which treatment is applied are highly important factors in determining the degree of success which may be expected. Success is frequently dependent upon follow-up treatment after the quantity and position of the resurrected cambium tissue are determined.

SLIME FLUX

Wounds sometimes bleed too profusely to permit immediate treatment with wound dressings. Tar compounds or asphalt emulsions are applicable to moist surfaces. Where the flow of sap is too rapid to permit the use of even this type of dressing or where the worker prefers to use some other material less applicable to use on wet wood, it becomes necessary to delay dressing the wound until bleeding has stopped. In such cases it is advisable to sterilize the cut with one of the antiseptic washes already referred to. This should be done both at the time the wound is made and again before applying the final dressing. If the wound is slow in drying up, it is often well to use an antiseptic wash every few days in an attempt to keep the surface as clean and sterile as possible.

If such wounds are not kept clean, the exuding sap is liable to fermentation by bacteria, yeasts, fungi, and certain low forms of animal life. At times such infections produce a diseased condition known as "slime flux." A slimy ooze flows from the wound. This is usually sour-smelling. It varies from bright pink to very dark blackish brown in color. The bark and wood in the immediate vicinity of the wound may be killed back and the wound made progressively larger by the slime flux as it flows down the trunk.

The treatment of such wounds is much the same as that recommended for the prevention of the conditions. Frequent cleaning and sterilization should be given in the hope that the wound will ultimately dry up enough to permit its final cleaning and dressing.

Often such treatment is futile. In some of these cases the trunk of the tree contains a large quantity of fermented sap under high pressure. It then becomes necessary to relieve the pressure before attempting to dry up the wound by surface sterilization. To do this, the water-soaked trunk must be drained by tapping. Generally the region affected extends to the base of the tree. For that reason it is best to first try tapping near the base of the trunk and directly under the part which is fluxing. This may be done by boring a hole to the center of the trunk with a ⅝-inch auger. The hole should be sloped slightly upward to the center of the tree for better drainage. If the waterlogged tissue is tapped, the sour sap should be discharged under pressure. If it is not located by the first drilling, additional holes should be bored higher on the trunk closer to the fluxing wound. When the affected region is located, a short piece of galvanized pipe having a driving fit is forced a couple of inches into the auger hole. The pipe should be long enough to carry the drip free of the trunk and root crown, so that there will be no further killing-back of the bark. If the pressure can be relieved, it is sometimes possible to dry up and treat the wounds, but many cases of slime flux will not respond to this treatment.

The preceding discussion refers to typical slime flux, which should not be confused with the small bleeding cankers occurring on maples and some other hardwood trees in some areas in New England.

GIRDLING ROOTS

Shade and ornamental trees are sometimes subject to girdling by their own roots. This is frequently caused by careless transplanting and may sometimes be aggravated by an excess of organic matter applied near the trunk. When young trees are set out, small roots may get wrapped about the trunk. As both the tree and the roots increase in diameter, the trunk becomes constricted. Natural root grafting tends to prevent injury. At times, however, this grafting takes place so slowly that strangling results. If the roots are above the ground, this condition is generally sufficiently obvious to be detected while still in its early stages and the damage prevented by the prompt removal of the girdling root (fig. 13). If the girdling takes place below ground, the trouble is more difficult to detect. It does not generally become obvious to the average tree owner until strangulation causes the tree to exhibit symptoms of being poorly buttressed on one or more sides or to show a general weakening of the top. Generally, if the girdling has advanced to this stage it becomes a problem of tree surgery rather than of preventive treatment. In such cases the soil should be pulled back from the root crown and the girdling root removed.

FROST CRACKS

Sudden severe cold frequently splits the trunks of trees These frost cracks occur longitudinally and are of varying length. They may occur at any point on the trunk but are most common on its south or southwest side. While the temperature is low, the cracks remain open; as the temperature rises, they close. During the growing season these cracks sometimes heal without treatment. In subsequent winters, however, they represent weak points in the trunk that are very apt to reopen. In some trees this repeated opening causes the callus growth on either side of the frost crack to become lipped, and the injury takes on a ridged appearance.

The treatment of frost cracks is not always advisable. Some trees can be helped by treatment. In other cases the trees may reopen during sudden extreme cold either along the treated splits or at new places on the trunks.

FIGURE 13.—A girdling root.

In many cases, it is best not to attempt treatment if the wound closes tightly during warm weather and appears to be healing without assistance

INSECTS AND DISEASES

GENERAL FEEDERS

5 times natural size.

Ants: Small insects ranging from less than 1/16 inch to ½ inch or more in length. Many different colors represented, including black, brown, yellow, and red. Three distinct body segments. Ordinarily live in colonies.

In many cases ants do not cause real damage in vegetable gardens, but their presence is annoying. In some instances, however, they feed on and injure seriously the leaves, stems, fruits, or roots of growing vegetables. In addition, their activities around the roots of plants cause excessive drying of the soil and indirect injury to affected plants.

Widely distributed and may cause serious damage in some localities.

Use one of the ready-prepared ant baits in the form sold by dealers. Follow directions given on the package in which it is sold. When small anthills are numerous, scatter thinly a mixture made up of ¼ ounce of paris green and ¼ pound of brown sugar on soil surface at the rate of 1 ounce per 500 square feet. Some kinds of ants respond to some types of baits, and their response may vary from time to time; therefore, they are not easy to control.

Slightly less than natural size of common species.

Cutworms: Dull-gray, fat worms, ¾ to 1¼ inches long.

Young plants cut at surface of ground.

Cutworms occur in all sections of the country and are particularly destructive during the early part of the season.

Use poison bait (poison bait 24) scattered lightly at base of plants. A collar of stiff cardboard rolled and set in the soil around the stem of transplants, such as cabbage or tomatoes, will aid in preventing cutworm injury. The collar, when in place, should be about ½ inch distant from the plant stem and should extend about 1 inch below and 2 inches above the soil.

About natural size.

Grasshoppers: Of many species, all with strong hind legs for jumping; most forms strong fliers.

Feed on any available vegetation, and when abundant may destroy a complete planting.

Widely distributed, but especially troublesome in the Central Northwest.

Use poisoned bait (poisoned bait 24) scattered thinly over the ground about, but not on, the growing plants. Apply in the morning as the grasshoppers become active.

GENERAL FEEDERS—Continued

Insect	Remedy
Japanese beetle (as a vegetable-garden pest): The parent, or beetle, is oval, nearly ½ inch long, about ¼ inch wide, and shining metallic green. Outer wings are coppery brown. The fully-grown grub, or larva, is about 1 inch long, with a white body and a brown head. This insect is a general feeder. Among the vegetables, the beetles are most likely to feed on the foliage of beans, asparagus, and rhubarb and on the silk and foliage of sweet corn. Grubs feed on the roots of various plants, including bean, tomato, beet, sweet corn, onion, and strawberry. Present in destructive abundance in many localities from southern New England to Virginia and eastern Ohio.	In the home garden the susceptible vegetables, such as string and lima beans, rhubarb, and asparagus, can be protected from injury by the beetles by dusting the plants thoroughly with a good grade of fine hydrated lime as often as necessary to maintain a good deposit. When rotenone-containing insecticides are used on beans for Mexican bean beetle control these insecticides also give fair protection against the Japanese beetle on this crop. The ears of sweet corn can be protected from serious beetle attack by dusting the tips of the ears with very fine hydrated lime 2 or 3 times at 3-day intervals early in the silking period. Ordinarily the grubs do not cause serious losses to vegetable crops. Carefully working the soil in the fall or spring and killing the larvae that are found or permitting chickens to run in the garden until seeding time is useful in controlling the grubs.

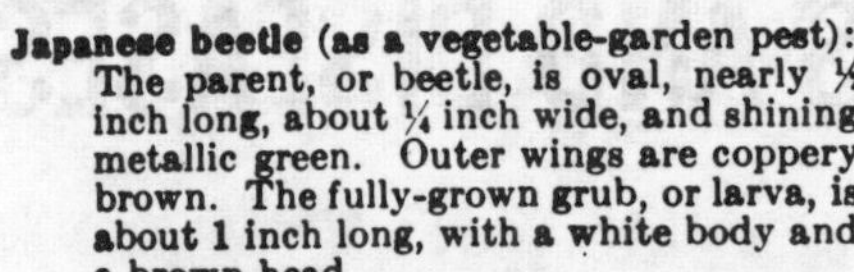

3 times natural size.

About natural size.

Insect	Remedy
Millipedes: Brown or grayish, hard-shelled, wormlike creatures, 1 to 1¼ inches long. Feed on roots, tubers, bulbs, and fleshy stems of plants and on seeds planted in soil. Found commonly under shelter, such as boards or flowerpots, or in decayed manure. Widely distributed.	Apply bait (poisoned bait 24) to infested premises. The sugar and paris green mixture recommended for sowbugs is also effective, as well as drenching infested soil with pyrethrum (spray mixture 6) Destroy or dispose of hiding places.

Slightly less than natural size.

Insect	Remedy
Mole crickets: Light-brown insects, 1½ inches long, faintly resembling field crickets. Large, beady eyes, and short, stout front legs bearing shovellike feet. Make burrows in upper inch or two of soil, like those of a small ground mole. Uproot seedlings. Destructive types of mole crickets occur in the coastal areas of North Carolina, South Carolina, Georgia, Alabama, and Mississippi and in Florida.	Use poisoned bait (poisoned bait 26) scattered lightly in all infested parts of garden. For best results apply bait in late afternoon following a rain or artificial application of water.

Less than natural size.

Insect	Remedy
Slugs and snails: Slugs as illustrated are black, shiny snails without shells. Eat leaves of small plants at night. Leave a glistening, slimy trail. Widely distributed and are particularly destructive on the West Coast.	Dust soil in infested parts of garden with hydrated lime. Spray plants with bordeaux mixture (spray mixture 8), and use poisoned bait (poisoned bait 24). Use commercially-prepared baits containing metaldehyde.

GENERAL FEEDERS—Continued

Insect | **Remedy**

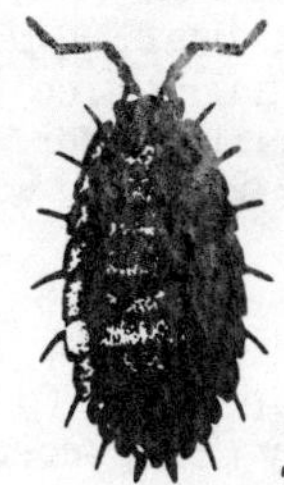

Twice natural size.

Sowbugs or pillbugs: Dark-gray, oval, flattened bodies, with seven pairs of legs, ½ inch long. Not true insects.
Feed upon roots and tender parts of plants.
Found in same situations and territory as millipedes.

Remedy: Sprinkle surface of infested soils with a dry mixture made up at the rate of 9 ounces of sugar and 1 ounce of paris green; or a mixture of 2 ounces of wheat flour, 2 ounces of sugar, and 1 ounce of paris green. Spray infested soil with nicotine sulfate (spray mixture 4) or pyrethrum (spray mixture 6).

4 times natural size

Vegetable weevil: Dull grayish-brown weevil ⅜ inch long, with 2 oval pale-gray marks on back. Larvae, or grub, ⅝ inch long, with light-green body and light-yellow to brown head.
Weevils and grubs feed on leaves and roots of many vegetables, including turnips, carrots, mustard, spinach, tomatoes, and potatoes.
Has been destructive in the Southern States and in limited coastal areas of California.

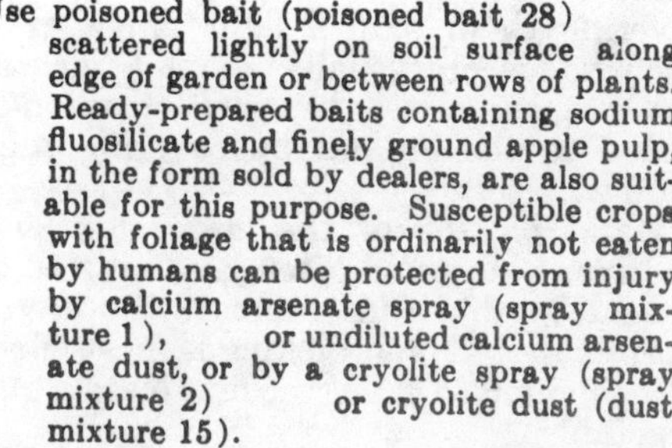

Remedy: Use poisoned bait (poisoned bait 28) scattered lightly on soil surface along edge of garden or between rows of plants. Ready-prepared baits containing sodium fluosilicate and finely ground apple pulp, in the form sold by dealers, are also suitable for this purpose. Susceptible crops with foliage that is ordinarily not eaten by humans can be protected from injury by calcium arsenate spray (spray mixture 1), or undiluted calcium arsenate dust, or by a cryolite spray (spray mixture 2) or cryolite dust (dust mixture 15).

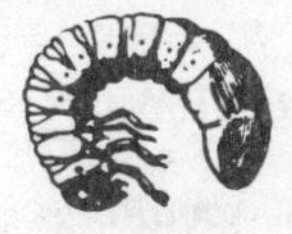

About natural size.

White grubs: Large white or light-yellow grubs, ½ to 1½ inches long, with hard brown or black heads. Live entirely in soil during larval stage. Usually found in curved position.
Feed on roots or underground stems of plants and on potato tubers.
Widely distributed and may cause severe damage in some localities.

Remedy: No remedy except prevention. Avoid abandoned or newly plowed grassland. If white grubs are found when spading or plowing the garden, sow an extra quantity of seed and thin out later. Plow or spade deeply in the late fall or during winter, if weather conditions permit.

About natural size.

Wireworms: Slender yellow to white worms, with dark head and tail, resembling a jointed wire.
Puncture and tunnel stems and roots.
Widely distributed and are more destructive in some areas than in others; particularly destructive in irrigated lands of Western States.

Remedy: Apply crude naphthalene flakes to soil surface, at rate of 1 ounce to each 5½ square feet. Spade or plow under 7 to 12 inches deep; follow by deep harrowing. Do not plant until 7 days after treatment. Avoid planting very susceptible crops in soils infested with wireworms. Deep cultivation in midsummer and heavy fertilization will help counteract wireworm damage.

General Methods of Insect and Disease Control

Although many of the control measures recommended in this publication include the use of insecticides and fungicides, there are other generally useful practices, such as those given in the following paragraphs, that aid in the control of insects and diseases attacking vegetables and do not require the use of insecticides or fungicides.

Insect Control—General Methods

Small seedlings may be protected from insects, excepting those living in the soil, by covering the plants with an inverted glass jar or completely covering them with a light paper or muslin hood. Such hoods are usually about 8 inches in diameter and are supported by wire or wooden hoops and sealed to the ground by covering the edge of the hood with soil.

Hand picking of the larger beetles, caterpillars, and plant bugs will often give satisfactory control in a small garden and eliminate the need for applying insecticides. Hand picking is most effective if begun early enough to catch the first insects attracted to the vegetables.

Disease Control—General Methods

Plant diseases can rarely be cured, but it is possible to prevent their occurrence and spread. Disease control should begin with the seed and continue until harvest. The control measures described in this section include directions for the preparation and use of the chemical seed treatments and sprays and dusts already mentioned.

Good Garden Practices

The methods of gardening essential to the production of good crops are also an aid in disease control. These practices include (1) the use of fertile, well-drained soils; (2) the proper application of fertilizers of a type suited to the soil and crop; (3) the planting of crops and varieties suited to the soil and climate; and (4) clean cultivation.

Sanitation

At the end of the season all diseased crop refuse, including the roots, should be disposed of by burning. Do not compost the remains of diseased plants. Keep down weeds in the vicinity of the garden, since they may harbor disease-producing viruses or fungi. The garden should be so planned that the same crop or related crops, such as cabbage and cauliflower or tomatoes, peppers, and eggplant, are not grown in the same spot in successive years.

Seed and Plant Selection

Obtain disease-free seed. Where certified seed is available, as with tomatoes and potatoes, endeavor to obtain it. Cabbage, cauliflower, bean, and pea seed grown in the far West is ordinarily free from certain disease-producing organisms. Never save seed from decayed or spotted fruits or from wilted plants.

When seedling plants are purchased, make sure they do not show swellings on the roots, stem cankers, or leaf spots. If southern-grown tomato plants are used, it is best to buy State-certified plants.

Use of Resistant Varieties

Resistant varieties offer the most effective means of disease control, but such varieties are as yet available in the case of only a few diseases of certain crops. The number of highly resistant varieties is also limited, but a larger group of disease-tolerant varieties exists, and these, while not entirely resistant, are comparatively slightly injured. Valuable examples of resistant varieties are available in cabbage, tomato, watermelon, beans, peas, and potatoes; and the names of many of these varieties are given in the lists of diseases. For a further list consult United States Department of Agriculture Leaflet 203, Disease-Resistant Varieties of Vegetables for the Home Garden.

Seed Treatment

Chemical seed treatments are used for two purposes, (1) protection against decay of seed in the soil and the damping-off of small seedlings, and (2) the disinfection of the seed to kill any parasitic fungi or bacteria that may be present on its surface (p. 27). The same treatment, however, does not necessarily serve both purposes. It must also be remembered that seed treatment does not insure the freedom of the plant from all diseases, although it is a very valuable means of disease control.

How to Prepare Insecticides and Fungicides for Garden-Pest Control [1]

Insecticides

The following formulas and directions are given for the preparation of spray and dust mixtures and poisoned baits needed for the control of the more common insects and related pests attacking vegetables in farm, suburban, city, and community gardens, as listed in this publication. These directions have been made as simple and as uniform as possible, with due regard to the saving of insecticides, such as rotenone and pyrethrum, which have been made scarce by war conditions. Small measures are given for each of the ingredients in order to guide the gardener in preparing small quantities of the finished insecticide.

Spray mixture 1: CALCIUM ARSENATE:

Calcium arsenate	1 ounce (5 level tablespoonfuls).
Hydrated lime	3 ounces.
Water	1 gallon.

Spray mixture 2: CRYOLITE:

Cryolite	1 ounce (8 level *teaspoonfuls*).
Water	1 gallon.

Do not use lime or bordeaux mixture with cryolite.

Spray mixture 3: PARIS GREEN:

Paris green	2 level *teaspoonfuls*.
Hydrated lime	3 level tablespoonfuls.
Water	1 gallon.

Spray mixture 4: NICOTINE SULFATE:

Nicotine sulfate (40 percent) [2]	1 tablespoonful.
Soap (mild laundry type)	1 cubic-inch cake (or 2 level tablespoonfuls of soap flakes).
Water	1 gallon.

Dissolve soap in 1 pint of warm water. Add nicotine sulfate. Stir this mixture and add enough water to make 1 gallon.

Spray mixture 5: ROTENONE:

Derris or cube root powder (5 percent rotenone content)	½ ounce (3 level tablespoonfuls).
Water	1 gallon.

If the available powder is of lower rotenone content, use proportionally more of it.

Mix the powder first with a small quantity of water, then add it to the rest of the water in the sprayer.

Spray mixture 6: PYRETHRUM:

Use a ready-prepared pyrethrum spray material at the dilution given on the package in which it is sold.

Spray mixture 7: NICOTINE-PYRETHRUM:

Add 1 tablespoonful of nicotine sulfate (40 percent) to 1 gallon of water containing spray mixture 6. Mix thoroughly. Stir well all spray mixtures during their preparation, and where a powder and liquid are mixed together, shake the sprayer from time to time during the spraying unless the sprayer is provided with an agitator.

[2] The strong nicotine sulfate solution (40 percent) is very poisonous, and care should be taken not to get it on the skin or about the eyes or mouth.

Dust mixture 14: CALCIUM ARSENATE:

Calcium arsenate	1 pound.
Hydrated lime	2–3 pounds.

Place the materials in a tight can or similar container. Add several stones 1 inch in diameter to aid mixing process. Place tightly fitting cover on can. Shake or rotate can for 5 minutes. Remove stones by passing mixture through sifter or screen.

Dust mixture 15: CRYOLITE:

Cryolite	2 pounds.
Talc	1 pound.

Do not use lime or bordeaux mixture with cryolite.

Dust mixture 16: PARIS GREEN:

Paris green	1 pound.
Hydrated lime	10 pounds.

Mix by same method as dust mixture 14.

Dust mixture 17: NICOTINE SULFATE (3 percent):

Nicotine sulfate (40 percent)	1 ounce (5 *teaspoonfuls*).
Hydrated lime	1 pound.

Sift lime to break up lumps. Put sifted lime in tight can. Add several stones 1 inch in diameter to aid mixing process. Pour nicotine sulfate over lime. Place tight-fitting cover on can. Shake or rotate can for 5 minutes. Remove stones by passing mixture through sifter or screen.

Dust mixture 18: ROTENONE:

Use a ready-prepared dust mixture containing at least 0.75 percent of rotenone in the form sold by the dealer.

Dust mixture 19: PYRETHRUM:

Use a ready-prepared pyrethrum dust or dust mixture in the form sold by the dealer. Follow directions given on the package in which it is sold.

To prepare a home-made pyrethrum dust mixture use—

Ground pyrethrum flowers (1.3 percent total pyrethrins content)	1 pound.
Talc, pyrophyllite, or tobacco dust	3 pounds.

Mix by same method as dust mixture 14 (above).

Dust mixture 20: NICOTINE-PYRETHRUM:

Mix thoroughly equal quantities of dust mixtures 17 and 19.

Spray mixture 8: BORDEAUX MIXTURE:

Bluestone (copper sulfate)	4 ounces.
Hydrated lime	4 ounces.
Water	3 gallons.

Dissolve the bluestone in a wooden, earthenware, or glass vessel (*never in metal*), using hot water. Dilute with half the total water specified. Make a paste of the lime in a small quantity of water, and add the rest of the water to this. Pour the diluted bluestone and lime solutions together and mix thoroughly. Strain the mixture through a fine cheesecloth directly into the sprayer, and it is ready for use.

This mixture should be made fresh each time it is used.

Spray mixture 9: BORDEAUX MIXTURE-CALCIUM ARSENATE:

Add 3 ounces of calcium arsenate to 3 gallons of bordeaux mixture, made according to directions just given. Mix thoroughly.

Spray mixture 10, which was described in Miscellaneous Publication 525, is no longer recommended.

Spray mixture 11: TARTAR EMETIC:

Tartar emetic	1 ounce (6½ level *teaspoonfuls*).
Brown sugar	2 ounces (6 tablespoonfuls).
Water	3 gallons.

Four tablespoonfuls of sirup or molasses may be substituted for the brown sugar.

Dissolve the sugar or sirup in a small quantity of water. Add the tartar emetic slowly while stirring the water. Then dilute with quantity of water required to make 3 gallons. This solution should be made fresh each time it is used.

Spray mixture 12: SOAP:

Soap (mild laundry type)	2 ounces (4 cubic-inch cakes or 8 level tablespoonfuls of soap flakes).
Water	1 gallon.

Cut cake soap into very small pieces. Dissolve soap in quart of hot water. Let cool. Add sufficient water to make 1 gallon. Use half strength on very tender plants such as young cabbage, garden peas, and beans.

Solution 13: CORROSIVE SUBLIMATE:

Corrosive sublimate (mercuric chloride)	⅒ ounce (six 7½-grain tablets).
Water	1 gallon.

Dissolve the corrosive sublimate in a pint of hot water in a glass or earthenware vessel. Then dilute with quantity of cold water required to make 1 gallon.

Calomel (mercurous chloride) may be substituted for corrosive sublimate at the rate of ⅒ ounce to 1 gallon of water.

Dust mixture 21: SULFUR-PYRETHRUM:

Dusting sulfur	1½ pounds.
Pyrethrum flowers (1.3 percent total pyrethrins content)	ounce (5 tablespoonfuls).

Do not use sulfur on squashes, melons, or cucumbers.

Mix by same method as dust mixture 14.

Dust mixtures 22 and 23, are no longer recommended.

Poisoned bait 24: CUTWORM AND SLUG BAIT:

Sodium fluosilicate or paris green	¼ pound.
Dry, flaky wheat bran	5 pounds (1 peck).
Water to moisten	3 or 4 quarts.

Mix thoroughly the poison and the dry bran. Then moisten the mixture with water until each flake of the bran has been wetted. Prepare this bait in the morning and apply it late in the day, so that it will be moist and attractive when the cutworms begin to feed in the evening. Scatter the bait lightly and evenly on the soil surface of the garden or around the bases of plants that have been set out. Repeat application, if necessary.

Poisoned bait 25: TOMATO FRUITWORM BAIT:

Cryolite	½ pound.
Corn meal	5 pounds.

Sift corn meal to break up or remove all lumps. Put one-fourth of corn meal in bucket or similar container. Add one-fourth of poison to corn meal. Mix thoroughly. Repeat process until entire quantity is mixed. Scatter the bait lightly and evenly over the leaves of tomato plants, especially the fruit clusters, growing tips, and outer leaves.

Poisoned bait 26: MOLE CRICKET BAIT:

Sodium fluosilicate	½ pound.
Dry wheat bran	5 pounds (1 peck).
Water	1 to 2 pints.

Mix by same general method as poisoned bait 24, but add only sufficient water to the dry bran and poison to cause the bait particles to cling together when squeezed in the hands. Scatter the bait lightly and evenly on the soil surface of infested gardens.

Poisoned bait 27: STRAWBERRY ROOT WEEVIL BAIT:

Calcium arsenate	½ pound.
Dry wheat bran	5 pounds (1 peck).
Water	2 quarts.

Mix by same method as poisoned bait 24. Scatter bait lightly and evenly around plants as soon as presence of insect is detected.

Poisoned bait 28: VEGETABLE WEEVIL BAIT:

Sodium fluoride	½ pound.
Fresh, finely chopped carrots or turnips	4 pounds.
Dry wheat bran	7 pounds.
Water to moisten	3 or 4 quarts.

Mix bait by method described for poisoned bait 24. Then mix chopped vegetables with the prepared bait. This bait is more attractive to the weevils if allowed to stand several hours before it is applied. Apply in the late afternoon. The bait is effective only late in the winter and in the spring, since at other times of year the weevils prefer growing crops.

FUNGICIDES

Treatments for Prevention of Seed Decay and Damping-Off

Seed decay and damping-off can be controlled by dusting the seed with various chemical compounds, some of which are listed below. Farmers' Bulletin 1862, Vegetable Seed Treatments, gives a more complete list of seed treatments and the details of their use with various crops. The treatments here described are generally effective, except as noted. The amount of dust needed for treating seed for even a large garden is so small that it will avoid wastage of valuable material to purchase the smallest package available and endeavor to share that with neighbors. In treating seed the dust and seed are placed in a closed container and shaken for 3 to 4 minutes, after which any excess dust is screened off and the seed is ready to plant. The following dusts give effective seed protection and aside from the exceptions noted may be used on any of the vegetable crop seeds where their use is not specifically mentioned.

Semesan.—An organic mercury compound which can be used on all vegetable seeds except lima bean. Directions for its use on various seeds come with the package.

Red copper oxide.—Red oxide of copper (Cuprocide) is commonly used for control of damping-off. It should never be used on cabbage, cauliflower, or related plants, or on onion seed or sets, or lima beans. Use as directed by the manufacturer. From one-fourth to one and one-half level teaspoonfuls are sufficient for a pound of seed, depending on the size of the seeds.

Spergon and *Arasan.*—These are compounds containing no mercury or copper which can be used on practically all vegetable seeds with good results. Spergon is effective on beans and peas. Use as especially directed by makers.

Seed Disinfectants

Various chemicals are used to destroy disease-producing organisms on the seed surface. Those here listed are generally effective when used as recommended. A more complete list is given in Farmers' Bulletin 1862, mentioned above. It is advisable to consult your county agent or State agricultural college if in doubt as to what to use on any crop.

Corrosive sublimate.—Some seed-borne organisms often can be controlled by treating the seed with a corrosive sublimate solution. This is used at various strengths as shown below. The seed is placed in a loose cloth bag and soaked for the time indicated. This chemical corrodes metal and must be used in earthenware, glass, or wooden containers. After the seed has been soaked it should be rinsed in running water or in several changes of water and dried at once. A 1:1,000 solution of corrosive sublimate (1 ounce to 7½ gallons of water) is usually used, and this can be made in small quantities by dissolving one of the prepared tablets sold by druggists in 1 pint of water. A 1:1,500 solution is prepared by using one tablet to 1½ pints of water. One tablet to 1 quart of water gives a 1:2,000 solution. Treat the seed as follows:

Cucumber, muskmelon, and *watermelon:* Soak seed 5 minutes in a 1:1,000 solution.

Eggplant: Soak seed 10 minutes in a 1:1,000 solution.

Pepper: Soak seed 2 minutes in a 1:1,000 solution.

Tomato: Soak seed 5 minutes in a 1:2,000 solution.

After treating any kind of seed, wash the seed for 15 minutes and dry it at once.

This treatment does not protect against damping-off, and if this protection is desired, the seed must be given a second treatment with one of the chemical protectants listed above.

Semesan.—A solution of Semesan in water can be used as a disinfectant for most vegetable seeds. The solution should be made according to the directions accompanying the package.

Spraying and Dusting

The use of sprays or dusts is of value in the control of many leaf-blight diseases, but only those parts of the plant are protected that are thoroughly coated with the material. Sprays often stick better than dusts and can be applied in light winds. On the other hand, dusts are easier to apply and the equipment is less expensive and requires less attention to keep it in working order. For the small garden, dusting is probably the more satisfactory method.

Many diseases are not controlled by sprays or dusts and there are many other diseases which frequently are not damaging enough to require spraying. Potatoes, celery, cucumbers, and melons commonly require the use of fungicides, but a number of other crops rarely require their use. The fungicides listed below are those generally recommended for vegetable crops.

Copper Sprays

Bordeaux mixture.—Bordeaux mixture is the copper spray in most common use and one of the most effective. It can be prepared in 3-gallon quantities as given on page 26. It should always be freshly prepared, as it will not keep from one day to the next. Always wash the sprayer well after use.

Prepared bordeaux can be purchased in convenient packages and is often most satisfactory for a very small garden, but the freshly prepared mixture is more effective and less expensive. Consult the section on Insecticides (p. 26) for directions as to combining an insecticide with bordeaux mixture.

Fixed copper sprays.—"Fixed" or "insoluble" copper sprays are on the market and are preferable to bordeaux mixture for tomatoes, cucumbers, and muskmelons, since they cause less damage to the foliage. They should be used as recommended by the manufacturer.

Copper Dusts

Copper-lime dust.—A dust composed of 20 parts of monohydrated copper sulfate and 80 parts of hydrated lime is often used on vegetable crops. It can be purchased ready mixed. This mixture should be applied when the foliage is wet.

Fixed copper dusts.—The fixed copper compounds mentioned above are often mixed with various inert materials and used as dusts. They are effective on many crops and can be purchased from dealers in agricultural supplies.

Sulfur Dusts

Sulfur dusts especially prepared for use on plants may be used for the control of powdery mildew of beans and sometimes bean rust. They are also of value in controlling some insects. *They should not be used on cucumbers or melons, as they are very damaging to these crops. For the treatment of a disease, sulfur should not be used unless it is recommended for this purpose.* Most vegetable diseases are best controlled by copper fungicides.

DDT INSECTICIDES

Insecticides containing DDT are available in four general types: (1) *Powders* to apply as a dust, (2) *wettable powders* or powders that will mix readily with water for spraying, (3) *emulsions* to be diluted with water and applied as a spray, and (4) *solutions* to be applied without further dilution. Of these four types the dusting powder and wettable powders are safest for use on plants, and the gardener interested in using DDT will find these powders suitable. DDT solutions are primarily for use against household pests and should not be applied to plants or animals. DDT emulsions may cause damage to some kinds of plants and, unless expert advice and supervision are available, they should not be used by the home gardener.

DDT will satisfactorily control various types of garden pests, but it is not a satisfactory remedy for some others, notably the Mexican bean beetle, some types of aphids, and red spider mites. DDT dust and wettable powders should not affect the growth of most vegetables; however, pumpkins and squash appear to be susceptible to the action of DDT. Isolated cases of injury to peas and tomatoes, apparently due to some local factor, have been reported.

Experimental work to date shows that DDT is poisonous to higher animals and man and therefore its usage in the garden on leafy vegetables is limited. See "Warning Regarding Poison Residues".

A dust mixture containing 3 percent of DDT is effective against the Colorado potato beetle, the potato flea beetles, potato and bean leafhopper, cabbage looper, the imported cabbage worm, the diamond-back moth larva, and some species of cutworms which feed on the foliage of cabbage. A higher strength of dust will be needed for the control of aphids on potatoes and thrips on onions.

While the indications are that DDT dust mixtures which contain at least 5 percent of DDT will kill the immature forms of squash bugs, as stated above, DDT has injured squash and pumpkins and may stunt the growth of other crops belonging to the same plant family.

The DDT content of commercial wettable powders varies; therefore, in their use the directions of the manufacturer should be followed.

Tables of Measures

The following tables of measures will be found convenient in preparing small quantities of insecticides for the garden:

Liquid measure:

3 *teaspoonfuls* = 1 tablespoonful.
2 tablespoonfuls = 1 fluid ounce
16 tablespoonfuls
or
8 fluid ounces = 1 cup.
2 cups = 1 pint.
2 pints = 1 quart.
4 quarts = 1 gallon.

Approximate quantities required to weigh 1 ounce:

1 ounce of calcium arsenate	5 level tablespoonfuls.
1 ounce of copper sulfate powder.	5 level *teaspoonfuls.*
1 ounce of corrosive sublimate powder.	1 level tablespoonful.
1 ounce of cryolite	8 level *teaspoonfuls.*
1 ounce of hydrated lime	3 level tablespoonfuls.
1 ounce of nicotine sulfate	5 *teaspoonfuls.*
1 ounce of paris green	1½ level tablespoonfuls.
1 ounce of pyrethrum flowers or powder.	5 level tablespoonfuls.
1 ounce of sulfur (dusting sulfur).	2½ level tablespoonfuls.
1 ounce of talc	3 level tablespoonfuls.
1 ounce of tarter emetic	6½ level *teaspoonfuls.*

Quantity of Sprays or Dusts to Apply

Sprays.—For small gardens, approximately 1 to 1½ quarts of liquid spray is required per 50 feet of row for each application to plants of medium size.

Dusts.—For small gardens, approximately 1 to 1½ ounces of dust mixture is required per 50 feet of row for each application to plants of medium size.

Spraying and Dusting Equipment

The effectiveness of an insecticide or fungicide depends to a large extent upon the thoroughness of the application of the material. The most effective way of applying an insecticide or fungicide is by the use of either sprayers or dusters manufactured expressly for the purpose.

Sprayers

Hand Atomizers (fig. 1).—The hand atomizer is probably the most familiar type of equipment used in applying liquid insecticides, as it has been commonly used for applying fly sprays in the home. Its capacity is from ½ pint to 2 quarts and it is useful for spraying small plantings, although the under sides of the leaves of the plant are difficult to reach.

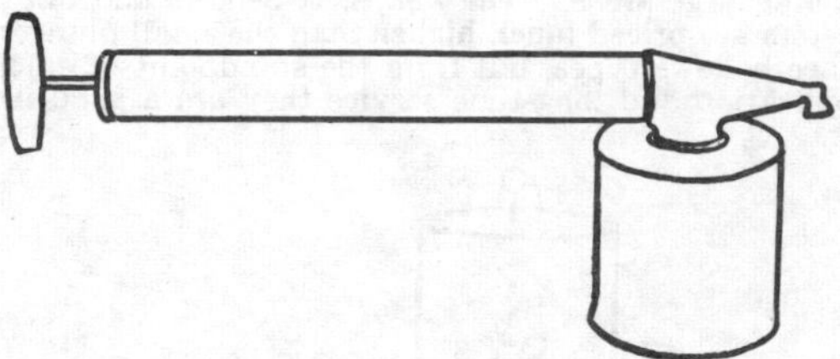

FIGURE 1.—Hand atomizer.

Compressed-air sprayers (fig. 2).—The compressed-air sprayer is the most satisfactory for the small garden, but its manufacture has been limited because of the shortage of metal. It is usually made of galvanized sheet steel and has a capacity of 1 to 5 gallons. Since these sprayers are not equipped with an agitator, it is necessary to keep the materials well mixed by shaking the tank frequently during the spraying operations.

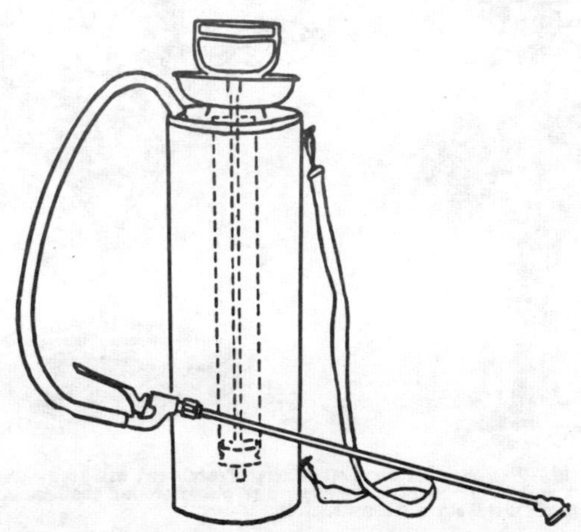

FIGURE 2.—Compressed-air sprayer.

Knapsack sprayers (fig. 3).—A knapsack sprayer is also a very useful piece of equipment for the home gardener. It costs more than the compressed-air sprayer but has an advantage over the compressed-air sprayer in that a higher and more uniform pressure can be maintained when the pump is kept in operation. An agitator is provided within the tank and operates with the movement of the pump handle.

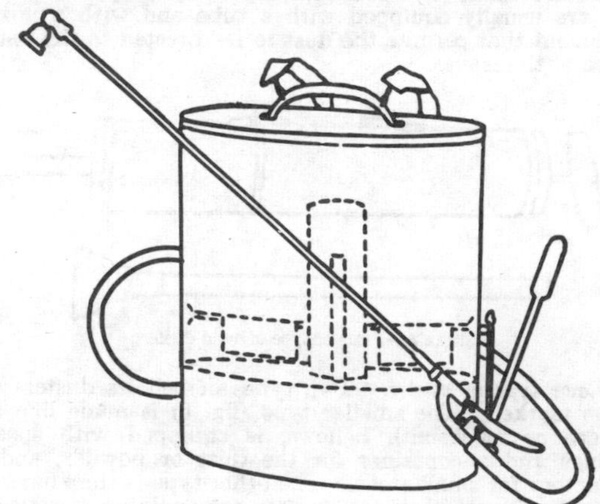

FIGURE 3.—Knapsack sprayer.

Bucket pump (fig. 4).—The bucket pump, or stirrup pump, was standard spray equipment prior to the war. The stirrup pump which has been manufactured and sold during the war period for fire-fighting purposes is not suitable for applying insecticides or fungicides without considerable modification as to nozzle and air chamber. It is necessary to have an air chamber in order to build up sufficient pressure, and a nozzle with a small opening to permit the spray to be applied in a fine mist. The most efficient operation of the bucket pump requires two persons—one to operate the pump and the other to manipulate the hose and nozzle.

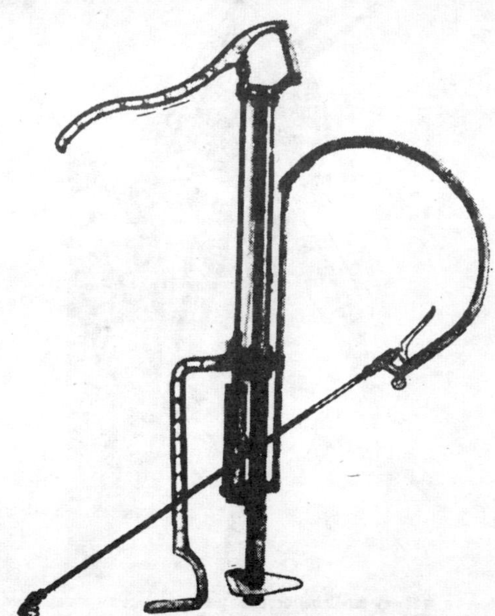

FIGURE 4.—Bucket pump with hose, extension rod, cut-off, and nozzle.

Dusters

Plunger type of duster.—The plunger type of duster (fig. 5), or dust gun, is the one most commonly manufactured for applying insecticides to small areas. Its dust-holding capacity ranges from 1 to 3 pounds. Prior to the war these dust guns were mostly of metal and equipped with metal or glass containers for the insecticide. The newer types placed on the market are made of wood and especially prepared paper. They are usually equipped with a tube and with a nozzle attachment that permits the dust to be directed to the under surface of the leaves.

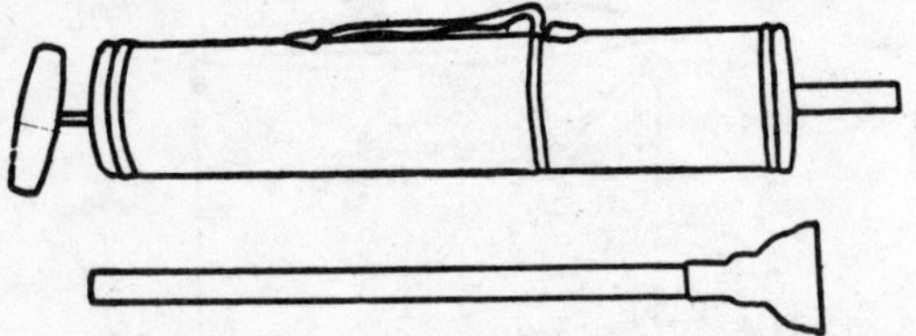

FIGURE 5.—Plunger type of hand duster.

Bellows type of duster.—Two types of bellows dusters are on the market. The smaller type (fig. 6) is made like the fireplace or blacksmith bellows, is equipped with special openings and a container for the dust or powder, and is satisfactory for small areas. The other type is the knapsack duster (fig. 7), which is satisfactory for applying insecticidal dust to both small and large gardens.

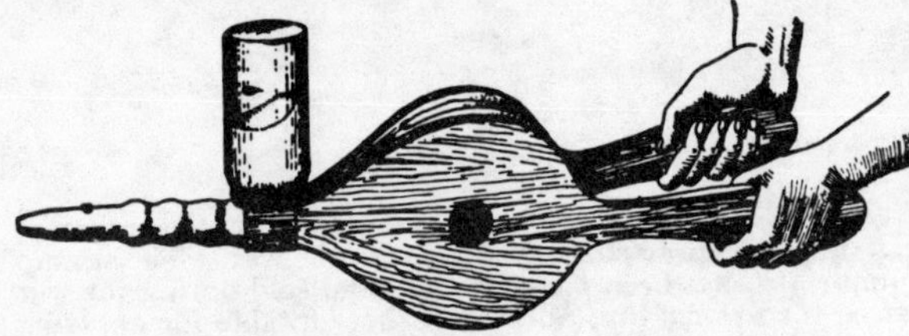

FIGURE 6.—Simple bellows type of duster.

FIGURE 9.—An ordinary medicine dropper used to inject oil among corn silks for earworm control.

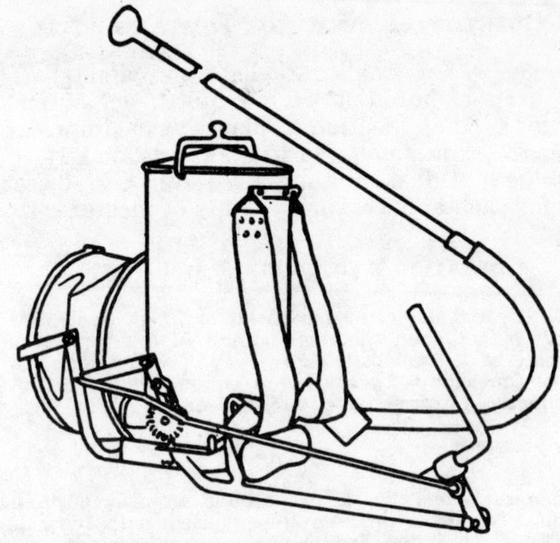

FIGURE 7.—Knapsack-bellows duster.

Fan or blower type of duster.—The fan or blower type of duster (fig. 8) is a satisfactory piece of equipment for both small and large areas. The knapsack-bellows and fan types of dusters are priced much higher than the small plunger and fireplace bellows types, but from the standpoint of efficiency of application and long-time service they are a good investment.

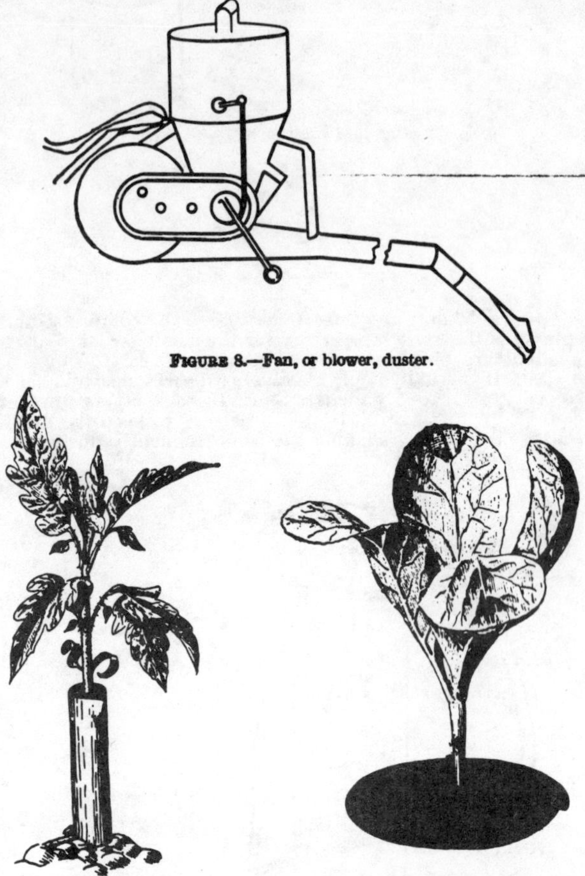

FIGURE 8.—Fan, or blower, duster.

FIGURE 10.—Protective devices: Left, a collar of cardboard will keep cutworms away from plants. Right, a tar paper disk placed around the base of each cabbage plant will aid in maggot control.

PART FOUR

Background and Study Material for the Exam

Final Advice

Practice Using Answer Sheets

Alter numbers to match the practice and drill questions in each part of the book.
Make only ONE mark for each answer. Additional and stray marks may be counted as mistakes.
In making corrections, erase errors COMPLETELY. Make glossy black marks.

1 A B C D E	1 A B C D E	1 A B C D E	1 A B C D E	1 A B C D E
2 A B C D E	2 A B C D E	2 A B C D E	2 A B C D E	2 A B C D E
3 A B C D E	3 A B C D E	3 A B C D E	3 A B C D E	3 A B C D E
4 A B C D E	4 A B C D E	4 A B C D E	4 A B C D E	4 A B C D E
5 A B C D E	5 A B C D E	5 A B C D E	5 A B C D E	5 A B C D E
6 A B C D E	6 A B C D E	6 A B C D E	6 A B C D E	6 A B C D E
7 A B C D E	7 A B C D E	7 A B C D E	7 A B C D E	7 A B C D E
8 A B C D E	8 A B C D E	8 A B C D E	8 A B C D E	8 A B C D E
9 A B C D E	9 A B C D E	9 A B C D E	9 A B C D E	9 A B C D E
0 A B C D E	0 A B C D E	0 A B C D E	0 A B C D E	0 A B C D E

1 A B C D E	1 A B C D E	1 A B C D E	1 A B C D E	1 A B C D E
2 A B C D E	2 A B C D E	2 A B C D E	2 A B C D E	2 A B C D E
3 A B C D E	3 A B C D E	3 A B C D E	3 A B C D E	3 A B C D E
4 A B C D E	4 A B C D E	4 A B C D E	4 A B C D E	4 A B C D E
5 A B C D E	5 A B C D E	5 A B C D E	5 A B C D E	5 A B C D E
6 A B C D E	6 A B C D E	6 A B C D E	6 A B C D E	6 A B C D E
7 A B C D E	7 A B C D E	7 A B C D E	7 A B C D E	7 A B C D E
8 A B C D E	8 A B C D E	8 A B C D E	8 A B C D E	8 A B C D E
9 A B C D E	9 A B C D E	9 A B C D E	9 A B C D E	9 A B C D E
0 A B C D E	0 A B C D E	0 A B C D E	0 A B C D E	0 A B C D E

1 A B C D E	7 A B C D E	13 A B C D E	19 A B C D E	25 A B C D E
2 A B C D E	8 A B C D E	14 A B C D E	20 A B C D E	26 A B C D E
3 A B C D E	9 A B C D E	15 A B C D E	21 A B C D E	27 A B C D E
4 A B C D E	10 A B C D E	16 A B C D E	22 A B C D E	28 A B C D E
5 A B C D E	11 A B C D E	17 A B C D E	23 A B C D E	29 A B C D E
6 A B C D E	12 A B C D E	18 A B C D E	24 A B C D E	30 A B C D E

TEAR OUT ALONG THIS LINE AND MARK YOUR ANSWERS AS INSTRUCTED IN THE TEXT

TECHNIQUES OF READING INTERPRETATION

In the following pages you'll find every proven technique for succeeding with the reading comprehension question, the pitfall of many a test-taker. These methods have worked beautifully for thousands of ambitious people and they are certain to help you. They are well worth all the time you can afford to devote to them.

The reading comprehension question is the pitfall of many a test-taker. He may do well in every other part of the examination, but "messes up" the comprehension part. If you don't want this to happen to you, you should make every effort to improve your ability to interpret a reading passage.

You can markedly upgrade your reading ability —but you must have a plan—a procedure—a method. First, let us understand that there are two aspects of success in reading interpretation:

1. **reading speed**
   and
2. **reading understanding**

There are many individuals who read with excellent comprehension, but who read too slowly. Remember, there is a time limit on your test. On the other hand, there are those who read rapidly but, for reasons that we shall cite later, do not thoroughly understand what they are reading. These exam-takers will answer few of the comprehension test questions correctly.

We must disagree with those who hold the mistaken belief that there is a causal relationship between speed of reading and comprehension of the material read. Each is important during an exam— speed and comprehension—but improvement in reading skill requires two different treatments: improvement in reading speed and improvement in reading comprehension. Let us, then, divide our discussion into two parts:

1. **increasing reading speed**
   and
2. **improving reading comprehension**

A great many people read very slowly and with little comprehension, yet are completely unaware of just how badly they do read. Some people pronounce the words to themselves as they read, saying each word almost as distinctly as though reading aloud; or they think each one separately.

You were probably taught to read letter by letter; gradually, as you matured, you learned to read word by word. As an adult, however, you should be able to read a complete phrase as quickly as you once read just one letter. If you cannot do this, or if you have trouble in understanding what you read, you should practice reading intensively.

There is no need to be discouraged if this is the case, however. Most students, with a little effort, can increase the speed of their reading significantly. Do not be afraid of not understanding what you read quickly. The old idea that slow readers make up for their slowness by better comprehension of what they read has been proven untrue. Your ability to comprehend what you read will keep pace with your increase in speed. You will absorb as many ideas per page as before, and get many more ideas per unit of reading time.

It has been demonstrated that those who read best also read quickly. This is probably due to the fact that heavier concentration is required for rapid reading; and concentration is what enables a reader to grasp important ideas contained in the reading material.

A good paragraph generally has one central thought—that is, a topic sentence. Your main task is to locate and absorb that thought while reading the paragraph. The correct interpretation of the paragraph is based upon that thought, and not upon personal opinions, prejudices or preferences. If a selection consists of two or more paragraphs, the correct interpretation is based on the central idea of the entire passage. The ability to grasp the central idea of a passage can be acquired by practice—practice that will also increase the speed with which you read.

An important rule to follow in seeking to improve your reading ability is to force yourself to increase your speed. Just as you once stopped reading letter by letter, now learn to stop reading word by word. Force yourself to read by whole phrases and sentences. Move your eyes rapidly across the line of type, skimming it. Don't permit your eyes to stop for individual words, but try to reconstruct the whole idea even if a word has been missed. Proceed quickly through the paragraph in this skimming fashion, without rereading or backtracking to a missed word.

If you find yourself failing to comprehend what you read, read it over several times rapidly, until you do understand. Do not slow down on rereading. At first, you may find yourself missing some of the ideas. Persistent practice, however, will result in stepping up both your reading speed and your ability to comprehend what you read.

If you are one of those who mouth over the words you read, or think each one separately in a similar process, your first step is to learn to overcome this handicap to rapid reading. Learn not to move your lips and not to pronounce the words you read. The habit will be almost automatically overcome if you learn to leap from phrase to phrase. Synchronize your eye movements with your mind. Your mind is a great deal nimbler than your lips. Consequently, your lips and vocal cords must not be permitted to intervene in the instantaneous interchange of ideas between eyes and mind.

Certain physical factors affect your reading. You should always read sitting in a comfortable position, erect, with head slightly inclined. The light should be excellent, with both an indirect and a direct source available; direct light should come from behind you and slightly above your shoulder, in such a way that the type is evenly illumined. Hold the reading matter at your own best reading distance and at a convenient height, so you don't stoop or squint. It goes without saying that, if you need glasses, you should certainly use them when reading.

To prepare for a test in reading comprehension, then, you should keep the above ideas firmly in mind. Practice reading, for practice will improve your skill. Never retreat to your older, easier method of reading, once you have grasped the way we have indicated here. In a very short time, you will find the new method of reading easier than the old. You will read faster. You will understand more of what you read. You will enjoy reading more. You will accomplish more reading in less time. It will no longer be a chore, but a pleasant and profitable relaxation.

INCREASING READING SPEED: CAUSES & CURES OF SLOW READING

Cause #1: ***Word-by-Word Reading.*** Our earliest reading, since it was done aloud, was of necessity word-by-word reading. Unfortunately, for many, this habit has become so firmly implanted that it often persists.

Cure: Use the *eye-span method.* Look at that first part of a sentence—the part which consists of a thought unit. Then look for the next thought unit, if there is one in the same sentence—then, look for still another thought unit. For example, consider this sentence:

> Reading maketh a full man, conference a ready man, and writing an exact man.

How many ideas are there in the sentence? You are right—three. Now, let us employ the eye-span method in reading this sentence:

Reading maketh a full man,

EYE-SPAN 1

conference a ready man,

EYE-SPAN 2

and writing an exact man.

EYE-SPAN 3

Cause #2: ***Vocalizing.*** Some readers move their lips or whisper while they read "silently." This practice slows down silent-reading time considerably.

Cure: You must consciously refrain from moving your lips or whispering during silent reading. Have someone watch you while you read. Are you vocalizing?

Cause #3: ***One-Speed Reading.*** One should vary his reading speed according to what he is reading.

Cure: The pace of your reading should change not only from book to book, but even within a reading selection. Flexibility should be employed so that the reader will change his speed from paragraph to paragraph, even from sentence to sentence.

IMPROVING YOUR READING COMPREHENSION: CAUSES AND CURES OF POOR COMPREHENSION

Cause #1: *Vocabulary Weakness.* You must know the meaning of every word in a passage in order to understand the passage thoroughly. The sentence context will sometimes help you to arrive at the meaning of a word, but the context method is not to be depended upon.

Cure: Increase your vocabulary systematically by taking these simple steps:

1. LEARN LATIN. Don't get scared. We are referring to Latin roots, prefixes, and suffixes. Remember that approximately 70 per cent of our English words are derived from Latin and Greek.

2. TAKE WORD TESTS. We recommend the best-selling "2300 Steps to Word Power" ($1.45—Arco) which tests your knowledge of words through programmed instruction, the revolutionary fast-learning method.

3. READ—not only novels. Non-fiction is good, too —and don't forget to read newspapers and magazines (the more literate type).

4. LISTEN—to people who speak well. Tune in to worthwhile TV programs, also.
5. PLAY WORD GAMES—like Anagrams, Scrabble, and do Crossword Puzzles.
6. USE THE DICTIONARY—frequently and extensively.

Cause #2: *Hint Neglect.* Examination points may be unnecessarily lost by ignoring the author's hints as to what *he* thinks is most important.

Cure: Be on the lookout for such phrases as "Note that . . ." "Of importance is . . ." These give clues to what the writer is stressing. So do topic sentences. Beware of negatives and all-inclusive statements. Watch particularly words like always, never, all, only, every, absolutely, completely, none, entirely.

Cause #3: *Background Lack.* Since most reading comprehension passages deal with science, literature, or social studies, a weakness in background may create much difficulty in interpretation.

Cure: Read widely. Acquaint yourself with various aspects of science, literature, and social studies.

TEN SUCCESS STEPS

Here are proven techniques for getting the right answer to *any* Reading Interpretation question.

1. Read the selection through quickly to get the general sense.
2. Reread the selection, concentrating on the central idea.
3. Can you now pick out the *topic sentence* in each paragraph?
4. If the selection consists of more than one paragraph, determine the *central idea* of the entire selection.
5. Examine the five choices carefully, yet rapidly. Eliminate immediately those choices which are *far-fetched, ridiculous, irrelevant, false,* or *impossible.*
6. Eliminate those choices which may be true, but which have nothing to do with the sense of the selection.
7. Check those few choices which now remain as possibilities.
8. Refer back to the original selection and determine which one of these remaining possibilities is best in view of

    a) specific information in the selection
    or
    b) implied information in the selection

9. Be sure to consider only the facts *given* or *definitely understood* some place in the selection.
10. Be especially careful of trick expressions or "catch-words" which sometimes destroy the validity of a seemingly acceptable answer. These include the expressions: "under all circumstances," "at all times," "never," "always," "under no conditions," "absolutely," "completely," and "entirely."

AVOID THE TRAPS

Trap #1—Sometimes the question cannot be answered on the basis of the stated facts. You may be required to make a deduction from the facts given.

Trap #2—Eliminate your personal opinions.

Trap #3—Search out significant details that are nestled in the paragraph. Reread the paragraph as many times as necessary (with an eye on your watch).

GET PLENTY OF PRACTICE

Read:

(a) Editorial pages of various newspapers.

(b) Book reviews (also drama and movie reviews).

(c) Magazine articles.

For each selection that you read, do the following:

(a) Jot down the main idea of the article.

(b) Look up the meanings of words that you don't know or that you aren't sure of.

A SAMPLE QUESTION ANALYZED

Here is a sample question followed by an analysis. Try to understand the process of arriving at the correct answer.

(Reading) "Too often, indeed, have scurrilous and offensive allegations by underworld creatures been sufficient to blast the career of irreproachable and incorruptible executives who, because of their efforts to serve the people honestly and faithfully, incurred the enmity of powerful political forces and lost their positions."

Judging from the contents of the preceding paragraph, you might best conclude that

(A) the larger majority of executives are irreproachable and incorruptible

(B) criminals often swear in court that honest officials are corrupt in order to save themselves

(C) political forces are always clashing with government executive

(D) underworld creatures make scurrilous and offensive allegations against incorruptible executives

(E) false statements by criminals sometimes cause honest officials the loss of their positions or the ruin of their careers.

Interpretation

(A) can generally be said to be a true statement, but it cannot be derived from the paragraph. Nothing is said in the paragraph about "the larger majority" of executives.

(B) may also be a true statement and can to a certain extent be derived from the paragraph. However, the phrase "in order to save themselves" is not relevant to the sense of the paragraph, and even if it were, this choice does not sum up its central thought.

(C) cannot be derived from the paragraph. The catch-word "always" makes this choice entirely invalid.

(D) This choice is true as derived from the sense of the paragraph. It is open, however, to two exceptions. First, this choice is in the form of a general statement whereas the paragraph starts with the restrictive phrase "too often," thereby precluding a generality. Secondly, this choice does not summarize the central idea of the paragraph which may be better expressed in the remaining choice.

(E) is the *best* conclusion that could be drawn from the contents of the paragraph in the light of the five choices given. It is open to no exceptions and adequately sums up the central thought of the paragraph.

USING THE "SUCCESS STEPS" WITH A PRACTICE PASSAGE

Let us, now, demonstrate with an actual exam-type reading interpretation selection how to apply the ten "success steps":

Vacations were once the prerogative of the privileged few, even as late as the 19th century. Now they are considered the right of all, except for such unfortunate masses as, for example, the bulk of China's and India's population, for whom life, save for sleep and brief periods of rest, is uninterrupted toil.

They are more necessary now than once because the average life is less well-rounded and has become increasingly departmentalized. I suppose the idea of vacations, as we conceive it, must be incomprehensible to primitive peoples. Rest of some kind has of course always been a part of the rhythm of human life, but earlier ages did not find it necessary to organize it in the way that modern man has done. Holidays, feast days, were sufficient.

With modern man's increasing tensions, with the stultifying quality of so much of his work, this break in the year's routine became steadily more necessary. Vacations became mandatory for the purpose of renewal and repair. And so it came about that in the United States, the most self-indulgent of nations, the tensest, and the most departmentalized, vacations have come to take a predominant place in domestic conversation.

1. The title below that best expresses the ideas of this passage is:
   a. Vacation Preferences
   b. Vacations: the Topic of Conversation
   c. Vacations in Perspective
   d. The Well-Organized Vacation
   e. Renewal, Refreshment and Repair

2. **We need vacations now more than ever before because we have**
   A. a more carefree nature
   B. much more free time
   C. little diversity in our work
   D. less emotional stability
   E. a higher standard of living

3. **It is implied in the passage that the lives of Americans are very**
   A. habitual
   B. ennobling
   C. patriotic
   D. varied
   E. independent

4. **As used in the passage, the word "prerogative" (line 1) most nearly means**
   A. habit
   B. distinction
   C. request
   D. demand
   E. hope

STEP 1—We read the selection through quickly to get the general sense.
STEP 2—We reread the selection concentrating on the central idea.
STEP 3—We discover that the topic sentence of each paragraph of this selection is the first sentence of each paragraph. This order is almost always the case: the topic sentence is the first sentence of a paragraph.
STEP 4—The central idea of the selection consists of various aspects of vacations.
STEP 5—Question 1. . . . We eliminate Choice D immediately because it is irrelevant. The selection refers in no way to organization of a vacation.
STEP 6—Eliminate Choice B. Vacations are often a topic of conversation—not so in this selection, however.
STEP 7—Since Choices A, C, and E remain as possible correct choices, we check them.
STEP 8—Choice C is an all-inclusive title. Choices A and E are not all-inclusive. Therefore, C is the correct choice as the best title for the passage.
STEP 9—In arriving at the correct answer, we have considered only the facts given or definitely understood.
STEP 10—We were on the alert for trick expressions and "catch-words." There were none in Question 1.

. . . .

Proceed in the same "10-Step" manner in answering the other questions 2, 3 and 4 of the sample selection.

. . . .

PRACTICE PASSAGE ANSWERS

1. C 2. C 3. A 4. B

GARDENER - ASSISTANT GARDENER

READING COMPREHENSION

READING TEST ONE

DIRECTIONS: Below each of the following passages, you will find questions or incomplete statements about the passage. Each statement or question is followed by lettered words or expressions. Select the word or expression that most satisfactorily completes each statement or answers each question in accordance with the meaning of the passage. Write the letter of that word or expression on your answer paper.

A FAIR SAMPLING OF THE QUESTIONS YOU'LL BE ASKED

Correct key answers to all these test questions will be found at the end of the test.

The standardized educational or psychological tests, that are widely used to aid in selecting, classifying, assigning, or promoting students, employees, and military personnel have been the target of recent attacks in books, magazines, the daily press, and even in Congress. The target is wrong, for in attacking the tests, critics divert attention from the fault that lies with ill-informed or incompetent users. The tests themselves are merely tools, with characteristics that can be measured with reasonable precision under specified conditions. Whether the results will be valuable, meaningless, or even misleading depends partly upon the tool itself but largely upon the user.

All informed predictions of future performance are based upon some knowledge of relevant past performance: school grades, research productivity, sales records, batting averages, or whatever is appropriate. How well the predictions will be validated by later performance depends upon the amount, reliability, and appropriateness of the information used and on the skill and wisdom with which it is interpreted. Anyone who keeps careful score knows that the information available is always incomplete and that the predictions are always subject to error.

Standardized tests should be considered in this context. They provide a quick, objective method of getting some kinds of information about what a person has learned, the skills he has developed, or the kind of person he is. The information so obtained has, qualitatively, the same advantages and shortcomings as other kinds of information. Whether to use tests, other kinds of information, or both in a particular situation depends, therefore, upon the empirical evidence concerning comparative validity, and upon such factors as cost and availability.

In general, the tests work most effectively when the traits or qualities to be measured can be most precisely defined (for example, ability to do well in a particular course or training program) and least effectively when what is to be measured or predicted cannot be well defined (for example, personality or creativity). Properly used, they provide a rapid means of getting comparable information about many people. Sometimes they identify students whose high potential has not been previously recognized. But there are many things they do not do. For example, they do not compensate for gross social inequality, and thus do not tell how able an underprivileged youngster might have been had he grown up under more favorable circumstances.

Professionals in the business and the conscientious publishers know the limitations as well as the values. They write these things into test manuals and in critiques of available tests. But they have no jurisdiction over users; an educational test can be administered by almost anyone, whether he knows how to interpret it or not. Nor can the difficulty be controlled by limiting sales to qualified users; some attempts to do so have been countered by restraint-of-trade suits.

In the long run it may be possible to establish better controls or to require higher qualifications. But in the meantime, unhappily, the demonstrated value of these tests under many circumstances has given them a popularity that has led to considerable misuse. Also unhappily, justifiable criticism of the misuse now threatens to hamper proper use. Business and government can probably look after themselves. But school guidance and selection programs are being attacked for using a valuable tool, because some of the users are unskilled.

—by Watson Davis, Sc.D., Director of Science Service (reprinted with permission)

1. The essence of this article on educational tests is:
   (A) These tests do not test adequately what they set out to test.
   (B) Don't blame the test—blame the user.
   (C) When a student is nervous or ill, the test results are inaccurate.
   (D) Publishers of tests are without conscience.
   (E) Educators are gradually losing confidence in the value of the tests

2. Tests like the College Entrance Scholastic Aptitude Test are, it would seem to the author,
   (A) generally unreliable
   (B) generally reliable
   (C) meaningless
   (D) misleading
   (E) neither good nor bad

3. The selection implies that, more often, the value of an educational test rests with
   (A) the interpretation of results
   (B) the test itself
   (C) the testee
   (D) emotional considerations
   (E) the directions

4. Which statement is not true, according to the passage, about educational tests?
   (A) Some students "shine" unexpectedly
   (B) Predictions do not always hold true
   (C) Personality tests often fail to measure the true personality
   (D) The supervisor of the test must be very well trained
   (E) Publishers cannot confine sales to highly skilled administrators

5. According to the passage, the validity of a test requires most of all
   (A) cooperation on the part of the person tested
   (B) sufficient preparation on the part of the applicant
   (C) clearcut directions
   (D) one answer—and ony one—for each question
   (E) specificity regarding what is to be tested

When television is good, nothing—not the theatre, not the magazines, or newspapers—nothing is better. But when television is bad, nothing is worse. I invite you to sit down in front of your television set when your station goes on the air and stay there without a book, magazine, newspaper, or anything else to distract you and keep your eyes glued to that set until the station signs off. I can assure you that you will observe a vast wasteland. You will see a procession of game shows, violence, audience participation shows, formula comedies about totally unbelievable families, blood and thunder, mayhem, more violence, sadism, murder, Western badmen, Western goodmen, private eyes, gangsters, still more violence, and cartoons. And, endlessly, commercials that scream and cajole and offend. And most of all, boredom. True, you will see a few things you will enjoy. But they will be very, very few. And if you think I exaggerate, try it.

Is there no room on television to teach, to inform, to uplift, to stretch, to enlarge the capacities of our children? Is there no room for programs to deepen the children's understanding of children in other lands? Is there no room for a children's news show explaining something about the world for them at their level of understanding? Is there no room for reading the great literature of the past, teaching them the great traditions of freedom? There are some fine children's shows, but they are drowned out in the massive doses of cartoons, violence, and more violence. Must these be your trademarks? Search your conscience and see whether you cannot offer more to your young beneficiaries whose future you guard so many hours each and every day.

There are many people in this great country, and you must serve all of us. You will get no argument from me if you say that, given a choice between a Western and a symphony, more people will watch the Western. I like Westerns and private eyes, too—but a steady diet for the whole country is obviously not in the public interest. We all know that people would more often prefer to be entertained than stimulated or informed. But your obligations are not satisfied if you look only to popularity as a test of what to broadcast. You are not only in show business; you are free to communicate ideas as well as to give relaxation. You must provide a wider range of choices, more diversity, more alternatives. It is not enough to cater to the nation's whims—you must also serve the nation's needs. The people own the air. They own it as much in prime evening time as they do at 6 o'clock in the morning. For every hour that the people give you—you owe them something. I intend to see that your debt is paid with service.

—excerpt from speech by Newton N. Minow, chairman of the Federal Communications Commission, before the National Association of Broadcasters.

6. The wasteland referred to describes
   (A) Western badmen and Western goodmen
   (B) average television programs
   (C) the morning shows
   (D) television shows with desert locales
   (E) children's programs

7. The author's attitude toward television is one of
   (A) sullenness
   (B) reconciliation (D) rage
   (C) determination (E) hopelessness

8. The National Association of Broadcasters probably accepted Minow's remarks with
   (A) considerable enthusiasm
   (B) shocked wonderment
   (C) complete agreement
   (D) some disagreement
   (E) absolute rejection

9. The Federal Communications Commission chairman is, in effect, telling the broadcasters that
   (A) the listener, not the broadcaster, should make decisions about programs
   (B) children's shows are worthless
   (C) mystery programs should be banned
   (D) television instruction should be a substitute for classroom lessons
   (E) they had better mend their ways

10. Concerning programs for children, Minow believes that programs should
   (A) eliminate cartoons
   (B) provide culture
   (C) be presented at certain periods during the day
   (D) eliminate commercials
   (E) not deal with the West

11. The statement that "the people own the air" implies that
   (A) citizens have the right to insist on worthwhile television programs
   (B) television should be socialized
   (C) the government may build above present structures
   (D) since air is worthless, the people own nothing
   (E) the broadcasters have no right to commercialize on television

12. It can be inferred from the passage in regard to television programming that the author believes
   (A) the broadcasters are trying to do the right thing but are failing
   (B) foreign countries are going to pattern their programs after ours
   (C) there is a great deal that is worthwhile in present programs
   (D) the listeners do not necessarily know what is good for them
   (E) 6 A.M. is too early for a television show

If Johnny can't write, one of the reasons may be a conditioning based on speed rather than respect for the creative process. Speed is neither a valid test of nor a proper preparation for competence in writing. It makes for murkiness, glibness, disorganization. It takes the beauty out of the language. It rules out respect for the reflective thought that should precede expression. It runs counter to the word-by-word and line-by-line reworking that enables a piece to be finely knit.

This is not to minimize the value of genuine facility. With years of practice, a man may be able to put down words swiftly and expertly. But it is the same kind of swiftness that enables a cellist, after having invested years of efforts, to negotiate an intricate passage from Haydn. Speed writing is for stenographers and court reporters, not for anyone who wants to use language with precision and distinction.

Thomas Mann was not ashamed to admit that he would often take a full day to write 500 words, and another day to edit them, out of respect for the most difficult art in the world. Flaubert would ponder a paragraph for hours. Did it say what he wanted it to say—not approximately but exactly? Did the words turn into one another with proper rhythm and grace? Were they artistically and securely fitted together? Were they briskly alive, or were they full of fuzz and ragged edges? Were they likely to make things happen inside the mind of the reader, igniting the imagination and touching off all sorts of new anticipations? These questions are relevant not only for the established novelist but for anyone who attaches value to words as a medium of expression and communication.

E. B. White, whose respect for the environment of good writing is exceeded by no word-artist of our time, would rather have his fingers cut off than to be guilty of handling words lightly. No sculptor chipping away at a granite block in order to produce a delicate curve or feature has labored more painstakingly than White in fashioning a short paragraph. Obviously, we can't expect our schools to make every Johnny into a White or a Flaubert or a Mann, but it is not unreasonable to expect more of them to provide the conditions that promote clear, careful, competent expression. Certainly the cumulative effort of the school experience should not have to be undone in later years.

—by Norman Cousins, Editor of *Saturday Review* (reprinted with permission)

13. According to the passage, competence in writing is
    (A) an art that takes practice
    (B) a skill that requires dexterity
    (C) a technique that is easy to learn
    (D) a result of the spontaneous flow of words
    (E) an inate ability that few people have

14. The main purpose of the passage is to
    (A) present an original idea
    (B) describe a new process
    (C) argue against an established practice
    (D) comment on a skill and its techniques
    (E) urge the reader to action

15. Our schools, according to the passage,
    (A) are providing proper conditions for good writing
    (B) should not stress writing speed on a test
    (C) should give essay tests rather than multiple-choice tests
    (D) teach good writing primarily through reading
    (E) correlate art and music with writing instruction

16. In describing White as a "word-artist," the author means that White
    (A) was also a cartoonist
    (B) illustrated his stories
    (C) was colorful in his descriptions
    (D) had artistic background
    (E) was a great writer

17. It can be inferred from the passage that the author values good literature primarily for its ability to
    (A) relieve the boredom of everyday life
    (B) accurately describe events as they occur
    (C) prevent disorder in society
    (D) communicate ideas and experience
    (E) provide individuals with skills for success

Correct Answers For The Foregoing Questions

To assist you in scoring yourself we have provided Correct Answers alongside your Answer Sheet. May we therefore suggest that while you are doing the test you cover the Correct Answers with a sheet of white paper.....to avoid temptation and to arrive at an accurate estimate of your ability and progress.

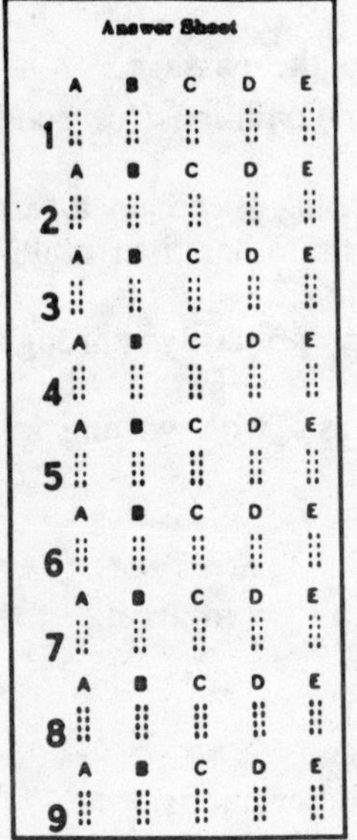
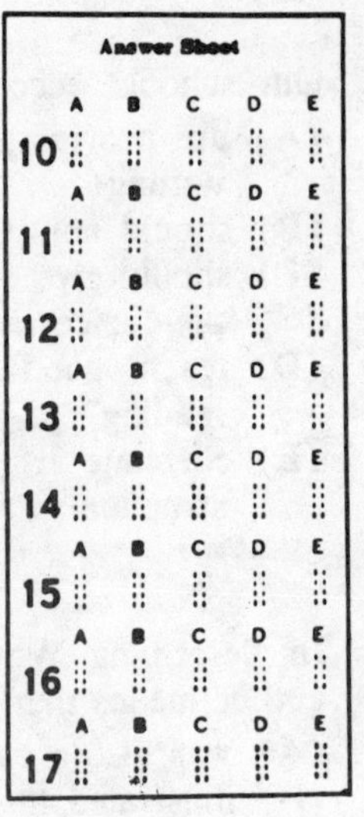
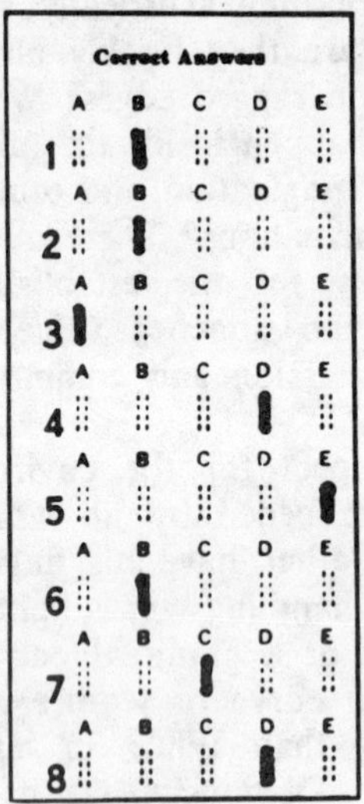
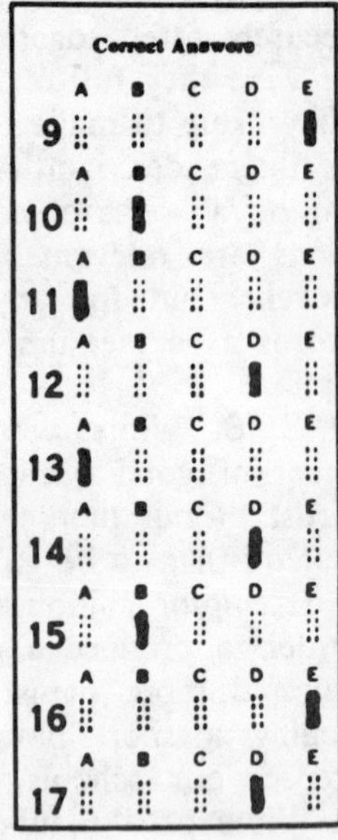

SCORE 1

.... %

NO. CORRECT

NO. OF QUESTIONS ON THIS TEST

SCORE 2

.... %

NO. CORRECT

NO. OF QUESTIONS ON THIS TEST

READING TEST TWO

DIRECTIONS: Below each of the following passages, you will find questions or incomplete statements about the passage. Each statement or question is followed by lettered words or expressions. Select the word or expression that most satisfactorily completes each statement or answers each question in accordance with the meaning of the passage. Write the letter of that word or expression on your answer paper.

A FAIR SAMPLING OF THE QUESTIONS YOU'LL BE ASKED

Correct key answers to all these test questions will be found at the end of the test.

Recent scientific discoveries are throwing new light on the basic nature of viruses and on the possible nature of cancer, genes and even life itself. These discoveries are providing evidence for relationships among these four subjects which indicate that one may be dependent upon another to an extent not fully appreciated heretofore. Too often one works and thinks within too narrow a range and hence fails to recognize the significance of certain facts for other areas. Sometimes the important new ideas and subsequent fundamental discoveries come from the borderline areas between two well-established fields of investigation. This will result in the synthesis of new ideas regarding viruses, cancer, genes and life. These ideas in turn will result in the doing of new experiments which may provide the basis for fundamental discoveries in these fields.

There is no doubt that of the four topics, life is the one most people would consider to be of the greatest importance. However, life means different things to different people and it is in reality difficult to define just what we mean by life. There is no difficulty in recognizing an agent as living so long as we contemplate structures like a man, a dog or even a bacterium, and at the other extreme a piece of iron or glass or an atom of hydrogen or a molecule of water. The ability to grow or reproduce and to change or mutate has long been regarded as a special property characteristic of living agents along with the ability to respond to external stimuli. These are properties not shared by bits of iron or glass or even by a molecule of hemoglobin. Now if viruses had not been discovered, all would have been well. The organisms of the biologist would have ranged from the largest of animals all the way down to the smallest of the bacteria which are about 200 millimicra. There would have been a definite break with respect to size; the largest molecules known to the chemist were less than 20 millimicra in size. Thus life and living agents would have been represented by those structures which possessed the ability to reproduce themselves and to mutate and were about ten times larger than the largest known molecule. This would have provided a comfortable area of separation between living and non-living things.

Then came the discovery of the viruses. These infectious, disease-producing agents are characterized by their small size, by their ability to grow or reproduce within specific living cells, and by their ability to change or mutate during reproduction. This was enough to convince most people that viruses were merely still smaller living organisms. When the sizes of different viruses were determined, it was found that some were actually smaller than certain protein molecules. When the first virus was isolated in the form of a crystallizable material it was found to be a nucleoprotein. It was found to possess all the usual properties associated with protein molecules yet was larger than any molecule previously described. Here was a molecule that possessed the ability to reproduce itself and to mutate. The distinction between living and non-living things seemed to be tottering. The gap in size between 20 and 200 millimicra has been filled in completely by the viruses, with some actual overlapping at both ends. Some large viruses are larger than some living organisms, and some small viruses are actuallly smaller than certain protein molecules.

Let us consider the relationship between genes and viruses since both are related to life. Both genes and viruses seem to be nucleoproteins and both reproduce only within specific living cells. Both possess the ability to mutate. Although viruses generally reproduce many times within a given cell, some situations are known in which they appear to reproduce only once with each cell division. Genes usually reproduce once with each cell division, but here also the rate can be changed. Actually the similarities between genes and viruses are so remarkable that viruses were referred to as "naked genes" or "genes on the loose."

Despite the fact that today viruses are known to cause cancer in animals and in certain plants, there exists a great reluctance to accept viruses as being of importance in human cancer. Basic biological phenomena generally do not differ strikingly as one goes from one species to another. It should be recognized that cancer is a biological problem and not a problem that is unique for man. Cancer originates when a normal cell suddenly becomes a cancer cell which multiplies widely and without apparent restraint. Cancer may originate in many differrent kinds of cells, but the cancer cell usually continues to carry certain traits of the cell of origin. The transformation of a normal cell into a cancer cell may have more than one kind of cause, but there is good reason to consider the relationships that exist between viruses and cancer.

Since there is no evidence that human cancer, as generally experienced, is infectious, many persons believe that because viruses are infectious agents they cannot possibly be of importance in human cancer. However, viruses can mutate and examples are known in which a virus that never kills its host can mutate to form a new strain of virus that always kills its host. It does not seem unreasonable to assume that an innocuous latent virus might mutate to form a strain that causes cancer. Certainly the experimental evidence now available is consistent with the idea that viruses as we know them today, could be the causative agents of most, if not all cancer, including cancer in man.

1. People were convinced that viruses were small living organism, because viruses
   (A) are disease-producing
   (B) reproduce within living cells
   (C) could be grown on artificial media
   (D) consist of nucleoproteins

2. Scientists very often do not apply the facts learned in one subject area to a related field of investigation because
   (A) the borderline areas are too close to both to give separate facts
   (B) scientists work in a very narrow range of experimentation
   (C) new ideas are synthesized only as a result of new experimentation
   (D) fundamental discoveries are based upon finding close relationships in related sciences

3. Before the discovery of viruses, it might have been possible to distinguish living things from non-living things by the fact that
   (A) animate objects can mutate
   (B) non-living substances cannot reproduce themselves
   (C) responses to external stimuli are characteristic of living things
   (D) living things were greater than 20 millimicra in size

4. The size of viruses is presently known to be
   (A) between 20 and 200 millimicra
   (B) smaller than any bacterium
   (C) larger than any protein molecule
   (D) larger than most nucleoproteins

5. That genes and viruses seem to be related might be shown by the fact that
   (A) both are ultra-microscopic
   (B) each can mutate but once in a cell
   (C) each reproduces but once in a cell
   (D) both appear to have the same chemical structure

6. Viruses were called "genes on the loose" because they
   (A) are able to reproduce very freely
   (B) like genes, seem to be able to mutate
   (C) seemed to be genes without cells
   (D) can loosen genes from cells

7. Cancer should be considered to be a biological problem rather than a medical one because
   (A) viruses are known to cause cancers in animals
   (B) at present, human cancer is not believed to be contagious
   (C) there are many known causes for the transformation of a normal cell to a cancer cell
   (D) results of experiments on plants and animals do not vary greatly from species to species

8. The possibility that a virus causes human cancer is indicated by
   (A) the fact that viruses have been known to mutate
   (B) the fact that a cancer-immune individual may lose his immunity
   (C) the fact that reproduction of human cancer cells might be due to a genetic factor
   (D) the fact that man is host to many viruses

9. The best title for this passage is
   (A) New Light on the Cause of Cancer
   (B) The Newest Theory on the Nature of Viruses
   (C) Viruses, Genes, Cancer and Life
   (D) On the Nature of Life

10. According to the passage, cancer cells are
   (A) similar to the cell of origin
   (B) mutations of viruses
   (C) unable to reproduce
   (D) among the smallest cells known
   (E) present in small amounts in all individuals

An action of apparent social significance among animals is that of migration. But several different factors are at work causing such migrations. These may be concerned with food-getting, with temperature, salinity, pressure and light changes; with the action of sex hormones and probably other combinations of these factors.

The great aggregations of small crustaceans, such as copepods found at the surface of the ocean, swarms of insects about a light, or the masses of unicellular organisms making up a part of the plankton in the lakes and oceans, are all examples of nonsocial aggregations of organisms brought together because of the presence or absence of certain factors in their environment, such as air currents, water currents, food or the lack of it, oxygen or carbon dioxide, or some other contributing causes.

Insects make long migrations, most of which seem due to the urge for food. The migrations of the locust, both in this country and elsewhere, are well known. While fish, such as salmon, return to the same stream where they grew up, such return migrations are rare in insects, the only known instance being in the monarch butterfly. This is apparently due to the fact that it is long-lived and has the power of strong flight. The mass migrations of the Rocky Mountain and the African species of locust seem attributable to the need for food. Locusts live, eat, sun themselves and migrate in groups. It has been suggested that their social life is in response to the two fundamental instincts, aggregation and imitation.

Migrations of fish have been studied carefully by many investigators. Typically the migrations are from deep to shallow waters, as in the herring, mackerel and many other marine fish. Fresh-water fish in general exhibit this type of migration in the spawning season. Spawning habits of many fish show a change in habitat from salt to fresh water. Among these are the shad, salmon, alewife and others. In the North American and European eels, long migrations take place at the breeding season. All these migrations are obviously not brought about by a quest for food, for the salmon and many other fish feed only sparingly during the spawning season, but are undoubtedly brought about by metabolic changes in the animal initiated by the interaction of sex hormones. If this thesis holds, then here is the beginning of social life.

Bird migrations have long been a matter of study. The reasons for the migration of the golden plover from the Arctic regions to the tip of South America and return in a single year are not fully explainable. Several theories have been advanced, although none have been fully proved. The reproductive "instinct," food scarcity, temperature and light changes, the metabolic changes brought about by the activity of the sex hormones and the length of the day, all have been suggested, and ultimately several may prove to be factors. Aside from other findings, it is interesting to note that bird migrations take place year after year on about the same dates. Recent studies in the biochemistry of metabolism, showing that there is a seasonal cycle in the blood sugar that has a definite relation to activity and food, seem to be among the most promising leads.

In mammals the seasonal migrations that take place, such as those of the deer, which travel from the high mountains in summer to the valleys in winter, or the migration of the caribou in the northern areas of Canada, are based on the factor of temperature which regulates the food supply. Another mystery is the migration of the lemming, a small ratlike animal found in Scandinavia and Canada. The lemming population varies greatly from year to year, and, at times when it greatly increases, a migration occurs in which hordes of lemmings march across the country, swimming rivers and even plunging into the ocean if it bars their way. This again cannot be purely social association of animals. The horde is usually made up entirely of males, as the females seldom migrate.

11. The migration of the lemmings cannot be considered one of social association since
(A) only males migrate
(B) migrations occur only with population increases
(C) it is probably due to the absence of some factor in the environment
(D) the migrants do not return

12. Animals which apparently migrate in quest of food are the
(A) fish (C) mammals
(B) birds (D) **insects**

13. A characteristic of migration is the return of the migrants to their former home areas. This is, however, not true of the
(A) birds (C) mammals
(B) **insects** (D) fish

14. The reproductive instinct is probably not a factor in the actual migration of
(A) shad (C) golden plover
(B) lemming (D) monarch butterfly

15. In paragraph 1, several probable factors causing migrations are given. None of these seem to explain the migrations of
(A) lemming (C) salmon
(B) caribou (D) locusts

16. The reasons for the migrations of birds may ultimately be determined by scientists working in the field of
(A) population studies
(B) ecology
(C) metabolism chemistry
(D) reproduction

17. According to the passage, the reproductive process seems to be a known factor in the migration of many
(A) fish (B) insects
(C) mammals (D) birds

18. Animals which migrate back and forth between the same general areas are
(A) locusts and salmon
(B) salmon and golden plover
(C) golden plover and lemming
(D) monarch butterfly and caribou

19. The shortest distance covered by any migrating group is taken by
(A) insects (C) birds
(B) fish (D) mammals

20. The main purpose of the passage is to
(A) show how a natural event effects change in different species
(B) present a new theory in regard to biological evolution
(C) teach the reader how to evaluate a natural phenomenon
(D) describe a phenomenon that has not yet been satisfactorily explained
(E) show how species behave similarly under the same conditions

21. Return migrations are usually associated with animals that
(A) make long migrations
(B) are long-lived
(C) migrate to spawn
(D) make short migrations

Correct Answers For The Foregoing Questions

To assist you in scoring yourself we have provided Correct Answers alongside your Answer Sheet. May we therefore suggest that while you are doing the test you cover the Correct Answers with a sheet of white paper.....to avoid temptation and to arrive at an accurate estimate of your ability and progress.

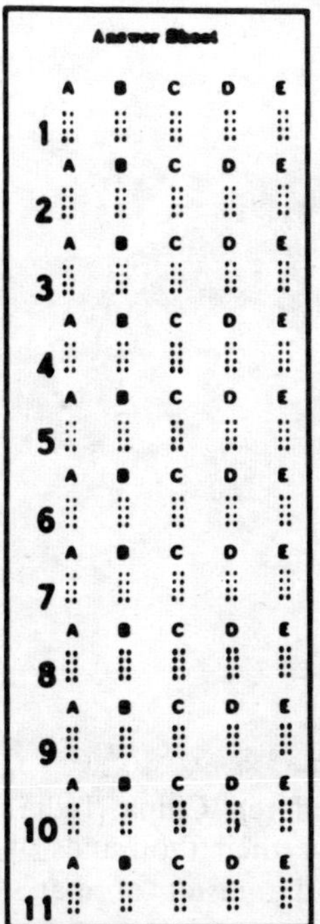

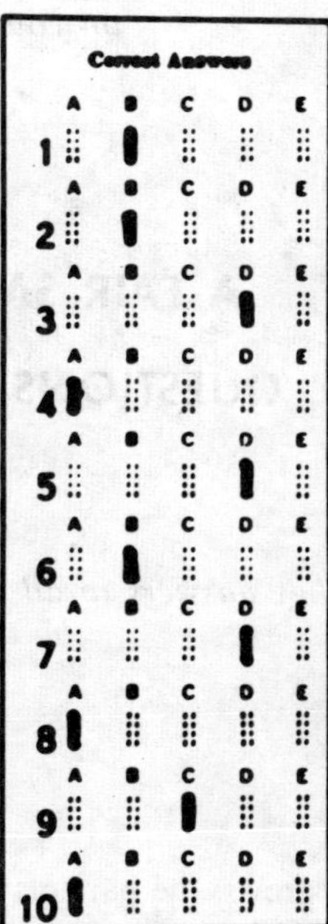

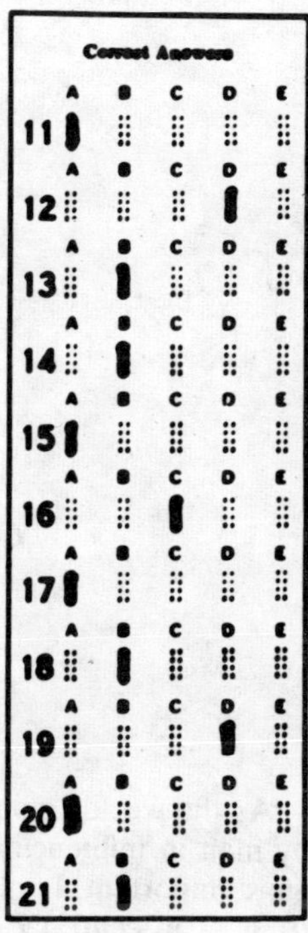

SCORE 1

.... %

NO. CORRECT

NO. OF QUESTIONS ON THIS TEST

SCORE 2

.... %

NO. CORRECT

NO. OF QUESTIONS ON THIS TEST

READING TEST THREE

DIRECTIONS: Below each of the following passages, you will find questions or incomplete statements about the passage. Each statement or question is followed by lettered words or expressions. Select the word or expression that most satisfactorily completes each statement or answers each question in accordance with the meaning of the passage. Write the letter of that word or expression on your answer paper.

A FAIR SAMPLING OF THE QUESTIONS YOU'LL BE ASKED

Correct key answers to all these test questions will be found at the end of the test.

As the world's population grows, the part played by man in influencing plant life becomes more and more important. In old and densely populated countries, as in central Europe, man determines almost wholly what shall grow and what shall not grow. In such regions, the influence of man on plant life is in large measure a beneficial one. Laws, often centuries old, protect plants of economic value and preserve soil fertility. In newly settled countries the situation is unfortunately quite the reverse. The pioneer's life is too strenuous a one for him to think of posterity.

Some years ago Mt. Mitchell, the highest summit east of the Mississippi, was covered with a magnificent forest. A lumber company was given full rights to fell the trees. Those not cut down were crushed. The mountain was left a wasted area where fire would rage and erosion would complete the destruction. There was no stopping the devastating foresting of the company, for the contract had been given. Under a more enlightened civilization this could not have happened. The denuding of Mt. Mitchell is a minor chapter in the destruction of lands in the United States; and this country is by no means the only or chief sufferer. China, India, Egypt, and East Africa all have their thousands of square miles of waste land, the result of man's indifference to the future.

Deforestation, grazing, and poor farming are the chief causes of the destruction of land fertility. Wasteful cutting of timber is the first step. Grazing then follows lumbering in bringing about ruin. The Caribbean slopes of northern Venezuela are barren wastes owing first to ruthless cutting of forests and then to destructive grazing. Hordes of goats have roamed these slopes until only a few thorny acacias and cacti remain. Erosion completed the devastation. What is there illustrated on a small scale is the story of vast areas in China and India, countries where famines are of regular occurrence.

Man is not wholly to blame, for Nature is often merciless. In parts of India and China, plant life, when left undisturbed by man, cannot cope with either the disastrous floods of wet seasons or the destructive winds of the dry season. Man has learned much; prudent land management has been the policy of the Chinese people since 2700 B. C., but even they have not learned enough.

When the American forestry service was in its infancy, it met with much opposition from legislators who loudly claimed that the protected land would in one season yield a crop of cabbages of more value than all the timber on it. Herein lay the fallacy, that one season's crop is all that need be thought of. Nature, through the years, adjusts crops to the soil and to the climate. Forests usually occur where precipitation exceeds evaporation. If the reverse is true, grasslands are found; and where evaporation is still greater, desert or scrub vegetation alone survives. The phytogeographic map of a country is very similar to the climatic map based on rainfall, evaporation, and temperature. Man ignores this natural adjustment of crops and strives for one "bumper" crop in a single season; he may produce it, but "year in and year out the yield of the grassland is certain, that of the planted fields, never."

Man is learning; he sprays his trees with insecticides and fungicides; he imports ladybugs to destroy aphids; he irrigates, fertilizes, and rotates his crops; but he is still indifferent to many of the consequences of his short-sighted policies. The great dust storms of the western United States are proof of this indifference.

In spite of the evidence to be had from this country, the people of other countries, still in the pioneer stage, farm as wastefully as did our own pioneers. In the interiors of Central and South American Republics, natives fell superb forest trees and leave them to rot in order to obtain virgin soil for cultivation. Where the land is hillside, it readily washes and after one or two seasons is unfit for crops. So the frontier farmer pushes back into the primeval forest, moving his hut as he goes, and fells more monarchs to lay bare another patch of ground for his plantings to support his family. Valuable timber which will require a century to replace is destroyed and the land laid waste to produce what could be supplied for a pittance.

How badly man can err in his handling of land is shown by the draining of extensive swamp areas, which to the uninformed would seem to be a very good thing to do. One of the first effects of the drainage is the lowering of the water-table, which may bring about the death of the dominant species and leave to another species the possession of the soil, even when the difference in water level is little more than an inch. Frequently, bog country will yield marketable crops of cranberries and blueberries but, if drained, neither these nor any other economic plant will grow on the fallow soil. Swamps and marshes have their drawbacks but also their virtues. When drained they may leave waste land, the surface of which rapidly erodes to be then blown away in dust blizzards disastrous to both man and wild beasts.

1. The best title for this passage is
(A) How to Increase Soil Productivity
(B) Conservation of Natural Resources
(C) Man's Effect on Soil
(D) Soil Conditions and Plant Growth

2. A policy of good management is sometimes upset by
(A) the indifference of man
(B) centuries-old laws
(C) floods and winds
(D) grazing animals

3. Areas in which the total amounts of rain and snow falling on the ground are greater than that which is evaporated will support
(A) forests
(B) grasslands
(C) scrub vegetation
(D) no plants

4. Pioneers do not have a long range view on soil problems since they
(A) are not protected by laws
(B) live under adverse conditions
(C) use poor methods of farming
(D) must protect themselves from famine

5. Phytogeographic maps are those that show
(A) areas of grassland
(B) areas of bumper crops
(C) areas of similar climate
(D) areas of similar plants

6. The basic cause of frequent famines in China and India is probably due to
(A) allowing animals to roam wild
(B) drainage of swamps
(C) over-grazing of the land
(D) destruction of forests

7. With a growing world population, the increased need for soil for food production may be met by
(A) draining unproductive swamp areas
(B) legislating against excess lumbering
(C) trying to raise bumper crops each year
(D) irrigating desert areas

8. What is meant by "the yield of the grassland is certain; that of the planted field, never" is that

(A) it is impossible to get more than one bumper crop from any one cultivated area
(B) crops, planted in former grassland, will not give good yields
(C) through the indifference of man, dust blizzards have occurred in former grasslands
(D) if man does not interfere, plants will grow in the most suitable environment

9. The first act of prudent land management might be to
(A) prohibit drainage of swamps
(B) use irrigation and crop rotation in planted areas
(C) increase use of fertilizers
(D) prohibit excessive forest lumbering

10. The results of good land management may usually be found in
(A) heavily populated areas
(B) areas not given over to grazing
(C) underdeveloped areas
(D) ancient civilizations

Regarding physical changes that have been and are now taking place on the surface of the earth, the sea and its shores have been the scene of the greatest stability. The dry land has seen the rise, the decline, and even the disappearance, of vast hordes of various types and forms within times comparatively recent, geologically speaking; but life in the sea is today virtually what it was when many of the forms now extinct on land had not yet been evolved. Also, it may be parenthetically stated here, the marine habitat has been biologically the most important in the evolution and development of life on this planet. Its rhythmic influence can still be traced in those animals whose ancestors have long since left that realm to abide far from their primary haunts. For it is now generally held as an accepted fact that the shore area of an ancient sea was the birthplace of life.

Still, despite the primitive conditions still maintained in the sea, its shore inhabitants show an amazing diversity, while their adaptive characters are perhaps not exceeded in refinement by those that distinguish the dwellers of dry land. Why is this diversity manifest? We must look for an answer into the physical factors obtaining in that extremely slender zone surrounding the continents, marked by the rise and fall of the tides.

It will be noticed by the most casual observer that on any given seashore the area exposed between the tide marks may be roughly divided into a number of levels each characterized by a certain assemblage of animals. Thus in proceeding from high- to low-water mark, new forms constantly become predominant while other forms gradually drop out. Now, provided that the character of the substratum does not change, these differences in the types of animals are determined almost exclusively by the duration of time that the individual forms may remain exposed to the air without harm. Indeed, so regularly does the tidal rhythm act on certain animals (the barnacles, for instance), that certain species have come to require a definite period of exposure in order to maintain themselves, and will die out if kept continuously submerged. Although there are some forms that actually require periodic exposure, the number of species inhabiting the shore that are able to endure exposure every twelve hours, when the tide falls, is comparatively few.

With the alternate rise and fall of the tides, the successive areas of the tidal zone are subjected to force of wave-impact. In certain regions the waves often break with considerable force. Consequently, wave-shock has had a profound influence on the structure and habits of shore animals. It is characteristic of most shore animals that they shun definitely exposed places, and seek shelter in nooks and crannies and such refuges as are offered under stones and seaweed; particularly is this true of those forms living on rock and other firm foundations. Many of these have a marked capacity to cling closely to the substratum; some, such as anemones and certain snails, although without the grasping organs of higher animals, have special powers of adhesion; others, such as sponges and sea squirts, remain permanently fixed, and if torn loose from their base are incapable of forming a new attachment. But perhaps the most significant method of solving the problem presented by the surf has been in the adaptation of body-form to minimize friction. This is strikingly displayed in the fact that seashore animals are essentially flattened forms. Thus, in the typically shore forms the sponges are of the encrusting type, the non-burrowing worms are leaflike, the snails and other mollusks are squat forms and are without the spines and other ornate extensions such as are often produced on the shells of many mollusks in deeper and quieter waters. The same influence is no less marked in the case of the crustaceans; the flattening is either lateral, as in the amphipods, or dorsoventral, as in the isopods and crabs.

In sandy regions, because of the unstable nature of substratum, no such means of attachment as indicated in the foregoing paragraph will suffice to maintain the animals in their almost ceaseless battle with the billows. Most of them must perforce depend on their ability quickly to penetrate into the sand for safety. Some forms endowed with less celerity, such as the sand dollars, are so constructed that their bodies offer no more resistance to wave impact than does a flat pebble.

Temperature, also, is a not inconsiderable factor among those physical forces constantly operating to produce a diversity of forms among seashore animals. At a comparatively shallow depth in the sea, there is small fluctuation of temperatures; and life there exists in surroundings of serene stability; but as the shore is approached, the influence of the sun becomes more and more manifest and the variation is greater. This variation becomes greatest between the tide marks where, because of the very shallow depths and the fresh water from the land, this area is subjected to wide changes in both temperature and salinity.

Nor is a highly competitive mode of life without its bearing on structure as well as habits. In this phase of their struggle for existence, the animals of both the sea and the shore have become possessed of weapons for offense and defense that are correspondingly varied.

Although the life in the sea has been generally considered and treated as separate and distinct from the more familiar life on land, that supposition has no real basis in fact. Life on this planet is one vast unit, depending for its existence chiefly on the same sources of supply. That portion of animal life living in the sea, notwithstanding its strangeness and unfamiliarity, may be considered as but the aquatic fringe of the life on land. It is supported largely by materials washed into the sea, which are no longer available for the support of land animals. Perhaps we have been misled in these considerations of sea life because of the fact that approximately three times as many major *types* of animals inhabit salt water as live on the land: of the major types of animals no fewer than ten are exclusively marine, that is to say, nearly half again as many as land-dwelling types together. A further interesting fact is that despite the greater variety in the form and structure of sea animals about three-fourths of all known *kinds* of animals live on the land, while only one-fourth lives in the sea. In this connection it is noteworthy that sea life becomes scarcer with increasing distance from land; toward the middle of the oceans it disappears almost completely. For example, the central south Pacific is a region more barren than is any desert area on land. Indeed, no life of any kind has been found in the surface water, and there seems to be none on the bottom.

Sea animals are largest and most abundant on those shores receiving the most copious rainfall. Particularly is this true on the most rugged and colder coasts where it may be assumed that the material from the land finds its way to the sea unaltered and in greater quantities.

11. **The best title for this passage is**
    (A) Between the Tides (C) The Tides
    (B) Seashore Life (D) The Seashore

12. Of the following adaptations, the one that would enable an organism to live on a sandy beach is
    (A) the ability to move rapidly
    (B) the ability to burrow deeply
    (C) a flattened shape
    (D) spiny extensions of the shell

13. The absence of living things in mid-ocean might be due to
    (A) lack of rainfall in mid-ocean
    (B) the distance from material washed into the sea
    (C) larger animals feeding on smaller ones which must live near the land
    (D) insufficient dissolved oxygen

14. A greater variety of living things exist on a rocky shore than on a sandy beach because
    (A) rocks offer a better foothold than sand
    (B) sandy areas are continually being washed by the surf
    (C) temperature changes are less drastic in rocky areas
    (D) the water in rock pools is less salty

15. Organisms found living at the high-tide mark are adapted to
    (A) maintain themselves in the air for a long time
    (B) offer no resistance to wave impact
    (C) remain permanently fixed to the substratum
    (D) burrow in the ground

16. The author holds that living things in the sea represent the aquatic fringe of life on land. This is so because
   (A) there are relatively fewer marine forms of animals than there are land-living forms
   (B) there is greater variety among land-living forms
   (C) marine animals ultimately depend upon material from the land
   (D) there are three times as many kinds of animals on land than there are in the sea

17. A biologist walking along the shore at the low-tide line would not easily find many live animals since
   (A) their flattened shapes make them indistinguishable
   (B) they are washed back and forth by the waves
   (C) they burrow deeply
   (D) they move rapidly

18. The intent of the author in the next to the last paragraph is to show that
   (A) the temperature and salinity of the sea determine the variety among shore animals
   (B) marine animals are vastly different from terrestrial organisms
   (C) colder areas can support more living things than warm areas
   (D) marine forms have the same problems as terrestrial animals

19. A scientist wishing to study a great variety of living things would do well to hunt for them
   (A) in shallow waters
   (B) on a rocky seashore
   (C) on a sandy seashore
   (D) on any shore between the tide lines

20. The most primitive forms of living things in the evolutionary scale are to be found in the sea because
   (A) the influence of the sea is found in land animals
   (B) the sea is relatively stable
   (C) many forms have become extinct on land
   (D) land animals are supposed to have evolved from sea organisms

Correct Answers For The Foregoing Questions

To assist you in scoring yourself we have provided Correct Answers alongside your Answer Sheet. May we therefore suggest that while you are doing the test you cover the Correct Answers with a sheet of white paper.....to avoid temptation and to arrive at an accurate estimate of your ability and progress.

Answer Sheet

	A	B	C	D	E
1	A	B	C	D	E
2	A	B	C	D	E
3	A	B	C	D	E
4	A	B	C	D	E
5	A	B	C	D	E
6	A	B	C	D	E
7	A	B	C	D	E
8	A	B	C	D	E
9	A	B	C	D	E
10	A	B	C	D	E

Answer Sheet

	A	B	C	D	E
11	A	B	C	D	E
12	A	B	C	D	E
13	A	B	C	D	E
14	A	B	C	D	E
15	A	B	C	D	E
16	A	B	C	D	E
17	A	B	C	D	E
18	A	B	C	D	E
19	A	B	C	D	E
20	A	B	C	D	E

Correct Answers

	A	B	C	D	E
1			C		
2			C		
3	A				
4		B			
5				D	
6				D	
7		B			
8				D	
9				D	
10	A				

Correct Answers

	A	B	C	D	E
11		B			
12	A				
13		B			
14		B			
15	A				
16			C		
17				D	
18				D	
19				D	
20		B			

SCORE 1

.... %

NO. CORRECT

NO. OF QUESTIONS ON THIS TEST

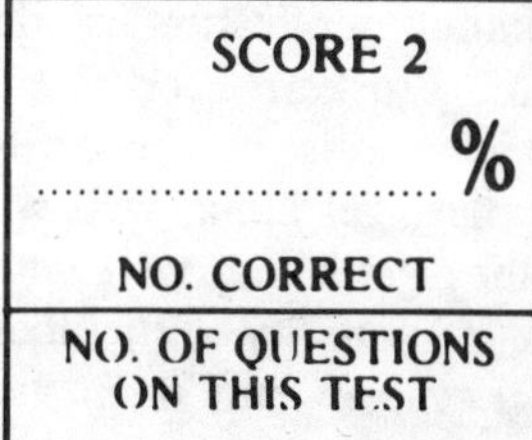

THE COMPLETE SUPERVISION QUIZZER

Supervision takes place whenever one person is made responsible for the work of others. Whether on the police force, in the fire department, in the office, stockroom, factory, among skilled mechanics or unskilled laborers, the requirements of supervision remain basically the same.

A supervisor is responsible for extracting a maximum return from the personnel and equipment allotted to him for performing his functions. He must train his subordinates to perform their work in the best possible manner, and condition their thinking so that they will cooperate with him in an effort to reach unit objectives. He must convince them that what is good for the organization is also good for them.

A supervisor cannot fulfill his function in an organization without the support and cooperation of his subordinates, and he can do this only through the skillful application of the science of human relations. Workers need the security and recognition which he is in the best position to give them. He must get along well with them and see to it that they get along well with each other by eliminating personality difficulties. He must listen to their grievances and show them that their efforts are recognized and appreciated.

In recent years there has been considerable development in the science of supervision. The resulting concepts are found to be applicable wherever supervision exists.

It is sometimes said that people are so different that they are all alike. This theory can be applied to supervision in general. When a sergeant is responsible for the performance of a patrolman or a foreman for a factory worker, certain conditions arise out of the supervisory relationship. If both subordinates are in need of training, the same fundamental concepts of teaching apply for each. If both are in need of disciplinary action, similar infractions probably require similar disciplinary action.

More and more questions on recent examinations for supervisory positions have been devoted to the science of supervision and administration. This type of question is a great evaluator of a person's judgment. The importance of proper supervision in an organization is also being widely recognized. It is an accepted theory that the type of supervision workers operate under plays a big part in establishing their level of morale. Employee morale and job efficiency are directly related. An organization cannot be efficient if its workers do not perform under proper supervisory techniques.

Working on the accepted theory that supervision is similar wherever it exists, Arco reviewed all examinations given recently and extracted questions of a supervisory nature. The questions were then categorized and put into sections in progressive order of difficulty. Every question is followed by the accepted answer and a brief explanation of the supervisory concept which it involves. These concepts make good study material not only because examination questions are derived from them, but because they also provide a firm base for the science of supervision. By studying the explanations you will note that a lot of plain common sense is involved together with the application of good human-relation practices.

If you are already a supervisor, use this book to improve your effectiveness. If you are not yet a supervisor, it will help you become one.

SUPERVISING UNSKILLED WORKERS

1. One of the men in your crew complains about having to do a hard job. The best thing for you to do is to

   (A) ignore him
   (B) explain to him that all men must do their fair share of the hard jobs
   (C) tell him that his next job will be an easy one
   (D) take him off this job

Answer: **(B)** It usually works out well to have the undesirable tasks rotated among all workers of equal rank. All tasks cannot be desirable, but all have to be performed.

2. Men will respect their supervisor most if he

   (A) acts sternly with them
   (B) does not show favoritism
   (C) is quick to criticize their errors
   (D) does not enforce all the rules and regulations

Answer: **(B)** A foreman is most likely to gain the respect of his men if he treats them impartially. A strict supervisor will not always gain his subordinate's respect; on the other hand, a lenient supervisor is even less likely to be respected. Criticism of subordinate's errors should always be handled with the greatest discretion.

3. The best supervisor is usually the

   (A) best mechanic
   (B) fastest worker
   (C) man in service the longest
   (D) ablest leader

Answer: **(D)** The successful supervisor must be a good leader of men. He must be able to gain their support in fulfilling the functions he is charged with. A good worker does not necessarily make a good supervisor. The same can be said of a fast worker. A man who has worked at his job for a long time does not necessarily acquire leadership ability.

4. One of your men offers a suggestion to improve the method of doing a job. The best thing to do is to tell the man

   (A) that the job has always been done the same way and therefore it must be the best way
   (B) that you will check his suggestion to see if it really is a better way of doing the job
   (C) to make the suggestion to the chief engineer
   (D) to discuss it with the other men, and if they agree with him you will try the suggested method

Answer: **(B)** Some of the most useful suggestions come from those closest to the actual work. All suggestions should be carefully evaluated by the supervisor. Even if the entire suggestion is not valid, it may have its good points. Besides, the supervisor will do much to maintain the morale of his group if he encourages suggestions.

5. Of the following, the statement that is correct is that

   (A) every worker can do the same amount of work
   (B) the man with the most seniority will work the fastest
   (C) the strongest man will do the most work
   (D) the amount of work a man does can be increased by improving morale

Answer: **(D)** Production and employee morale are directly related. When morale is high, production will be high; when morale is low, production will be poor.

6. Of the following, the best way for a supervisor to get his men to follow his orders and directives willingly is to

   (A) ask for volunteers
   (B) explain the reasons behind the orders and directives
   (C) issue them in the form of a request or in a mild tone of voice
   (D) take part in carrying them out

Answer: **(B)** A worker will be more likely to perform well when he knows why he is carrying out a particular task.

7. Inefficient scheduling of work should be suspected when one notes that there are several men
   (A) absent from work
   (B) in the rest room
   (C) loading a truck
   (D) waiting to use equipment

Answer: **(D)** The fact that equipment is not available when necessary is usually indicative of poor scheduling of work. Workers who must wait around for equipment are losing valuable time.

8. Whenever you give an assignment to one of your experienced men, he asks you a great many questions about it although he has successfully performed similar assignments in the past. The time you spend in answering his many questions about minor details takes you away from more important work. Under these circumstances, you should probably *first*
   (A) answer his questions in such a way that he will be discouraged from asking further questions
   (B) ask the man to ask his questions of one of his fellow employees
   (C) assure the man of your confidence in his ability to carry out the assignment properly and suggest that he proceed with his assignment
   (D) tell the man that if the assignment is too difficult you will give it to someone who does not raise so many questions

Answer: **(C)** This man is needlessly wasting the time of his supervisor. Apparently he lacks confidence in himself. The supervisor should attempt to instill self-confidence in this man through encouragement and praise whenever justified.

9. A supervisor should think of himself primarily as a
   (A) boss of his crew
   (B) part of the top management team
   (C) skilled maintenance and repair man in various fields
   (D) mechanic first and as a boss second

Answer: **(A)** A supervisor is paid to supervise. His aim should be to achieve maximum production from the men assigned to him and the attainment of his unit's objectives.

10. If, after you have been a supervisor for several years, you find that your men never complain to you about working conditions or assignments, this is most probably a sign that
   (A) there is poor communication between you and your men
   (B) the men are interested mainly in their rate of pay
   (C) the men have nothing to complain about
   (D) you are a very good supervisor

Answer: **(A)** It is perfectly normal for workers to have some complaints. If a supervisor never receives any, the reason probably is that his manner does not encourage them. His attitude should be such as will make it easy for his men to come to him with work problems.

11. "The number of subordinates directly reporting to a superior should not be greater than he can supervise competently." This could be an acceptable definition of
   (A) chain of command
   (B) span of control
   (C) specialized functions
   (D) unity of command

Answer: **(B)** The concept of span of control relates to the number of subordinates any supervisor can effectively handle. This number may increase or decrease, depending on the type of work being performed, how effectively the subordinates are trained, the conditions they perform the work under, etc.

12. A characteristic which a supervisor should consider most desirable in a worker is
   (A) willingness to work as much overtime as possible
   (B) keeping aloof from his co-workers
   (C) the ability to carry out assignments properly
   (D) the readiness to report gang gossip back to the foreman

Answer: **(C)** A worker is most valuable to his organization if he performs his duties with the greatest possible efficiency. How valuable can a worker make himself solely on his willingness to work overtime if he does not perform his regular duties well? Personality traits are not important unless they tend to interfere with work performance.

13. If a supervisor's crew continues to work effectively when he is out sick for a day or two, it would most probably indicate that

(A) he has their full cooperation
(B) the supervisor apparently serves no useful function with this crew
(C) the men are trying to curry favor
(D) the job is not too difficult

Answer: **(A)** When a crew functions as well in the absence of the supervisor as when he is present, it is an indication that a high degree of morale exists. The men are well trained and cooperative and fully behind their supervisor in attainment of unit objectives.

14. A supervisor would be personally to blame for inefficiency resulting from

(A) improper planning of work assignments
(B) unforeseen delays in delivery of material
(C) departmental policy of job rotation
(D) frequent labor turnover

Answer: **(A)** Poor planning causes delays in work through idle labor, lack of needed supplies, and improper staffing.

15. A supervisor is most likely to be held in high regard by his men if he makes it a practice to

(A) exchange advice with them on personal problems
(B) be outspoken when pointing out their faults
(C) expect them all to carry out any job he gives them with equal proficiency
(D) observe the same rules of conduct that he expects them to observe

Answer: **(D)** A supervisor will be respected by his subordinates if he observes the same rules of conduct that he expects them to follow. The exchange of advice on personal problems is a practice fraught with danger. If the advice does not have good results, it is bound to cause friction. An effective supervisor will use discretion while criticizing his subordinates. Criticism should do good, not harm.

16. A supervisory practice which is most likely to lead to confusion and inefficiency is for the supervisor to

(A) issue orders only in writing
(B) relay his orders to the men through co-workers
(C) follow up his orders after issuing them
(D) give orders verbally directly to the man assigned to the job

Answer: **(B)** Aside from the chance that a verbal order will not be relayed accurately, there is also the risk that some workers will resent being given an order by a fellow worker.

17. Several of the men in your crew start a discussion during working hours of rumored changes in working conditions. This discussion can best be stopped by telling the men that

(A) existing conditions are satisfactory
(B) you will check on the rumor
(C) working conditions do not concern them
(D) they should wait and see if the working conditions are changed

Answer: **(B)** Uncertainty based on rumors of change can be demoralizing. As supervisor, you should assure the men that you will find out if the rumor is valid and report back to them.

18. It has been said that the success of a unit performing routine work rests on the unit supervisor. If the supervisor wants to prevent boredom and to stimulate their interest in their duties, it would generally be best for him to

(A) set an easy pace for his subordinates so that they will not become bored because of having to learn too much too rapidly
(B) set the pace for his subordinates so that the task is never too easy but is a constant challenge calling for more and better work
(C) inspect his subordinates on the job at irregular intervals in order to determine whether they are performing their duties properly
(D) see to it that the objectives and goals of the department are properly communicated and interpreted to his subordinates

Answer: **(B)** A good work standard is not easily attained. A worker must be made to extend himself to some degree or he is prone to becoming easily bored.

19. Frequently when you, as a supervisor, have given instructions to your crew on how to do a job, a certain crew member has made a suggestion to you concerning a better way in which to do the job. The next time he does this, you should

(A) listen to his suggestion, thank him, and adopt it if it seems good
(B) listen to his suggestion, thank the man, but don't adopt it
(C) ask him whether he is trying to embarrass you
(D) tell the man to put it in writing, so that you and your superior can examine and discuss it fully

Answer: **(A)** If the man really suggests a better method for performing the job, by all means take advantage of it. This is bound to benefit the unit.

20. You, as a supervisor, are given an engineer's sketch of a certain trench to be excavated and a small piece of curbing to be removed from your area. This work is to be done by you and your crew. You do not fully understand the sketch. You should

(A) first ask whether any member of the crew understands it
(B) first ask your supervisor for help
(C) do the work the best you can without seeking advice
(D) wait until an engineer visits the job site and then request an explanation of the sketch

Answer: **(B)** This goes for everyone, workers and supervisors alike. When in doubt about working instructions, ask questions. It is better to ask questions before starting the job than after it is done wrong.

21. One of the men in your crew who is a good worker prefers to be alone and rarely mixes with other crew members. As a supervisor you should

(A) respect as far as possible his apparent desire to be alone
(B) team him up whenever possible with the most sociable members of the crew
(C) urge other crew members to find out why he seldom talks with others
(D) try to discover if there is anything abnormal in the man's personal life

Answer: **(A)** As long as he does good work, permit him to be by himself if it does not interfere with unit objectives.

22. A subordinate assigned to your ten-man crew asks you to excuse him from lifting any heavy objects for a period of one week to permit a sore thumb and index finger to heal. It would be best for you to

(A) grant this request
(B) ask him for a medical certificate before granting the request
(C) suggest that he arrange with another crew member to do any heavy lifting work for him
(D) tell him he will have to take his chances that no heavy lifting work will be required of him during that week

Answer: **(A)** There is nothing in the question to indicate the man is a malingerer; therefore why not grant his request?

23. Since his subordinates must carry out every order he issues, it is the responsibility of the supervisor to

(A) issue orders that are justified and clearly understood
(B) issue orders sparingly
(C) issue very important orders in writing
(D) justify to his men the need for an order when he issues it

Answer: **(A)** It is important indeed that a supervisor gives orders which are not only valid but which are workable. He must make sure that he issues them in a manner which makes them easily understood.

24. If you are assigned to be supervisor over a crew of men which includes several employees who have been unfriendly to you in the past, the best course of action for you to take is to

(A) give some excuse to be relieved of this assignment
(B) supervise these men more closely than the others
(C) tell these men right at the start that you will not tolerate any nonsense from them
(D) treat them the same as you do the others under your supervision

Answer: **(D)** Initially this situation calls for no special action at all. All should be treated exactly alike. However, if these men do pose a problem, your position should be made quite clear. You will not tolerate any attitude that will interfere with satisfactory work performance. The fact that a supervisor is not liked by his subordinates is not as important as that he commands their respect.

25. It is most important for a supervisor to

(A) acknowledge good work on the part of his men
(B) know when a situation requires a decision from higher authority than his own
(C) make discipline strict but not lacking in personal sympathy
(D) rotate the unpleasant work assignments

Answer: **(B)** All supervisors should be aware of where their authority begins and ends. Without this information it is impossible for them to fulfill their functions properly. When a situation arises that calls for a decision to be made by a higher authority, the supervisor involved should not hesitate to consult that authority.

26. Some management authorities propose that work assignments be made by assigning a varied set of tasks to a group of employees and then allowing the group to decide for itself how to organize the work to be done. This method of assigning work is called "job enlargement." The one of the following which is considered to be the chief advantage of job enlargement is that it

(A) encourages employees to specialize in the work they are assigned to do
(B) reduces the amount of control that employees have over their work
(C) increases the employees' job satisfaction
(D) reduces the number of skills that each employee is required to learn

Answer: **(C)** This situation results in the absence of specific orders to perform work. If the employee is given the opportunity to have at least some say in the work he is to perform, he is bound to receive greater satisfaction from its performance.

27. When you ask one of your men to do some work from a high ladder, he asks for another assignment because he is bothered by working in high places. In this case it would be best for you to

(A) give the man another assignment as requested
(B) insist that the man do the job originally assigned
(C) ask the man to try to exchange assignments with another man
(D) tell the man to return to his reporting quarters while you start disciplinary action against him

Answer: **(A)** There is nothing in the question to make one believe that the man has any other reason for asking to be excused from the task aside from a fear of height. If at all possible, the supervisor should assign this task to another man.

28. Although there is a normal disparity between successive ranks of employees in an organization, the greatest disparity and change in rank occur when a worker becomes a first-line supervisor. This is true chiefly because the first-line supervisor

(A) must be better informed than his subordinates
(B) becomes responsible for the first time for the job performance of others
(C) must learn to assume new and more complex duties
(D) has greater responsibility and authority than the subordinates under his supervision

Answer: **(B)** There is a great difference in being responsible for your own work and being responsible for the work of others. A first-line supervisor makes this transition when he assumes his new job.

29. If one of your workers informs you of an obvious error in a written order issued by you it would be best for you to

(A) tell him it is of no consequence and the order still stands since its intent is evident
(B) point out that all orders issued by supervision must be carried out without questioning their accuracy
(C) request him to say nothing to the other men in order to keep their respect
(D) immediately change the order to correct the obvious error

Answer: **(D)** A supervisor should not only have an open mind, but he should be a "big person." If an obvious error is brought to the attention of a supervisor by any one of his subordinates, he should take immediate remedial action. This is bound to result in the fostering of good relations between him and his subordinates.

30. In setting up a work schedule for a special job, it is least important for you to know

(A) the pay rate of the various men assigned to you
(B) when the employees will be available

(C) the approximate time required to complete the job
(D) when the material for the job will be available

Answer: **(A)** The pay rate is the least important of the choices. When scheduling a job the availability of labor and material is most important. When the job is to be completed is also pertinent. Although you are a supervisor, you are not required to know the pay rates of the various workers who will perform the work. You are not determining the cost of the job.

31. In measuring the work of his subordinates, the supervisor of a unit performing routine work began by observing his subordinates at work. If a subordinate seemed to be busy, then the supervisor concluded that the subordinate was producing a great deal of work. On the other hand, the supervisor concluded that a subordinate was not producing much work if he did not seem to be busy. The supervisor's work measurement method was faulty chiefly because

(A) it did not use a standard against which a subordinate's work could be measured
(B) the type of work performed by his subordinates did not lend itself to accurate measurement
(C) his subordinates may not have worked at their normal rates if they were aware that their work was being observed
(D) the supervisor may not have observed a subordinate's work for a long enough period of time

Answer: **(A)** Observation in itself is a poor method of measuring work performance. What is lacking in this situation is the absence of the finished product. A supervisor should inspect the finished product for accuracy and then measure the amount done against a predetermined standard. Quantity of work performed may be easily measured by assigning a specific amount to be done during a set amount of time.

32. You find that your superior has a tendency to issue written orders which lack sufficient detail and clarity. As supervisor it is best that you

(A) request that he issue all his orders verbally
(B) complain to the superior about the condition
(C) ask for clarification on receiving the orders
(D) use your own judgment

Answer: **(C)** It is imperative that when an order is received it be thoroughly understood. If the recipient of an order is not sure of everything about it, he should ask for immediate clarification before he undertakes to carry out the order.

33. In acquainting a new man with his duties, it would be improper for a supervisor to talk about the

(A) shortcomings of the men in the crew
(B) proper method of making inspection reports
(C) rules and regulations of the department
(D) special safety precautions

Answer: **(A)** Obviously this is the one thing a supervisor must not do. The information in the other choices would all be proper to orient a new worker.

34. "Supervisory authority implies the acceptance of responsibility." For a supervisor this should mean chiefly that he should

(A) be accountable for his own actions
(B) not give authority to members of his crew
(C) not give advice to his subordinates
(D) keep complete records of serious errors

Answer: **(A)** A supervisor should realize that he holds a position of responsibility and that his actions will be scrutinized very carefully by his subordinates and his superiors alike.

35. You are a supervisor and you learn that a certain subordinate is soon to be transferred to your crew. You know that he has a reputation for being hard to handle and inclined to be belligerent. The one of the following that would be the *least* desirable thing for you to do as a supervisor would be to

(A) make reference to his reputation as soon as he joins the crew and tell him you will not tolerate the slightest misbehavior
(B) ask him about the kind of work he has done
(C) try to discover whether his bad reputation is deserved or not
(D) welcome him into the crew as just another member

Answer: **(A)** This employee must be given a chance to prove himself in spite of his reputation. Perhaps his bad reputation was gained because of conditions which were beyond his control.

36. If a supervisor has a subordinate in his crew who is constantly blaming his co-workers when jobs that this subordinate works on turn out unsatisfactorily, then it would be best for the supervisor to try to

(A) assign him to jobs which will fix responsibility on him alone
(B) reassign this man so that he works with different individuals
(C) refer this man to your superior for appropriate action
(D) say or do nothing but give him a less-than-satisfactory service rating

Answer: **(A)** This subordinate must be assigned to jobs where he could be held strictly responsible for their proper performance. In fact, it may be necessary to assign him to tasks that he would have to perform entirely on his own. He would not be able to blame anyone but himself if they were not properly done.

37. A worker, Jones, complains to you that you are giving another worker, Smith, more than his share of good details. Jones mentions what he believes are a half dozen specific examples of this. As their supervisor, it would be best for you to tell Jones

(A) when he's a supervisor, he'll make the assignments
(B) why you have been giving these details to Smith
(C) you will give Smith fewer such details in the future
(D) you will give Jones more such details in the future than you will give Smith

Answer: **(B)** Employee Jones is specific in his grievance and he does deserve an explanation. He cannot be "put off" with a general denial. There is probably a good explanation for your assigning these duties to Smith. If your reasons are good, an explanation will probably alleviate the situation. The other three choices contain courses of action which are either arbitrary or not in the best interests of the unit.

38. As a supervisor, you realize that a subordinate who is a good employee has failed to carry out an assignment properly because he apparently did not thoroughly understand your instructions. The man is aware that he did not carry out the assignment properly but has concealed this from you and has not come to talk it over. As a supervisor, it would be best for you to

(A) ask one of his "buddies" to speak to him and try to develop his confidence in you
(B) give him a mild reprimand
(C) overlook this in view of the man's record
(D) try to establish a better relationship with this man

Answer: **(D)** This situation indicates that the subordinate is reluctant to communicate with his supervisor. The reason is probably based on a poor relationship between the two. Action should be taken to alleviate this.

39. One of the duties of a supervisor is to see to it that quality standards of work are maintained. An example of a standard of quality would be

(A) how well a task had been performed
(B) how fast the task had been performed
(C) how many units of work were performed in a specific time
(D) how long it took to fill out the reports connected with the work

Answer: **(A)** The measurement of the quality of work performance will show how well work was performed. The other three choices contain examples of quantity performance.

40. For a supervisor to question a worker about his personal problems would be most justified when the supervisor feels that

(A) he can help solve such problems
(B) he himself has had similar problems in the past
(C) the job performance of the worker is affected by such problems
(D) the worker has a negative attitude toward such problems

Answer: **(C)** Modern supervisory practice dictates that a supervisor is not to become involved in personal problems of his subordinates unless the problems are affecting work performance.

41. It may happen sometimes that a supervisor will doubt the wisdom of an order he has received from a superior. However, in issuing this order to *his* subordinates for execution, should the supervisor let them know about his doubts?

(A) no, because the supervisor can never be sure his own views are entirely correct
(B) yes, because the supervisor owes it to his men to be completely frank with them

(C) no, because criticism of such orders by the supervisor will create indecision among the men
(D) yes, because the men may have some valuable suggestions to offer

Answer: **(C)** A supervisor should support his superiors if he expects his subordinates to support him. It is a very poor practice indeed for the supervisor to show any disrespect of his superiors to his subordinates.

42. A certain supervisor, when he gives an order, frequently accompanies it with a warning that disciplinary action will follow if the order is not carried out as directed. This practice is

(A) desirable because it makes for a tightly knit, well-disciplined force
(B) undesirable because it is likely to antagonize the men and result in loss of their cooperation
(C) desirable because the men expect this type of supervision
(D) undesirable because the warning will lose its effect eventually

Answer: **(B)** This is a classic example of negative discipline. This type of action is designed to make subordinates work lest they be punished. It is seldom used at the present time because it cannot possibly have worthwhile results.

43. Your crew consistently performs more work than the crew headed by another supervisor. The other supervisor tells you that the high performance of your crew makes his crew look bad. Under these circumstances, it would be best for you to

(A) ignore the matter and have your crew continue working as before
(B) report the matter to your superior for disciplinary action
(C) slow your crew down somewhat to show the other supervisor that you are willing to cooperate with him
(D) slow your crew down to the level of the other crew

Answer: **(A)** It would be a poor practice indeed for the supervisor to slow up his more efficient crew so that the less efficient crew can compare favorably with it. It should work the other way around. The supervisor of the less efficient crew should institute the necessary training so that his crew can catch up with the more efficient one.

44. You have reason to believe that one of the men in your crew gossips about you behind your back. Under these circumstances, it is usually best to

(A) attempt to find out which of your men believes the gossip
(B) find out what the man's weak points are and bring them to the attention of your crew
(C) ignore the matter
(D) speak to the man about it and tell him to stop

Answer: **(C)** The supervisor in this instance must make himself "big." He should ignore the matter until it becomes a problem.

45. One of your subordinates tells you that he wants to submit a suggestion to the Suggestion Program regarding the operation of the unit, but that he wants your advice first. The most advisable course of action for you to take is to

(A) advise him that any suggestions concerning the unit should be made directly to you
(B) give him advice provided he includes your name on the suggestion
(C) give him the advice he needs
(D) tell him that it would not be fair if you were to give him any help

Answer: **(C)** A suggestion program operates on the basis that suggestors should be encouraged to contribute ideas for operational improvement. It is not wise for the supervisor to show any animosity towards a contributor even though it concerns the work of his unit. Let the suggestor receive any credit that may be coming to him and feel that you are flattered that he has sought your advice.

46. A task has to be performed. You issue instructions to your crew as to how this should be done. One of your men strongly objects and says that your instructions are wrong. You listen to his reasons but you still think that you are right. Under these circumstances, you should

(A) ask for opinions from the other men in the crew as to how the job should be done
(B) contact another worker to get his opinion
(C) refer the matter to your supervisor for his decision
(D) tell the man to perform the job in accordance with your instructions

Answer: **(D)** It is the function of the supervisor to make decisions as to how work is to be performed. The supervisor in this question has acted correctly by listening to this worker who had another way to do the job. However, if after listening to this worker the supervisor is still of the opinion that his way is best, he should order his subordinates to proceed immediately to do the work according to his instructions.

47. You tell a man to separate and store supplies in a certain way. The man then asks you, "Why do you want me to do it this way?" You should answer his question by
    (A) advising him to figure out the reason himself
    (B) explaining to him why you want it done in that particular way
    (C) repeating your instructions more slowly
    (D) telling him to follow your instructions without asking any questions

Answer: **(B)** A worker will function more effectively if he can understand the reason why a job is performed in a particular manner. If he doubts the validity of the reason, he may consider the order arbitrary and be less likely to function effectively.

48. Assume that an employee shows you that you have made an error in issuing certain instructions. You admit your error. Such action on your part is desirable primarily because
    (A) the job may be done correctly
    (B) your men will be encouraged to make similar corrections in the future
    (C) you will gain a reputation for fairness
    (D) your men will realize that you will not make errors of this type in the future

Answer: **(A)** This question states that the supervisor has been in error while issuing instructions. Of primary importance is that these instructions be corrected so that the work can be performed accurately. It is the responsibility of the supervisor to see that the work of his unit is accomplished in the most effective way.

49. Suppose that you are the supervisor of a small unit in an agency. One of your subordinates tells you that he is dissatisfied with his work assignment and that he wishes to discuss the matter with you. The employee is obviously very angry and upset. Of the following, the course of action that you should take first in this situation is to
    (A) postpone discussion of the employee's complaint, explaining to him that the matter can be settled more satisfactorily if it is discussed calmly
    (B) have the employee describe his complaint, correcting him whenever he makes what seems to be an erroneous charge against you
    (C) permit the employee to present his complaint in full, withholding your comments until he has finished describing his complaint
    (D) promise the employee that you will review all the work assignments in the unit to determine whether or not any changes should be made

Answer: **(C)** Many employee grievances are disposed of by merely permitting the aggrieved to have his say and get something off his chest. His dissatisfaction may or may not be justified. In any case, the supervisor, by giving the subordinate the opportunity to state his complaint in full, will then be able to determine its validity.

50. Assume that the operations of a certain unit enable the supervisor to allow each of his subordinates wide discretion in selecting the kind and amount of work he chooses to do. However, in evaluating the work of his subordinates, the supervisor places more emphasis on some areas of their work than on others. Factors such as number of applications processed and number of letters written are given great weight in evaluation, while factors such as number of papers filed and number of forms checked are given little weight. Hence, a subordinate who processes a large number of applications would receive a high evaluation even if he checked very few forms. The supervisor's method of evaluation would most likely result in
    (A) an increase in the amount of time spent on processing each application
    (B) a backlog of papers waiting to be filed
    (C) an improvement in the quality of letters written
    (D) a decline in output in all areas of work

Answer: **(B)** This situation is a poor one indeed. Workers would tend to spend time on work that the supervisor evaluated highly and neglect the work which the supervisor did not assign credit for.

51. As the newly appointed supervisor of a unit in an agency, you are about to design a system for measuring the quantity of work produced by your subordinates. The one of the following which is the first step that you should take in designing this system is to

(A) establish the units of work measurement to be used in the system
(B) determine the actual advantages and disadvantages of the system
(C) determine the abilities of each of your subordinates
(D) ascertain the types of work done in the unit

Answer: **(D)** The first step in a program designed to measure the quantity (amount) of work performed by your subordinates is a determination of the different types of work being performed which are measurable.

52. "It has been said that the best supervisor is the one who gives the fewest orders." The one of the following supervisory practices that would be most likely to increase the number of orders that a supervisor must give to get out the work is to

(A) set general goals for his subordinates and give them the authority for reaching the goals
(B) train subordinates to make decisions for themselves
(C) establish routines for his subordinates' jobs
(D) introduce frequent changes in the work methods his subordinates are using

Answer: **(D)** When the performance of a job is not changed frequently, standard operating procedures can be set up, thus cutting down the amount of orders which are given by the supervisor. If the workers are aware of just what has to be done and how it should be done, the necessity for orders will be few. However, if the work procedures are changed frequently, it will require more orders by the supervisor and closer supervision.

53. The one of the following supervisory practices that would be most likely to give subordinates in a unit of a public agency a feeling of satisfaction in their work is to

(A) establish work goals that take a long time to achieve
(B) show the subordinates how their work goals are related to the goals of the agency
(C) set work goals higher than subordinates can achieve
(D) refrain from telling subordinates that they are failing to meet their work goals

Answer: **(B)** A worker who performs only part of a function should be shown just how his work contributes to the major goals of his agency. Only in this way will he be able to feel a sense of accomplishment.

54. For a supervisor to listen to the personal problems which his subordinates bring to him is generally

(A) desirable; it is likely that the supervisor has broader experience in solving personal problems than do his subordinates
(B) undesirable; the supervisor may be unable to solve such problems
(C) desirable; the supervisor can better understand his subordinates' behavior on the job
(D) undesirable; permitting a subordinate to talk about his personal problems may only make them seem worse

Answer: **(C)** A supervisor should take an interest in a subordinate's personal problems when they are affecting his work.

55. Suppose that you are the supervisor of a small unit. You have given one of your subordinates, Mr. Smith, an assignment which must be completed by the end of the day. Because he is unfamiliar with the assignment, Mr. Smith will be unable to complete it on time. Your other subordinates are too busy to help Mr. Smith, but you have the time to help him complete the assignment. For you to help Mr. Smith complete the assignment would be

(A) desirable because a supervisor is expected to be familiar with his subordinates' work
(B) undesirable because Mr. Smith will come to depend on you to help him do his work
(C) desirable because Mr. Smith is likely to appreciate your help and give you his cooperation when you need it
(D) undesirable because a supervisor should not perform the same type of work as his subordinates do

Answer: **(C)** A supervisor is paid primarily to supervise his subordinates. However, helping in the work of one of his men is justified when it is necessary to accomplish an objective and when there is no other way of getting the job done.

56. The one of the following which is generally the basic reason for using standard procedures in an agency is to

(A) provide sequences of steps for handling recurring activities
(B) facilitate periodic review of standard practices
(C) train new employees in the agency's policies and objectives
(D) serve as a basis for formulating agency policies

Answer: **(A)** The key word in this question is *recurring*. If a function is going to be performed again and again in the future, why not set up a standard procedure for its performance? This will eliminate a great deal of instructional time.

57. Miss Green is assigned to type weekly reports to be submitted to her supervisor, Mr. Brown. Before she begins working on the reports, he tells her that they should be neat in appearance. The first two reports she submits are unsatisfactory to Mr. Brown because they contain a few erasures, and he tells her that they are unsatisfactory. The next two reports she submits are unsatisfactory because they contain many erasures. Mr. Brown accepts these two reports without criticizing them. The fifth report she submits contains fewer erasures than the previous reports but, it, too, is unsatisfactory because of its erasures. In order to prevent the submission of unsatisfactory reports in the future, Mr. Brown criticizes the erasures in her fifth report. She seems puzzled and upset by his criticism. Mr. Brown's handling of Miss Green was faulty chiefly because

(A) he did not give her sufficient opportunity to correct the work herself
(B) she may not have been capable of doing neat work
(C) he was inconsistent in his criticism of her work
(D) he should have criticized the reports containing many erasures rather than the reports with only a few erasures

Answer: **(C)** The acceptance of unsatifactory work at one time and the rejection of it at another time will undermine the standards that should be set for an employee. Miss Green will never know what is expected of her. Standards should be consistent.

58. Assume that you are the head of a unit in an agency. From time to time, your subordinates are assigned to other units to do reception work and other duties. You receive a note from Mr. Jones, the head of one of these other units, stating that the work of Miss Smith, one of your subordinates, was unsatisfactory when she worked for him, and asking you not to assign her to him again. Although Miss Smith has worked in your unit for a long time, this is the first time that anyone has complained about her work. The one of the following actions that you should take first in this situation is to ask

(A) the heads of the other units for whom Miss Smith has worked whether or not her work has been satisfactory
(B) Mr. Jones in what way Miss Smith's work has been unsatisfactory
(C) Miss Smith to explain in what way her work for Mr. Jones was unsatisfactory
(D) Mr. Jones which of your subordinates he would prefer to have assigned to him

Answer: **(B)** Avoid general complaints of unsatisfactory work. They should always be specific so that, if valid, corrective measures can be taken.

59. Assume that in an office, correspondence is filed according to the date received, in 12 folders, one for each month of the year. On January 1 of each year, correspondence dated through December 31 of the preceding year is transferred from the active to the inactive files. New folders are then inserted in the active files to contain the correspondence to be filed in the next year. The one of the following which is the chief disadvantage of this method of transferring correspondence from active to inactive files is that

(A) the inactive files may lack the capacity to contain all the correspondence transferred to them
(B) the folders prepared each year must be labeled the same as the folders in preceding years
(C) some of the correspondence from the preceding year may not be in the active files on January 1
(D) some of the correspondence transferred to the inactive files may be referred to as frequently as some of the correspondence in the active files

Answer: **(D)** In this instance, material only a month old—and probably still very much current—would be placed in the inactive files.

60. "There are disadvantages as well as advantages in using statistical controls to measure specific aspects of subordinates' jobs." The one of the following which can least be considered to be an advantage of statistical controls to a supervisor is that such controls may

(A) reduce the need for close, detailed supervision
(B) give the supervisor information that he needs for making decisions
(C) stimulate subordinates whose work is measured by statistical controls to improve their performance
(D) encourage subordinates to emphasize aspects being measured rather than their jobs as a whole

Answer: **(D)** The workers would tend to work well in areas which could be revealed by the statistics. They would be less likely to give full effort to tasks for which they would not receive statistical credit.

61. In setting the work standard for a certain task, a unit supervisor took the total output of all the employees in the unit and divided it by the number of employees. He thus established the average output as the work standard for the task. The method that the supervisor used to establish the work standard is generally considered to be

(A) proper since the method takes into account the output of the outstanding, as well as of the less productive employees
(B) improper since the average output may not be what could reasonably be expected of a competent, satisfactory employee
(C) proper since the standard is based on the actual output of the employees who are to be evaluated
(D) improper since all the employees in the unit may be successful in meeting the work standard

Answer: **(B)** The average of anything is seldom good enough. It is determined by the worst as well as the best, and there may be more employees below a reasonable standard than are above it.

62. Assume that a system of statistical reports designed to provide information about employee work performance is put into effect in a unit of an agency. There is some evidence that the employees of this unit are working below their capacities. The information obtained from the system is to be used by management to improve employee work performance and to evaluate such performance. The employees whose work is to be recorded by the reports resent them. Nevertheless, the employees' work performance improves substantially after the reporting system is put into effect, and before management has put the information to use. The one of the following which is the most accurate conclusion to be drawn from this situation is that

(A) a statistical reporting system may fail to provide the information it is designed to provide
(B) low employee morale may have been the cause of the employees' former level of work performance
(C) a statistical reporting system designed only to provide information about problems may also help to solve the problems
(D) willing employee cooperation is essential to the success of a system of statistical reports

Answer: **(C)** In this instance the workers knew they were producing below their normal capacities and that as soon as the reporting system went into effect the finger would be pointed at them. As a result, they improved their work performance.

TRAINING AND RATING EMPLOYEES

1. You find that one of the men in your crew constantly consults with his fellow workers on how to do the work to which he has been assigned. As his supervisor it would be best for you to

   (A) commend him for securing the cooperation of his fellow workers
   (B) tell the men to let this man learn by his mistakes
   (C) give this man a job which is easy to do
   (D) see to it that the man learns his job

Answer: **(D)** This man is either insufficiently trained or he is unsure of himself. Training not only will prepare him to carry out his duties with greater efficiency, but it will also serve to give him the confidence he seems to be lacking.

2. Of the following, the one which can most easily be increased or improved in an employee by his supervisor is

   (A) ability to learn
   (B) aptitude
   (C) common sense
   (D) knowledge

Answer: **(D)** Knowledge may be acquired through education. Ability to learn, common sense, and aptitude are all to some extent inborn.

3. After you have given a newly-appointed subordinate complete instructions on how to use a piece of equipment, you should usually

   (A) assign him to work with another subordinate
   (B) go over the instructions once more
   (C) let him use the equipment while you watch him
   (D) tell him about the importance of the work

Answer: **(C)** One of the best methods for training people is to let them perform a job under close supervision until they have mastered it. Then let them proceed on their own.

4. You assign a man to take inventory of a certain item. The man gives you a figure which seems too high. Of the following, the best course of action for you to take is to

   (A) accept the figure given to you by the man if he is willing to initial it
   (B) accompany the man while he takes inventory again
   (C) ask the man to take inventory again and tell him why
   (D) take inventory yourself

Answer: **(C)** This choice will not only give you a double-checked figure but will also give the man valuable training.

5. Upon being assigned to an important job on which he will work alone, a worker insists that he knows exactly how to proceed and that no instructions or explanations by his supervisor are necessary. The best way for the supervisor to handle this situation is to

   (A) let the worker proceed without instructions
   (B) report the worker to your superior for not listening to instructions
   (C) remain present while the worker does the job
   (D) question the worker briefly as to his intended procedure

Answer: **(D)** This situation is not uncommon. The worker could have had previous experience at this job or at a similar job. However, since the supervisor will retain the ultimate responsibility for seeing that the job is performed correctly, he should question the worker briefly on the assignment before it is begun, and should follow this up with a check from time to time of how the work is progressing.

6. When conducting training, a supervisor made an effort to devote approximately the same amount of time to each member of the group. This procedure generally is

(A) good because the members will realize that they all are receiving equal treatment
(B) bad because some members require more training than others
(C) good because the supervisor is less likely to neglect any member
(D) bad because the supervisor has to devote too much effort to keeping track of the time spent with each member

Answer: **(B)** It is unusual for any two people to be able to absorb training material in exactly the same length of time. For that reason it would be wise for the supervisor to compensate for the differences in learning capacities of his men by giving more time to those in need of it.

7. The most logical reason for a supervisor to rotate job assignments among the men in his crew would be to

(A) improve maintenance procedures
(B) make sure that absences do not slow up the work too much
(C) determine which of his men are not readily adaptable
(D) reduce absenteeism

Answer: **(B)** Note that there was no mention of the type of job assignments which were to be rotated. Assuming that there is a variety of different jobs, rotation will give the workers a degree of skill in handling any of them. If one worker were to be absent on any given day, there would be another available to fill in without prior training. Therefore you would have a flexible unit in which one worker could fill in for another whenever necessary.

8. Assume that one of your subordinates made an error. It was found and corrected, but your subordinate seems rather depressed about the matter. Of the following, the most advisable course of action for you to take is to

(A) ignore the entire situation unless it happens again
(B) praise him
(C) reprimand him mildly
(D) show him how he can avoid such a mistake in the future

Answer: **(D)** Everybody is likely to make errors at one time or another. Of the four courses of action depicted in the choices, the only sensible one would be to show the subordinate how he can avoid similar errors is the future.

9. A training program for workers assigned to the information section should include actual practice in simulated interviews under simulated conditions. The one of the following educational principles which is the chief justification for this statement is that

(A) the workers will remember what they see better and longer than what they read or hear
(B) the workers will learn more effectively by actually doing the act themselves than they would learn from watching others do it
(C) the conduct of simulated interviews once or twice will enable them to cope with the real situation with little difficulty
(D) a training program must employ methods of a practical nature if the workers are to find anything of lasting value in it

Answer: **(B)** The best way of teaching a new task is to permit the trainee to perform it under close supervision, correct his errors, and when he masters it permit him to work on his own.

10. A newly appointed worker has been assigned to your crew. Of the following, the best practice to follow with this man is to

(A) immediately put him to work with the crew, since laboring requires no special skill
(B) allow him to do only the type of work he says he is capable of doing until he can learn the other jobs
(C) instruct the man as to how the job should be done before putting him to work
(D) give the man the most difficult job, since the best method of learning is by doing

Answer: **(C)** An effective way to train a new worker is to have him do the work under close supervision until he is ready to perform it on his own. This is usually preceded by a demonstration on the correct method of performance, and is followed by a checkup of the finished product.

11. At a training session involving the use of a new piece of equipment, the supervisor, after demonstrating one of the uses of the equipment, calls upon a subordinate to operate it. The subordinate makes several mistakes, but the supervisor says nothing to him until the operation is completed. Then the supervisor points out the mistakes and once again demonstrates the correct method of operation. The supervisor's method of teaching was

(A) good, mainly because the subordinate was permitted to complete the operation without frequent interruptions
(B) bad, mainly because the subordinate's errors were not corrected immediately
(C) good, mainly because the supervisor demonstrated thorough knowledge of the equipment
(D) bad, mainly because the supervisor did not call upon other subordinates to correct the errors and demonstrate the correct method of operation

Answer: **(B)** For best and most lasting results all errors made by workers should be corrected immediately, especially during the training process. The actions of the supervisor in this training session were indeed faulty.

12. For a worker to carry out an order most effectively, it is important that he

(A) be aware of the reasons for the order and understand his own exact role in the department's organization structure
(B) know what the order is about and be convinced in his own mind of the necessity for the order
(C) respect the superior's authority and have confidence in the superior's ability
(D) understand the order thoroughly and have the necessary skills to carry it out

Answer: **(D)** Every worker must thoroughly understand all orders that are given to him. Unless he does, he cannot perform his tasks effectively.

13. In conducting a meeting to pass along information to his subordinates, a supervisor may talk to his subordinates without giving them the opportunity to interrupt him. This method is called one-way communication. On the other hand, the supervisor may talk to his subordinates and give them the opportunity to ask questions or make comments while he is speaking. This method is called two-way communication. It would be more desirable for the supervisor to use two-way communication rather than one-way communication at a meeting when his primary purpose is to

(A) avoid, during the meeting, open criticism of any mistake he may make
(B) conduct the meeting in an orderly fashion
(C) pass along information quickly
(D) transmit information which must be clearly understood

Answer: **(D)** The supervisor must permit his subordinates to ask questions on material that is transmitted to them and which must be thoroughly understood. In the absence of this opportunity, subordinates could not be held responsible for work performance because they were not afforded the opportunity to clear up any questionable matter. This could be used as an excuse for poor work performance.

14. A worker tries hard, but his work is still not up to that of the other men. This worker most probably needs

(A) a sharp reprimand
(B) a medical examination
(C) a transfer to another section where standards aren't as high
(D) more training

Answer: **(D)** The man is willing enough. Therefore his poor work must be due to insufficient training.

15. In breaking in a group of new men placed under your supervision, it is important to keep in mind that they will probably learn most by

(A) attending well-prepared lectures
(B) studying printed instructions
(C) seeing training films
(D) doing the work under close supervision

Answer: **(D)** There is no better way to teach a new task than to have the worker perform the task under direct supervision until he has learned it well enough to perform it on his own.

16. A supervisor should acquaint a new worker about all the following matters *except* the

(A) correct use of tools and equipment
(B) dangers of the job
(C) departmental rules and regulations as they affect the worker
(D) peculiarities of his co-workers

Answer: **(D)** A new employee, while undergoing orientation, should not be told of the peculiarities of the men he will work with. He will find out soon enough on his own. This information is certainly not essential to getting him started.

GARDENER - ASSISTANT GARDENER

ESTABLISHING DISCIPLINE

1. If, as a disciplinary measure, you wish to reprimand a worker for some improper act or neglect of duty, it would *not* be good practice to

   (A) allow yourself a cooling-off period of several days before you administer the reprimand
   (B) give him a chance to reply to your criticism
   (C) be very specific about the particular act or neglect of duty for which you are reprimanding him
   (D) reprimand him when you are alone with him

Answer: **(A)** The longer the cooling-off period, the more the infraction will tend to be separated from the resultant discipline in the mind of the employee. A reprimand, or any other disciplinary measure, should take place as soon after the infraction as possible.

2. Before you recommend that charges be preferred against one of your men for an alleged infraction of the rules and regulations, you should make absolutely sure that

   (A) the charges will be sustained at the hearing
   (B) your superior will give his approval to your recommendation
   (C) the man's fellow employees will give testimony favorable to your side of the case
   (D) you have all the pertinent information on the case

Answer: **(D)** Disciplinary action is a very serious matter. You are instituting a procedure which may result in something being taken away from a person. The supervisor should precede disciplinary action with a thorough investigation and collection of pertinent facts. A missing fact can throw a different light on the situation.

3. The one of the following which would *not* be an acceptable practice for a supervisor to observe when criticizing a subordinate is to

   (A) focus attention on the act to be criticized instead of on the person
   (B) express the criticism in general rather than specific terms
   (C) refer to previous instances of poor performance
   (D) avoid humor or sarcasm when making the criticism

Answer: **(B)** The purpose of criticism of work performance is to point out specifically where it may be improved. If the criticism were general and not specific, the worker would not know what corrective action to take.

4. You are informed by another supervisor that some of your men who have been assigned to work by themselves are loafing on the job. You should handle this situation by

   (A) telling the supervisor that it is none of his business as they are not his men
   (B) calling the men together to your office and reprimanding them
   (C) changing the men's assignment so that they work under your direct supervision at all times
   (D) arranging to visit the men on the job at more frequent intervals

Answer: **(D)** There is nothing in the question that may lead to your suspecting the motives of the informant as being anything but good. If you have reason to believe they or any other workers are guilty of loafing, you have only one course of action, closer and more direct supervision.

5. If one of your crew comes to work obviously drunk, the best thing to do is to

   (A) give the man an easy job where he can't hurt himself
   (B) let the man "sleep it off" in the morning and put him to work when the effects have apparently worn off
   (C) send the man home
   (D) give the man a hard job where he can "sweat it out"

Answer: **(C)** The action that a supervisor should take when one of his crew reports for work drunk is quite clear. Send him home because he is unfit to perform his duties.

6. The best way for a supervisor to handle a chronic troublemaker in a section is to

   (A) give him closer supervision and if this is not enough take disciplinary action
   (B) let the troublemaker know that he is watching him very closely so he can get something specific on him
   (C) rely on the other men in the section to bring him into line
   (D) assign him to the most undesirable details

Answer: **(A)** A chronic troublemaker is bad for any organization. If close supervision does not help, more positive disciplinary action should be taken.

7. If a supervisor finds that he must frequently take disciplinary action against his men, he should

   (A) ask for a new assignment for the good of the service and to avoid a further clash of personalities
   (B) examine his supervisory practices to see whether they are at fault
   (C) realize that he has a "tough bunch" to supervise and not consider it unusual
   (D) understand that this is sometimes necessary in order to keep a disciplined force.

Answer: **(B)** Faulty practices by a supervisor are among the most common causes for the necessity of frequent disciplinary action. If the supervisor finds disciplinary problems a frequent occurrence, he should examine his supervisory practices first to see if they are at fault. If they are not, he should look elsewhere for the answer to his problem.

8. Two of your men frequently argue with each other so that the work of your crew is disrupted. You should *first*

   (A) attempt to find out why the men argue with each other
   (B) speak to the two men privately regarding their possible transfer to another crew
   (C) submit a report to your superior setting forth the facts
   (D) tell both men that unless they stop arguing you will see that they are given below-standard service ratings

Answer: **(A)** If the work of a crew is being disrupted by repeated arguments between two workers, it is the function of the supervisor first of all to discover the cause of the arguments and then to take immediate corrective measures.

9. Although you have frequently spoken to one of your men regarding the proper way of lifting objects, he persists in ignoring your instructions. He says that he knows the proper way of lifting, that you do not, and that he does not intend to hurt himself by following your instructions. Of the following, the best course of action for you to take is to

   (A) assign the man to tasks which do not involve heavy lifting
   (B) ignore the matter as long as the man does not hurt himself
   (C) put your instructions on how to lift in writing and give a copy of your instructions to each man in the crew
   (D) report the matter to your superior

Answer: **(D)** The subordinate in this question is taking an unreasonable attitude. The supervisor is the boss and his orders should be obeyed because he is responsible for the performance of the work and all of the ramifications that may result from it. Choice (A) depicts an escape from reality, as does choice (B). Choice (C) unnecessarily involves others who have been obeying the instructions of the supervisor. Choice (D) depicts the only logical course of action to be followed.

10. "It is only when an individual in the crew gets out of line that disciplinary action should be taken and then only to re-establish the proper working relationships of the whole crew." The use of disciplinary action as discussed in this sentence suggests that disciplinary action should have as its main goal

    (A) forgiveness
    (B) punishment
    (C) correction
    (D) sympathetic understanding

Answer: **(C)** The primary basis of disciplinary action is to train workers to correct their job performance and deportment, not to punish those guilty of rule infractions.

11. One of the members of your crew sometimes overstays his lunch period to the extent that he is interfering with the work of the entire crew. Of the following, the most desirable action you should take *first* is to

(A) assign him to less desirable details whenever you get a chance
(B) warn the man of his failure to observe time regulations
(C) report his lateness in returning from lunch for disciplinary action
(D) arrange his lunch hour at a time different from that of the other men

Answer: **(B)** Your *first* action should be a warning. His work is interfering with the output of the entire crew. If the warning does not work, more drastic and positive measures should be taken.

12. You have in your section a subordinate who is a good worker but who very often complains about Department policies. As a supervisor, you should

(A) arrange to transfer this man to another section where he may make a better adjustment
(B) give this man department material explaining the reasons for such policies
(C) talk to this man privately to try to change his mind and to stop his complaints
(D) tell the other subordinates to ignore him since he is such a good worker

Answer: **(C)** A worker who constantly complains about departmental policies creates a bad situation. A private talk with this individual may help to change his outlook. The supervisor may be able to convince him that there are good reasons for departmental policies.

13. You have reason to believe that one of your men is taking merchandise which does not belong to him from the storehouse. You question the man about this. He tells you that he borrowed the merchandise and intends to return it. Under these circumstances, you should probably

(A) disregard the matter until such time as you have evidence which will stand up in court
(B) offer to accompany the man to his home to pick up the property in question
(C) report the matter to your superior
(D) tell the man to return the property as soon as he has finished using it

Answer: **(C)** This man has removed merchandise from the premises without permission. This is a serious matter. If he intended to borrow it, he should have asked for permission to do so. In view of his admission, choices (A), (B) and (D) offer no acceptable course of action. Choice (C) would be the wisest to take on the basis of the evidence given.

14. The one of the following which is usually the *poorest* reason for transferring a worker is to

(A) grant a doctor's request that he work nearer his home
(B) discipline the man
(C) relieve the monotony of work assignments
(D) take care of changes in workload

Answer: **(B)** A transfer which takes place solely for disciplinary reasons is a poor practice indeed. Nothing is being done to solve the problem. What is actually being done is to transfer one supervisor's problem to another supervisor.

15. You have observed that a subordinate in your crew does good work only when he is under close supervision. Whenever he is not being carefully supervised he tends to loaf on the job. The most important consequence of this observation for you as a supervisor should be to

(A) try to change his attitude and warn him of possible disciplinary action
(B) let him work alone without supervision and visit him at unexpected intervals
(C) let him work with another man and ask this other man periodically whether the subordinate does a good day's work
(D) order him to produce as much work as the others

Answer: **(A)** A worker who performs well under close supervision only is not particularly valuable. The cost of supervising him closely may not be worthwhile. Therefore it is up to his supervisor to change his attitude in any way he can.

MAKING REPORTS

1. To be most effective, a report should be
   - (A) simple and concise
   - (B) long and impressive
   - (C) written with perfect grammar and punctuation
   - (D) typed instead of written

Answer: **(A)** A report should be easily understood—both complete and concise.

2. In a well-written report, the length of each paragraph should be
   - (A) varied according to the content
   - (B) not over 300 words
   - (C) pretty nearly the same
   - (D) gradually longer as the report is developed and written

Answer: **(A)** In any report the length of the paragraphs should be entirely dependent on what is to be said in each paragraph. A new thought calls for a new paragraph.

3. A supervisor should realize that the most usual reason for writing a report is to
   - (A) give orders and follow up their execution
   - (B) establish a permanent record
   - (C) raise questions
   - (D) supply information

Answer: **(D)** Reports form the basis of many supervisory and administrative decisions by bringing to light conditions worthy of attention.

4. Supervisors are required to submit written reports of all unusual occurrences promptly. The best reason for such promptness is that
   - (A) there is always a tendency to do a better job under pressure
   - (B) the employee will not be as likely to forget to make the report
   - (C) the report will tend to be more accurate as to facts
   - (D) the report may be too long if made at an employee's convenience

Answer: **(C)** The sooner a report is made after an occurrence, the more likely it is that it will be accurate because the facts are still fresh in the mind of the reporter. For this reason a report should be made as soon after the occurrence as practical.

5. The use of an outline to help in writing a report is
   - (A) desirable in order to insure a good organization and coverage
   - (B) necessary so it can be used as an introduction to the report itself
   - (C) undesirable since it acts as a straight jacket and may result in an unbalanced report
   - (D) desirable if you know your immediate supervisor reads reports with extreme care and attention

Answer: **(A)** An outline prepared before the actual report is written would contain all of the information that the reporter wishes to be included. The outline then could be juggled around so that the actual report would contain all of the information in the most logical sequence.

6. Before turning in a report of an investigation you have made, you discover some additional information you didn't know about when writing the report. Whether or not you rewrite your report to include this additional information should depend mainly on the
   - (A) length of the report
   - (B) established policy covering the subject matter of the report
   - (C) bearing this new information will have on the conclusions of the report
   - (D) number of people who will eventually review the report

Answer: **(C)** A report should be complete. If any pertinent information is missing, it may change the conclusions that are to be based on it. If you feel that the missing information may be important, by all means add it.

7. The greatest benefit the supervisor will have from keeping complete and accurate records of section operations is that

(A) he will find it easier to run his section efficiently
(B) he will need less equipment
(C) he will need less manpower
(D) the section will run smoothly when he is out

Answer: **(A)** Records are not an end in themselves but a means to an end. Much can be learned by analyzing them and they may be referred to before making decisions concerning the work of the section. Records may also be used to validate requests for more help or more material.

8. As a supervisor you have prepared a report to your superior and are ready to send it forward. But on rereading it, you think some parts are not clearly expressed and your superior may have difficulty getting your point. Of the following, it would be best for you to

(A) give the report to one of your men to read, and if he has no trouble understanding it send it through
(B) forward the report and call your superior the next day to ask if it was all right
(C) forward the report as is; higher echelons should be able to understand any report prepared by subordinates
(D) do the report over, rewriting the sections you are in doubt about

Answer: **(D)** Never forward a report that you are not entirely satisfied with. It will do you no credit, and it may not clearly convey the required information.

9. Conclusions and recommendations are usually better placed at the end rather than at the beginning of a report because

(A) the person preparing the report may decide to change some of the conclusions and recommendations before he reaches the end of the report
(B) they are the most important part of the report
(C) they can be judged better by the person to whom the report is sent after he reads the facts and investigations which come earlier in the report
(D) they can be referred to quickly when needed without reading the rest of the report

Answer: **(C)** They are a natural outgrowth of the content of the report.

10. When a supervisor submits a periodic report to his superior he should realize that the chief importance of such a report is that it

(A) is the principal method of checking on the efficiency of the supervisor and his subordinates
(B) is something to which frequent reference will be made
(C) eliminates the need for any personal follow-up or inspection by higher echelons
(D) permits the superior to exercise his functions of direction, supervision, and control better

Answer: **(D)** A report is submitted so that supervisory and administrative decisions can be based on its contents.

11. The use of the same method of record keeping and reporting by all offices in a decentralized agency is

(A) desirable, mainly because it saves time in operations
(B) undesirable, mainly because it kills the initiative of the individual supervisor
(C) desirable, mainly because it will be easier for the administrator to evaluate and compare the work output of the various offices
(D) undesirable, mainly because operations vary from office to office and uniform record keeping and reporting is not appropriate

Answer: **(C)** If all sections doing the same type of work keep similar reports, it will be much easier to compare the work of these sections.

12. A supervisor becomes aware that one of her very competent experienced workers *never* takes notes during an interview with a client except to note an occasional name, address, or date. When asked about this practice by the supervisor, the worker states that she has a good memory for important details and has always been able satisfactorily to record an interview after the client has left. It would generally be best for the supervisor to handle this situation by

(A) discussing with her that more extensive note-taking may sometimes be desirable with a client who believes note-taking to be evidence that his problem will receive serious consideration

(B) agreeing with this practice since note-taking interferes with the establishment of a proper worker-client relationship

(C) explaining that, since interviewing is an art form rather than an exact science, a good worker must devise her own personal rules for interviewing and not be bound by general principles

(D) warning the worker that memory is too uncertain a thing to be relied upon and, therefore, notes of all matters should be taken during an interview

Answer: **(A)** The worker probably has a better memory, and her past reports based on interviews have been satisfactory and complete. There is no point at this stage for insisting that the interviewer take extensive notes at all her interviews. This choice is better then choice (D) simply because the course of action described there is too positive. It mentions interviews of *all* matters. An interview may consist of but one or two questions or produce no relevant material.

13. A division chief gives one of his supervisors, newly assigned to his office, the responsibility for preparing an important monthly report. He explains the procedure in detail to the supervisor, and stresses the need for accuracy and timely submission. To understand the full details requires several days of careful explanation. The supervisor understands it thoroughly. However, before he has a chance to prepare the first report, the supervisor asks for leave and is told he can have it provided someone else is trained to prepare the report. The supervisor turns it over to a subordinate who turns in a report with numerous errors. The fault lies chiefly with

(A) all three, who were equally responsible for submission of the inaccurate report

(B) the division chief who should have taught the procedure to several subordinates in the time it took to train one

(C) the supervisor who should have been sure that the subordinate he assigned to do the report in his absence could do it before he went on leave

(D) the subordinate who was assigned to do the report while the supervisor was on leave and who should have insisted on more training before he undertook to do the report

Answer: **(C)** The supervisor was duly informed by the division chief of the importance of an accurate report. His leave was granted on the basis that someone else would be adequately trained by him to do it. The supervisor retains the responsibility for the poor report. He should have taken more precautions to make sure that his subordinate was adequately trained to turn in an accurate report.

14. An organization has six operating bureaus whose work is highly specialized and only loosely related. The chief executive has found it difficult to keep sufficiently informed about the work being performed by these bureaus. The one of the following administrative practices which would generally be most effective in obtaining for the chief executive the knowledge he needs is his

(A) instituting a system of statistical reports to indicate the amount of work completed by each bureau

(B) requiring bureau chiefs to program their work and submit periodic progress reports on all programs

(C) requiring all bureau chiefs to report, in detail, all the work their bureaus are performing

(D) holding regular staff meetings at which the bureau chiefs furnish detailed reports on work in process

Answer: **(B)** An organization such as the one described in the question must operate under predetermined programs and the chief executive must be advised of the progress that is being made towards attaining organization goals through the medium of periodic reports.

15. A supervisor finds that reports reaching him from his subordinates tend to exaggerate the favorable, and minimize the unfavorable, aspects of situations existing within the division. The one of the following which would be the most valid conclusion to draw is that

(A) the supervisor has been overly severe with subordinates and has instilled fear in them

(B) there is a normal tendency for persons to represent themselves and their actions in the best possible light
(C) members of the department tend to be optimists
(D) the supervisor has not been sufficiently critical of previous reports and has not been alert to conditions in the division

Answer: **(B)** Most people tend to build themselves up, not knock themselves down. They tend to relate their good points and keep their weak points under cover.

16. Assume that as supervisor you are recommending in a report to your superior that a radical change in a standard maintenance procedure should be adopted. Of the following, the most important information to be included in this report is
(A) a list of the reasons for making the change
(B) a complete description of the old procedure
(C) the names of the men who favor the change
(D) the number of instruction sheets needed for the new procedure

Answer: **(A)** Change in itself is not always beneficial. However, the supervisor here is more or less requesting permission to make a radical change in a standard maintenance procedure, and to get permission to do so he must show just what the change is to accomplish and just where the present procedure falls short.

17. The clerk who is responsible for receiving periodic reports complains to you about the way in which you are filling out a certain report. It would be best for you to
(A) tell the clerk that you are following official procedures in filling out the report
(B) ask to be referred to the clerk's superior
(C) ask the clerk exactly what is wrong with the way in which you are filling out the report
(D) tell the clerk that you are following the directions of your superior

Answer: **(C)** If the complaint is justified and you are convinced of it, you can do your job best by cooperating fully with the clerk.

18. An important report which is being prepared by you, a supervisor, will soon be due on the desk of your superior. No typing help is available at this time. For you to write out this report in longhand in such a situation would be
(A) bad; such a report would not make the impression a typed report would
(B) good; it is important to get the report in on time
(C) bad; your superior should not be required to read longhand reports
(D) good; it would call attention to the difficult conditions under which your unit must work

Answer: **(B)** This course of action should first be identified as good. Choice (B) is better then choice (D) because the question states that the report is very important and will soon be due. A report written in longhand which is submitted when due is better than no report at all.

19. If a supervisor is assigned to assemble information on a problem he must be especially careful to
(A) be impartial in collecting and presenting the information
(B) secure his information only from those in supervisory positions
(C) present the information in such a manner as to substantiate his superior's ideas on the subject
(D) discard information which seems inconsistent with previous information relating to this problem

Answer: **(A)** It is a common human failure in assembling information relative to a problem to omit information which might lead to a conclusion other than the one you hold. At times omissions are deliberate and other times omissions become subconscious acts. When you assemble material, include all pertinent matter. It is not your job to determine what is relevant to the matter; someone else will probably be assigned to that task. Do not let personal opinions interfere with the task you are to perform.

20. The most reliable of the following methods for detecting errors in a statistical report is to
(A) compare it with reports from similar units
(B) examine it for internal inconsistency
(C) compare it with reports, from the same unit, for previous periods
(D) examine it for unusual or unexpected data

Answer: **(B)** Errors in a statistical report are usually revealed through an inconsistency. When an inconsistency is noted it is indicative of one of two things. A drastic change in activity (which should be common knowledge) or an error in reporting.

SAFEGUARDING EMPLOYEES

(Check your answers with these that we provide. You should find considerable correspondence between them. If not, you'd better go back and find out why.
Please go over them carefully because they may be quite useful in helping you pick up extra points on the exam.)

1. A supervisor can most effectively develop proper safety habits in his men by
   (A) letting them learn from their own mistakes
   (B) invoking severe penalties for any accident
   (C) calling for immediate correction of unsafe practices observed in their daily work
   (D) explaining the necessity for securing safety awards

Answer: **(C)** A supervisor should not tolerate any delay in the correction of a hazardous procedure that he has spotted. Even the smallest accident is costly in manpower lost and human suffering.

2. A new helper with no previous experience is assigned to your crew. Normally this man should first be
   (A) made familiar with the layout of the entire agency
   (B) taught to perform the simplest routine procedures
   (C) informed of all the safety and other rules immediately applicable to him
   (D) familiarized with the departmental organization

Answer: **(C)** A worker should *first* be made familiar with all of the rules that will apply to him. This should be done before any formalized instruction begins. The key word in the question is *first.*

3. The one of the following which would be the best starting point for an accident reduction and prevention program would be to
   (A) determine the number, kinds, and causes of accidents that have occurred
   (B) improve working conditions so as to prevent most, if not all, accidents
   (C) promote an inter-departmental safety and safe practices contest
   (D) start a crash safety program to eliminate all accidents caused by carelessness

Answer: **(A)** An accident reduction program is always initiated with a compilation of the facts dealing with previous accidents. The data can then be fully analyzed and after the causes of the accidents are determined, effective steps can be taken to eliminate the causes.

4. A supervisor should approach the problem of safety with the idea that
   (A) a certain number of accidents are unavoidable
   (B) most accidents are preventable
   (C) all employees are safety conscious
   (D) the best way to stop accidents is to post a set of safety rules for all to follow

Answer: **(B)** When workers are mentally alert, accidents are few and far between. Careful planning with foresight towards accident prevention will identify hazardous situations which can then be corrected or eliminated.

5. A helper made a blunder which resulted in an injury to one of your experienced workers. As a supervisor you should certainly
   (A) recommend the dismissal of the helper
   (B) ignore the incident unless it recurs
   (C) study the accident for remedial action
   (D) have the helper transferred

Answer: **(C)** A blunder may be excused; everyone is capable of making one at one time or another. However, when an accident occurs, the cause of it must be determined so that future similar accidents may be avoided.

6. If a supervisor sees that one of his men is doing an assigned job by an unsatisfactory procedure, he should
   (A) tell the man the proper procedure to use before allowing him to continue

(B) make no comment until the job is finished
(C) reassign the job to another man
(D) reprimand the man and make sure not to assign this type of job to him again

Answer: **(A)** There is only one course of action to take here, and that is immediate correction of the improper work performance.

7. When a supervisor tells a subordinate to be more careful in an effort to avoid accidents, such a statement

(A) is sufficient; after all, the subordinate is assumed to be a responsible adult
(B) is not sufficient; the supervisor should be more specific in his directions
(C) is sufficient; the subordinate should be guided by his own self-interest to avoid accidents
(D) is not suffiicient; accident prevention is everybody's business

Answer: **(B)** A worker should have the dangerous aspects of his job pointed out to him and the safe method of performing these functions demonstrated to him.

8. Of the following, the main reason for a supervisor to stress safety is to

(A) develop a respect for danger in all members
(B) replace ignorance with practical knowledge leading to the elimination of unfounded fears
(C) establish a safety-conscious work atmosphere in which the men seek safer operating methods
(D) reduce the degree to which experienced members express impatience and contempt for "restrictive" safety practices

Answer: **(C)** Accidents are costly in man-hours lost and in personal suffering. All workers should be made safety-conscious, especially in a hazardous occupation. This is one of the primary responsibilities of a supervisor.

9. "Many accidents are caused by lack of attention to the job that is being done." This means most nearly that

(A) accidents are a major cause of inefficiency
(B) every job is a potential cause of accidents
(C) it pays to keep your mind on what you are doing
(D) no one should ever work at a speeded-up pace

Answer: **(C)** Most accidents are caused by workers who are not mentally alert. Mental alertness will go a long way towards eliminating accidents even in dangerous situations.

10. A supervisor severely criticized one of his men who was working on a scaffold with the crew because the man was repeatedly disregarding specific safety instructions relating to scaffold work. This action by the supervisor was

(A) improper because of the presence of the rest of the crew
(B) proper because the man's actions were deliberate
(C) improper because the supervisor exceeded his authority
(D) proper because it would serve as a warning to the rest of the crew

Answer: **(B)** The action of the supervisor should first be evaluated as proper. The key word is *repeatedly*. Because the man is continuing to disregard instructions, the situation calls for drastic measures, especially as the safety of the entire crew may be involved.

11. Safety experts generally regard attempting to determine who is to blame when investigating accidents to be a

(A) good practice, mainly because a violation of safety rules should not go unpunished
(B) poor practice, mainly because an attitude of covering up makes it difficult to uncover the facts
(C) good practice, mainly because persons involved in accidents through no fault of their own want to be exonerated
(D) poor practice, mainly because the multitude of factors that cause accidents generally makes it difficult, if not impossible, to fix the blame

Answer: **(B)** The main purpose of accident investigation is to discover the cause of the accident, not the individual who was responsible. If the emphasis is to be fixed on the discovery of the responsible party rather then on the cause, workers would tend to cover up when an accident occurs.

12. A supervisor observes one of his experienced men handling equipment in an unsafe manner. This hazard can be overcome through the use of an additional piece of equipment which may be obtained at the toolshed. Of the following, the best procedure for the supervisor to follow is to

    (A) question the man to find out whether he knows a better and safer way to perform this work
    (B) assign the man to other duties and assign another member of the crew to complete the job
    (C) advise the man that if the equipment he is working on is damaged he will be subject to charges for abusing department property
    (D) order the man to get the necessary equipment to do the job properly

Answer: **(D)** One of the primary functions of a supervisor is to correct improper work performance. Not only must a worker know the correct method of work performance; he must be conditioned to work in a safe and efficient manner.

13. Which one of the following would be considered the most worthwhile result of the investigation of an accident?

    (A) Data was obtained which will help prevent similar accidents.
    (B) Department equipment was found to be only slightly damaged.
    (C) No unfavorable publicity damaging to the Department was circulated.
    (D) The other party agreed not to press any claims against the Department.

Answer: **(A)** The primary purpose of accident reports is to provide data so that accidents of a similar nature do not occur in the future. If the cause of the accident is determined, corrective measures can be taken to eliminate it.

14. An accident-prone worker should be assigned to dangerous tasks

    (A) as few times as possible
    (B) as often as possible to cure the mental block that causes accident proneness
    (C) as often as the other workers but with clear-cut and positive instructions
    (D) frequently but only with maximum supervision

Answer: **(A)** This question leaves no doubt that the man is accident prone. If this is so, he should be kept away from tasks which involve danger.

15. The most effective safety campaign is a campaign which stresses

    (A) the safety record of the shop or section
    (B) how the loss from accidents is increasing
    (C) how safe practices protect the worker
    (D) the value of safety to the section or shop

Answer: **(C)** A worker will be most likely to be cooperative in a safety campaign if he can be made to realize that he will benefit from it, and that he will suffer personally from any accident in which he may be involved.

16. Suppose that a worker who has injured himself on the job because of his carelessness informs his supervisor of the accident. The supervisor has been newly appointed to his job and is anxious to keep accidents to a minimum. The action taken by the supervisor is to criticize the subordinate for his carelessness and to tell him that he is holding him responsible for the accident. Of the following, it would be most reasonable to conclude that, as a result of the supervisor's action, his subordinates may

    (A) tend to withhold information from him about future accidents
    (B) be critical of him, in turn, if he himself is injured on the job
    (C) expect him to supervise them more closely in the future
    (D) attempt to correct hazardous job conditions without his knowledge

Answer: **(A)** The supervisor in this instance has definitely not followed the correct course of action. The workers under him will hesitate to communicate freely with him in the future.

17. The most important thing for a supervisor to bear in mind in trying to establish a good safety record is that

    (A) a certain number of accidents will happen to his men regardless of the precautions taken
    (B) a way can be found to prevent most accidents
    (C) accident-prone individuals will defeat all measures taken to protect them
    (D) accidents are unavoidable if quality work is to be maintained

Answer: **(B)** Most accidents can be prevented by proper foresight. Before a job is actually begun, a safety-conscious supervisor will examine the component parts of the job with a view towards eliminating possible hazardous conditions.

18. If a harmful chemical solution should accidentally splash into the eyes of a workman the *immediate* first-aid measure to be employed should be to

(A) bandage the eyes firmly to protect them from the light
(B) wash out the eyes with large amounts of clean water
(C) make tears flow by any non-injurious means
(D) blot the eyes and eyelids with a clean, white, soft towel

Answer: (B) When any injurious solution enters the eye, the first thing to do is to attempt to wash it out with a large amount of clean water. This should be followed up by medical attention as soon as possible.

19. "Avoid letting the patient see his own injury." This first-aid advice is generally

(A) bad; otherwise the patient will fail to learn good safety practices from the accident
(B) good; it may frighten the patient and his condition may become worse
(C) bad; since the patient himself may suggest suitable first-aid procedures
(D) good; since he could later sue the first-aider for poor first-aid treatment

Answer: (**B**) A wound may look a lot worse than it actually is and sight of it would needlessly increase the patient's shock. And if the wound is serious, he should be spared becoming frightened while waiting for the doctor to arrive.

20. If you notice a worker starting to do a job in an unsafe manner and he tells you it is the procedure that he was taught by his former supervisor, you should

(A) speak to the other supervisor and find out if the worker was telling the truth
(B) reprimand the worker for violating safety rules
(C) question the worker to see if he knows the safe way to do this job
(D) show the worker the safe way to do this job and see that he follows your directions

Answer: (**D**) You are the boss now. After you demonstrate the way you want the job performed, it must be impressed upon the worker that your method will best insure his safety. Of course it is your responsibility to see that he follows your directions.

SUPERVISOR-SUPERIOR RELATIONSHIPS

1. Assume that your superior has issued orders for a change in work procedures that your men disagree with. As a supervisor it would be best for you to tell your men that

(A) nothing can be done about it at this time, even if their complaints are justified
(B) they should complain to your superior not to you
(C) you did not like the changes yourself and tried to talk your superior out of them
(D) you will take up their complaints with your superior

Answer: **(D)** The best you can do here is to pass on the complaints if you think they are justified. However, you should support the actions of your superior at all times. If you do not show the proper respect for your superior's authority, you cannot expect your subordinates to respect your authority.

2. A supervisor, realizing the importance of harmonious relationships within his command, made a practice of unobtrusively intervening in any conflict situation between subordinates. Whenever friction seemed to be developing, he would attempt to soothe ruffled feelings, remove the source of difficulty by rescheduling activities or reassigning personnel, etc. His efforts were always behind-the-scenes, and unknown to the subordinates involved. Although this method of operation produces some good results, its chief drawback is that it

(A) violates the chain of command principle
(B) involves the supervisor in personal relationships which are not properly his concern
(C) requires confidential sources of information about relationships within the division which borders on spying
(D) permits subordinates to engage in unacceptable practices without correction

Answer: **(D)** This supervisor played the role of the "great pacifier." His motto was peace at any cost. His actions permitted incidents which required corrective measures to be covered up.

3. A supervisor's superior entered the office while a division meeting was being held. The major items on the agenda were a new office procedure, the office's unsatisfactory safety record, and the wasteful use of office supplies. During the course of the meeting, the superior took over the discussion, frequently to amplify the remarks of the supervisor, to impart information about policies which had been adopted by management but not yet disseminated, and to modify or correct possible misinterpretations of the supervisor's remarks. The superior's actions in this situation were

(A) proper, mainly because the staff was given the latest and most accurate information concerning departmental policies
(B) improper, mainly because the supervisor was placed in a difficult position
(C) proper, mainly because the superior had an obligation to support and assist the supervisor
(D) improper, mainly because the superior did not completely take over the meeting

Answer: **(B)** The supervisor was made to look inadequate in the eyes of his subordinates. The superior should have remained an observer until he was called upon by the supervisor to partake in the discussion.

4. If one of your men goes directly to your superior with a simple grievance and your superior, improperly in your opinion, acts without first checking with you, you should

(A) discuss the matter with your superior
(B) ignore this man's grievances in the future

(C) ask for the man's transfer out of your department
(D) ask your superior to assign you to another department

Answer: **(A)** It is important that you first discuss this matter with your superior. Perhaps he was not aware of correct protocol, or perhaps your attitude does not encourage your men to relate their grievances to you.

5. Your superior complains to you that he could not find you at your assigned location and that the men under your supervision were idle while you were away. In this case it is most important for you to

(A) improve your supervisory practices
(B) explain why you were away
(C) disregard such an unreasonable complaint
(D) make certain you are rarely away from your assigned location

Answer: **(A)** If your subordinates are idle during your absence, it is due either to poor planning or, more likely, to the fact that they need much closer supervision than they are receiving.

6. The one of the following instances when it is most important for an upper-level supervisor to follow the chain of command is when he is

(A) communicating decisions
(B) communicating information
(C) receiving suggestions
(D) seeking information

Answer: **(A)** The communication of decisions should be relayed on a formal basis and should adhere strictly through the chain of command. The other choices contain matters which may be handled on a more informal basis.

7. Your superior gives you an assignment which you believe you cannot do since you do not have a sufficient number of men. You explain this to him, but he tells you to get the job done. You should

(A) do the best you can and keep him informed of the progress you are making
(B) report the matter to your main office
(C) insist that he give you his instructions in writing
(D) wait until he gives you more men before taking any action to carry out the assignment

Answer: **(A)** You have given your superior your viewpoint and he has told you to go ahead with the job. Your only course of action is to get on with the work in the best possible manner and keep him informed of your progress.

8. You receive a memorandum from your superior in which he instructs you to make a large number of changes in the procedures for storing materials. The best way to bring these changes to the attention of your crew is to

(A) post the memorandum on the bulletin board where everyone can read it
(B) meet individually with each member of your staff to discuss the changes
(C) hold a meeting with your crew and explain the changes to them
(D) see to it that the memorandum is circulated to and initialled by each member of the crew

Answer: **(C)** These changes would be more readily accepted if you explained the reasons for them to the men.

9. Your subordinates tell you that, in your absence, your superior gave them orders which differed from those which you had given them. In this case, you should

(A) discuss the matter with your subordinates to determine which orders are correct
(B) discuss the matter with your superior
(C) tell your subordinates to follow your orders
(D) tell your subordinates to follow your superior's orders

Answer: **(B)** The only sensible course of action to take in this instance is to discuss the matter with your superior and find out his reasons for the change. Perhaps his ideas are better then yours, or perhaps there was some misunderstanding that you can straighten out. The situation calls for a discussion.

10. Assume that you have just been promoted to supervisor. Your superior gives you detailed oral instructions as to how a job should be done. At the conclusion of his instructions, you realize that you do not fully understand him. Under these circumstances, you should

(A) ask an experienced worker to clarify your superior's instructions

(B) ask your superior to clarify anything that you do not understand
(C) ask your superior to put his instructions in writing
(D) carry out your superior's instructions as best you can

Answer: **(B)** If a worker or supervisor does not fully understand instructions, he should immediately seek clarification before going ahead with the work.

11. Assume that you are in charge of one section of a storehouse. When the man in charge of an adjoining section resigns, you are asked to assume that job in addition to your own. After several weeks, you find that it is impossible for you to provide adequate supervision for both sections. Of the following, the best course of action for you to take is to

(A) ask your superior for a transfer
(B) assign one subordinate in each section the job of supervision
(C) divide your time between the two sections
(D) inform your superior of the facts

Answer: **(D)** It is the function of all employees, whether they be supervisor or not, to report to their superior the fact that they are unable to perform their duties in the manner expected of them. In this way appropriate action can be taken before the work is performed in an ineffective manner.

12. You, as a supervisor, believe that your superior is demanding too much work of you and your staff. In such a situation it would be best for you to

(A) speak to the company head before you speak to your superior himself
(B) speak to members of your staff to see whether they have the same feeling
(C) talk to your superior and tell him how you feel about the matter
(D) wait until a conference is held and then discuss the matter with your superior and the other supervisors present

Answer: **(C)** There is no reason for you to be reluctant to express your feelings to your superior in this situation. This situation calls for immediate action and should not be put off or a morale problem may develop. It is never a good idea to go over somebody's head.

13. Your superior tells you, a supervisor, that he does not like the way you have been keeping your various official records. As a supervisor, your best course of action would be to

(A) ask him specifically how he wants you to keep such records
(B) explain the difficulties involved [illegible]p-ing so many required records without any clerical help being assigned
(C) tell him that you never knew how to keep records properly
(D) tell him that your previous superior never found fault with them

Answer: **(A)** A general complaint is not enough for you to revise your procedures. He should be specific about whatever aspects of your record keeping he thinks should be changed. It is also his function to make known just how he desires the records to be kept if the present method is unsatisfactory.

14. "You can pass the buck up but you can't pass it down." This statement implies most directly that a supervisor

(A) is not responsible for the acts of his subordinates
(B) is responsible for the acts of his subordinates
(C) is responsible for the acts of his superiors
(D) must take the blame for anything he does wrong

Answer: **(B)** You as a supervisor cannot transfer your responsibilities to any of your workers, and you must assume full responsibility for every one of their actions as far as the work is concerned.

15. You as a supervisor are summoned to a private conference with your superior where he informs you that your unit is not keeping up with the work schedules. He remarks that he believes you are saddled with a poor group of men and he suggests you push them harder to get the work done. You sincerely believe that you and your crew have done the best possible job with the equipment available. In this situation, you should

(A) assume full responsibility and blame since you are the supervisor
(B) explain the circumstances and point out why you feel that you and the men are doing a good job

(C) suggest to your superior that he himself speak to the men about the problem
(D) tactfully remind your superior that you are closer to the problem than he is

Answer: **(B)** You as supervisor honestly believe your men are doing a good job and so it is up to you to stand up for them and explain why they are doing the best they can under the particular set of circumstances.

16. A supervisor is assigned a group of temporary workers to complete a special assignment. It would be most important for him to know

(A) previous work experience of each temporary employee
(B) length of time the assignment is likely to last
(C) nature and extent of the supervisory duties to be assumed
(D) reasons why emergency employees are not as dependable as regular employees

Answer: **(C)** This factor can hold true for any assignment whether or not it is of a supervisory nature. When a worker is to assume an assignment, he should be made aware of the extent of his duties.

17. Your superior notifies you that several of your men have complained to him about your harsh supervisory methods. You should

(A) promise to ease up on the men
(B) ask him if it is fair for him to permit these men to go over your head
(C) tell him that production is always the main consideration
(D) ask him what specific acts have been considered harsh

Answer: **(D)** A complaint of "strict supervisory methods" in general is not enough. The complaints must be specific and involve definite instances.

18. You have noticed that your superior when under pressure has a habit of giving you oral orders which are not always clear and often lack sufficient detail. The best procedure for you to follow in such a case would be to

(A) ask your superior to put his orders in writing
(B) consult your superior often in the course of doing the job so as to get the details required to finish the job
(C) have these orders clarified by asking him for needed details at the time you receive such orders
(D) review past orders of a similar nature to discover the probable intent of the superior

Answer: **(C)** If you do not clearly understand orders given to you by your superior, you should immediately ask for clarification. There is no point in proceeding on an operation you do not fully understand. This particular concept goes for all workers, whether or not they are acting in a supervisory capacity.

19. When an experienced supervisor does not agree personally with some of the policies or objectives of his superior, it would be most correct for him to

(A) continue to operate his unit in accordance with the superior's policies and regulations
(B) direct his subordinates to follow the superior's policies and regulations, but indicate the weaknesses therein and be somewhat more lenient in the supervision of these duties
(C) seek to change the superior's policies through use of grievance procedures
(D) develop his own policies and apply them to the work of his unit on a trial basis

Answer: **(A)** A supervisor may not agree with all of the actions of his superior, but he should carry out the orders to the best of his ability. He should realize that it is very unlikely that all of his own subordinates agree with all of his actions, yet he expects them to carry out his orders.

20. A generally accepted concept of management is that the authority given to a person should be commensurate with his

(A) responsibility
(B) ability
(C) seniority
(D) dependability

Answer: **(A)** Delegated responsibility must be accompanied by appropriate authority to carry out the assigned function.

21. A complex problem has arisen. You as a division chief find it necessary to confer with the worker closest to the problem. After the discussion is over, the worker informs you that his immediate supervisor is much too strict in the handling of the subordinates under his direct supervision. The one of the following actions which is generally best for you to take is to

(A) advise the worker in a friendly fashion to apply for a transfer to a unit which has a more lenient supervisor
(B) caution the worker that complaining about a fellow employee behind his back is frowned upon by higher authority as it is a sign of disloyalty
(C) inform the worker that you will investigate the complaint to determine whether or not it has any validity
(D) tell the worker that the closer and stricter a supervisor is, the better and more completely trained will be her subordinate staff

Answer: **(C)** A complaint of strict discipline is always worthy of an investigation to determine the true facts. A promise that this action will take place is sufficient at this time; no further comment should be made without some other substantiation of the charges.

22. During a visit to your section, your superior criticizes the method being used by one of your clerks to prepare a certain report and orders him to modify the method. This change is in direct conflict with the specific orders given by you to the clerk. The clerk comes to you and asks you what to do. In this situation it would be best for you to

(A) advise the clerk to ignore the orders of your superior because your method is better
(B) tell the clerk to change his method of preparing the report to meet the specifications of your superior
(C) tell the clerk to hold off on changing the method of preparing the report until you have had a chance to discuss the proposed change with your superior
(D) devise a third method of preparing the report which will incorporate the better points of both methods

Answer: **(B)** You must show the same respect and support for your superior that you expect your subordinates to give to you.

23. In order to maintain a proper relationship with a worker who is assigned to staff rather than line functions, a line supervisor should

(A) accept all recommendations of the staff worker
(B) include the staff worker in the conferences called by the supervisor for his subordinates
(C) keep the staff worker informed of developments in the area of his staff assignment
(D) require that the staff worker's recommendations be communicated to the supervisor through the supervisor's own superior

Answer: **(C)** If a staff member is responsible for a certain function and the supervisor withholds pertinent information about this function, the staff member will not only work under extremely intolerable conditions, but it is most likely to result in a strained relationship between the two.

24. Of the following, the greatest disadvantage of placing a worker in a staff position under the direct supervision of the supervisor whom he advises is the possibility that the

(A) staff worker will tend to be insubordinate because of a feeling of superiority over the supervisor
(B) staff worker will tend to give advice of the type which the supervisor wants to hear or finds acceptable
(C) supervisor will tend to be mistrustful of the advice of a worker of subordinate rank
(D) supervisor will tend to derive little benefit from the advice because to supervise properly he should know at least as much as his subordinate

Answer: **(B)** Staff employees who act in an advisory capacity should present a detached viewpoint. This worker would be in a difficult position. He would be reluctant to advise anything which he knows might not be in line with his supervisor's thinking.

GARDENER - ASSISTANT GARDENER

TEST – TAKING MADE SIMPLE

Having gotten this far, you're almost an expert test-taker because you have now mastered the subject matter of the test. Proper preparation is the real secret. The pointers on the next few pages will take you the rest of the way by giving you the strategy employed on tests by those who are most successful in this not-so-mysterious art.

BEFORE THE TEST

T-DAY MINUS SEVEN

You're going to pass this examination because you have received the best possible preparation for it. But, unlike many others, you're going to give the best possible account of yourself by acquiring the rare skill of effectively using your knowledge to answer the examination questions.

First off, get rid of any negative attitudes toward the test. You have a negative attitude when you view the test as a device to "trip you up" rather than an opportunity to show how effectively you have learned.

APPROACH THE TEST WITH SELF-CONFIDENCE. Plugging through this book was no mean job, and now that you've done it you're probably better prepared than 90% of the others. Self-confidence is one of the biggest strategic assets you can bring to the testing room.

Nobody likes tests, but some poor souls permit themselves to get upset or angry when they see what they think is an unfair test. The expert doesn't. He keeps calm and moves right ahead, knowing that everyone is taking the same test. Anger, resentment, fear . . . they all slow you down. "Grin and bear it!"

Besides, every test you take, including this one, is a valuable experience which improves your skill. Since you will undoubtedly be taking other tests in the years to come, it may help you to regard this one as training to perfect your skill.

Keep calm; there's no point in panic. If you've done your work there's no need for it; and if you haven't, a cool head is your very first requirement.

Why be the frightened kind of student who enters the examination chamber in a mental coma? A test taken under mental stress does not provide a fair measure of your ability. At the very least, this book has removed for you some of the fear and mystery that surrounds examinations. A certain amount of concern is normal and good, but excessive worry saps your strength and keenness. In other words, be prepared EMOTIONALLY.

Pre-Test Review

If you know any others who are taking this test, you'll probably find it helpful to review the book and your notes with them. The group should be small, certainly not more than four. Team study at this stage should seek to review the material in a different way than you learned it originally; should strive for an exchange of ideas between you and the other members of the group; should be selective in sticking to important ideas; should stress the vague and the unfamiliar rather than that which you all know well; should be businesslike and devoid of any nonsense; should end as soon as you get tired.

One of the *worst* strategies in test taking is to do *all* your preparation the night before the exam. As a reader of this book, you have scheduled and spaced your study properly so as not to suffer from the fatigue and emotional disturbance that comes from cramming the night before.

Cramming is a very good way to *guarantee poor test results.*

However, you would be wise to prepare yourself factually by *reviewing your notes* in the 48 hours preceding the exam. You shouldn't have to spend more than two or three hours in this way. Stick to salient points. The others will fall into place quickly.

Don't confuse cramming with a final, calm review which helps you focus on the significant areas of this book and further strengthens your confidence in your ability to handle the test questions. In other words, prepare yourself FACTUALLY.

Keep Fit

Mind and body work together. Poor physical condition will lower your mental efficiency. In preparing for an examination, observe the common-sense rules of health. Get sufficient sleep and rest, eat proper foods, plan recreation and exercise. In relation to health and examinations, two cautions are in order. Don't miss your meals prior to an examination in order to get extra time for study. Likewise, don't miss your regular sleep by sitting up late to "cram" for the examination. Cramming is an attempt to learn in a very short period of time what should have been learned through regular and consistent study. Not only are these two habits detrimental to health, but seldom do they pay off in terms of effective learning. It is likely that you will be *more confused* than better prepared on the day of the examination if you have broken into your daily routine by missing your meals or sleep.

On the night before the examination go to bed at your regular time and try to get a good night's sleep. Don't go to the movies. Don't date. In other words, prepare yourself PHYSICALLY.

T-HOUR MINUS ONE

After a very light, leisurely meal, get to the examination room ahead of time, perhaps ten minutes early . . . but not so early that you have time to get into an argument with others about what's going to be asked on the exam, etc. The reason for coming early is to help you get accustomed to the room. It will help you to a better start.

Bring all necessary equipment . . .

. . . pen, two sharpened pencils, watch, paper, eraser, ruler, and any other things you're instructed to bring.

Get settled . . .

. . . by finding your seat and staying in it. If no special seats have been assigned, take one in the front to facilitate the seating of others coming in after you.

The test will be given by a test supervisor who reads the directions and otherwise tells you what to do. The people who walk about passing out the test papers and assisting with the examination are test proctors. If you're not able to see or hear properly notify the supervisor or a proctor. If you have any other difficulties during the examination, like a defective test booklet, scoring pencil, answer sheet; or if it's too hot or cold or dark or drafty, let them know. You're entitled to favorable test conditions, and if you don't have them you won't be able to do your best. Don't be a crank, but don't be shy either. An important function of the proctor is to see to it that you have favorable test conditions.

Relax . . .

. . . and don't bring on unnecessary tenseness by worrying about the difficulty of the examination. If necessary wait a minute before beginning to write. If you're still tense, take a couple of deep breaths, look over your test equipment, or do something which will take your mind away from the examination for a moment.

If your collar or shoes are tight, loosen them.

Put away unnecessary materials so that you have a good, clear space on your desk to write freely.

You Must Have **TO GIVE YOUR Best Test PERFORMANCE**

(1) A GOOD TEST ENVIRONMENT

(2) A COMPLETE UNDERSTANDING OF DIRECTIONS

(3) A DESIRE TO DO YOUR BEST

WHEN THEY SAY "GO" — TAKE YOUR TIME!

Listen very carefully to the test supervisor. If you fail to hear something important that he says, you may not be able to read it in the written directions and may suffer accordingly.

If you don't understand the directions you have heard or read, raise your hand and inform the proctor. Read carefully the directions for *each* part of the test before beginning to work on that part. If you skip over such directions too hastily, you may miss a main idea and thus lose credit for an entire section.

Get an Overview of the Examination

After reading the directions carefully, look over the entire examination to get an over-view of the nature and scope of the test. The purpose of this over-view is to give you some idea of the nature, scope, and difficulty of the examination.

It has another advantage. An item might be so phrased that it sets in motion a chain of thought that might be helpful in answering other items on the examination.

Still another benefit to be derived from reading all the items before you answer any is that the few minutes involved in reading the items gives you an opportunity to relax before beginning the examination. This will make for better concentration. As you read over these items the first time, check those whose answers immediately come to you. These will be the ones you will answer first. Read each item carefully before answering. It is a good practice to read each item at least twice to be sure that you understand it.

Plan Ahead

In other words, you should know precisely where you are going before you start. You should know:

1. whether you have to answer all the questions or whether you can choose those that are easiest for you;
2. whether all the questions are easy; (there may be a pattern of difficult, easy, etc.)
3. The length of the test; the number of questions;
4. The kind of scoring method used;
5. Which questions, if any, carry extra weight;
6. What types of questions are on the test;
7. What directions apply to each part of the test;
8. Whether you must answer the questions consecutively.

Budget Your Time Strategically!

Quickly figure out how much of the allotted time you can give to each section and still finish ahead of time. Don't forget to figure on the time you're investing in the overview. Then alter your schedule so that you can spend more time on those parts that count most. Then, if you can, plan to spend less time on the easier questions, so that you can devote the time saved to the harder questions. Figuring roughly, you should finish half the questions when half the allotted time has gone by. If there are 100 questions and you have three hours, you should have finished 50 questions after one and one half hours. So bring along a watch whether the instructions call for one or not. Jot down your "exam budget" and stick to it INTELLIGENTLY.

EXAMINATION STRATEGY

Probably the most important single strategy you can learn is to do the easy questions first. The very hard questions should be read and temporarily postponed. Identify them with a dot and return to them later.

This strategy has several advantages for you:

1. You're sure to get credit for all the questions you're sure of. If time runs out, you'll have all the sure shots, losing out only on those which you might have missed anyway.
2. By reading and laying away the tough ones you give your subconscious a chance to work on them. You may be pleasantly surprised to find the answers to the puzzlers popping up for you as you deal with related questions.
3. You won't risk getting caught by the time limit just as you reach a question you know really well.

A Tested Tactic

It's inadvisable on some examinations to answer each question in the order presented. The reason for this is that some examiners design tests so as to extract as much mental energy from you as possible. They put the most difficult questions at the beginning, the easier questions last. Or they may vary difficult with easy questions in a fairly regular pattern right through the test. Your survey of the test should reveal the pattern and your strategy for dealing with it.

If difficult questions appear at the beginning, answer them until you feel yourself slowing down or getting tired. Then switch to an easier part of the examination. You will return to the difficult portion after you have rebuilt your confidence by answering a batch of easy questions. Knowing that you have a certain number of points "under your belt" will help you when you return to the more difficult questions. You'll answer them with a much clearer mind; and you'll be refreshed by the change of pace.

Time

Use your time wisely. It's an important element in your test and you must use every minute effectively, working as rapidly as you can without sacrificing accuracy. Your exam survey and budget will guide you in dispensing your time. Wherever you can, pick up seconds on the easy ones. Devote your savings to the hard ones. If possible, pick up time on the lower value questions and devote it to those which give you the most points.

Relax Occasionally and Avoid Fatigue

If the exam is long (two or more hours) give yourself short rest periods as you feel you need them. If you're not permitted to leave the room, relax in your seat, look up from your paper, rest your eyes, stretch your legs, shift your body. Break physical and mental tension. Take several deep breaths and get back to the job, refreshed. If you don't do this you run the risk of getting nervous and tightening up. Your thinking may be hampered and you may make a few unnecessary mistakes.

Do not become worried or discouraged if the examination seems difficult to you. The questions in the various fields are purposely made difficult and searching so that the examination will discriminate effectively even among superior students. No one is expected to get a perfect or near-perfect score.

Remember that if the examination seems difficult to you, it may be even more difficult for your neighbor.

Think!

This is not a joke because you're not an IBM machine. Nobody is able to write all the time and also to read and think through each question. You must plan each answer. Don't give hurried answers in an atmosphere of panic. Even though you see a lot of questions, remember that they are objective and not very time-consuming. Don't rush headlong through questions that must be thought through.

Edit, Check, Proofread . . .

. . . after completing all the questions. Invariably, you will find some foolish errors which you needn't have made, and which you can easily correct. Don't just sit back or leave the room ahead of time. Read over your answers and make sure you wrote exactly what you meant to write. And that you wrote the answers in the right place. You might even find that you have omitted some answers inadvertently. You have budgeted time for this job of proofreading. PROOFREAD and pick up points.

One caution, though. Don't count on making major changes. And don't go in for wholesale changing of answers. To arrive at your answers in the first place you have read carefully and thought correctly. Second-guessing at this stage is more likely to result in wrong answers. So don't make changes unless you are quite certain you were wrong in the first place.

FOLLOW DIRECTIONS CAREFULLY

In answering questions on the objective or short-form examination, it is most important to follow all instructions carefully. Unless you have marked the answers properly, you will not receive credit for them. In addition, even in the same examination, the instructions will not be consistent. In one section you may be urged to guess if you are not certain; in another you may be cautioned against guessing. Some questions will call for the best choice among four or five alternatives; others may ask you to select the one incorrect or the least probable answer.

On some tests you will be provided with worked out fore-exercises, complete with correct answers. However, avoid the temptation to skip the directions and begin working just from reading the model questions and answers. Even though you may be familiar with that particular type of question, the directions may be different from those which you had followed previously. If the type of question should be new to you, work through the model until you understand it perfectly. This may save you time, and earn you a higher rating on the examination.

If the directions for the examination are written, read them carefully, at least twice. If the directions are given orally, listen attentively and then follow them precisely. For example, if you are directed to use plus (+) and minus (−) to mark true—false items, then don't use "T" and "F". If you are instructed to "blacken" a space on machine-scored tests, do not use a check (✓) or an "X". Make all symbols legible, and be sure that they have been placed in the proper answer space. It is easy, for example, to place the answer for item 5 in the space reserved for item 6. If this is done, then all of your following answers may be wrong. It is also very important that you understand the method they will use in scoring the examination. Sometimes they tell you in the directions. The method of scoring may affect the amount of time you spend on an item, especially if some items count more than others. Likewise, the directions may indicate whether or not you should guess in case you are not sure of the answer. Some methods of scoring penalize you for guessing.

Cue Words. Pay special attention to qualifying words or phrases in the directions. Such words as *one, best reason, surest, means most nearly the same as, preferable, least correct,* etc., all indicate that *one* response is called for, and that you must select the response which best fits the qualifications in the question.

Time. Sometimes a time limit is set for each section of the examination. If that is the case, follow the time instructions carefully. Your *exam budget* and your watch can help you here. Even if you haven't finished a section when the time limit is up, pass on to the next section. The examination has been planned according to the time schedule.

If the examination paper bears the instruction "Do not turn over page until signal is given," or "Do not start until signal is given," follow the instruction. Otherwise, you may be disqualified.

Pay Close Attention. Be sure you understand what you're doing at all times. Especially in dealing with true-false or multiple-choice questions it's vital that you understand the meaning of every question. It is normal to be working under stress when taking an examination, and it is easy to skip a word or jump to a false conclusion, which may cost you points on the examination. In many multiple-choice and matching questions, the examiners deliberately insert plausible-appearing false answers in order to catch the candidate who is not alert.

Answer clearly. If the examiner who marks your paper cannot understand what you mean, you will not receive credit for your correct answer. On a True-False examination you will not receive any credit for a question which is marked both true and false. If you are asked to underline, be certain that your lines are under and not through the words and that they do not extend beyond them. When using the separate answer sheet it is important *when you decide to change an answer,* you erase the first answer completely. If you leave any graphite from the pencil on the wrong space it will cause the scoring machine to cancel the right answer for that question.

Watch Your "Weights." If the examination is "weighted" it means that some parts of the examination are considered more important than others and rated more highly. For instance, you may find that the instructions will indicate "Part I, Weight 50; Part II, Weight 25, Part III, Weight 25." In such a case, you would devote half of your time to the first part, and divide the second half of your time among Parts II and III.

A Funny Thing . . .

. . . happened to you on your way to the bottom of the totem pole. You *thought* the right answer but you marked the *wrong* one.

1. You *mixed answer symbols*! You decided (rightly) that Baltimore (Choice D) was correct. Then you marked *B* (for Baltimore) instead of *D*.
2. You *misread* a simple instruction! Asked to give the *latest* word in a scrambled sentence, you correctly arranged the sentence, and then marked the letter corresponding to the *earliest* word in that miserable sentence.
3. You *inverted digits!* Instead of the correct number, 96, you wrote (or read) 69.

Funny? Tragic! Stay away from accidents.

Record your answers on the answer sheet one by one as you answer the questions. Care should be taken that these answers are recorded next to the appropriate numbers on your answer sheet. It is poor practice to write your answers first on the test booklet and then to transfer them all at one time to the answer sheet. This procedure causes many errors. And then, how would you feel if you ran out of time before you had a chance to transfer all the answers.

When and How To Guess

Read the directions carefully to determine the scoring method that will be used. In some tests, the directions will indicate that guessing is advisable if you do not know the answer to a question. In such tests, only the right answers are counted in determining your score. If such is the case, don't omit any items. If you do not know the answer, or if you are not sure of your answer, then *guess.*

On the other hand, if the directions state that a scoring formula *will* be used in determining your score or that you are *not to guess,* then *omit* the question if you do not know the answer, or if you are not sure of the answer. When the scoring formula is used, a percentage of the *wrong* answers will be subtracted from the number of *right* answers as a correction for haphazard guessing. It is improbable, therefore, that mere guessing will improve your score significantly. *It may even lower your score.* Another disadvantage in guessing under such circumstances is that it consumes valuable time that you might profitably use in answering the questions you know.

If, however, you are uncertain of the correct answer but have *some* knowledge of the question and are able to eliminate one or more of the answer choices as wrong, your chance of getting the right answer is improved, and it will be to your advantage to *answer* such a question rather than *omit* it.

BEAT THE ANSWER SHEET

Even though you've had plenty of practice with the answer sheet used on machine-scored examinations, we must give you a few more, last-minute pointers.

The present popularity of tests requires the use of electrical test scoring machines. With these machines, scoring which would require the labor of several men for hours can be handled by one man in a fraction of the time.

The scoring machine is an amazingly intricate and helpful device, but the machine is not human. The machine cannot, for example, tell the difference between an intended answer and a stray pencil mark, and will count both indiscriminately. The machine cannot count a pencil mark, if the pencil mark is not brought in contact with the electrodes. For these reasons, specially printed answer sheets with response spaces properly located and properly filled in must be employed. Since not all pencil leads contain the necessary ingredients, a special pencil must be used and a heavy solid mark must be made to indicate answers.

(a) Each pencil mark must be heavy and black. Light marks should be retraced with the special pencil.

(b) Each mark must be in the space between the pair of dotted lines and entirely fill this space.

(c) All stray pencil marks on the paper, clearly not intended as answers, must be completely erased.

(d) Each question must have only one answer indicated. If multiple answers occur, all extraneous marks should be thoroughly erased. Otherwise, the machine will give you *no* credit for your correct answer.

Be sure to use the special electrographic pencil!

HERE'S HOW TO MARK YOUR ANSWERS ON MACHINE-SCORED ANSWER SHEETS:

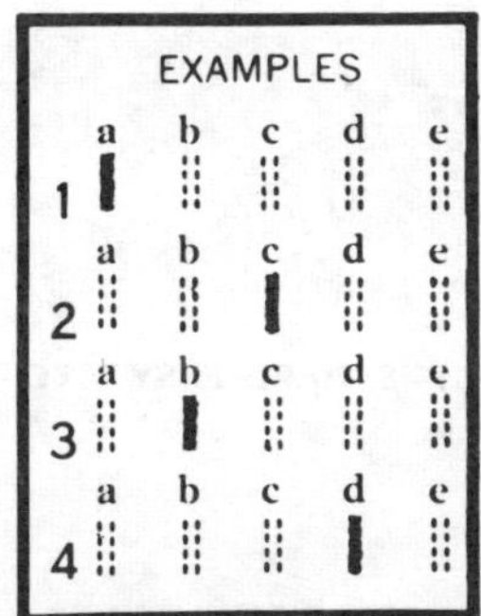

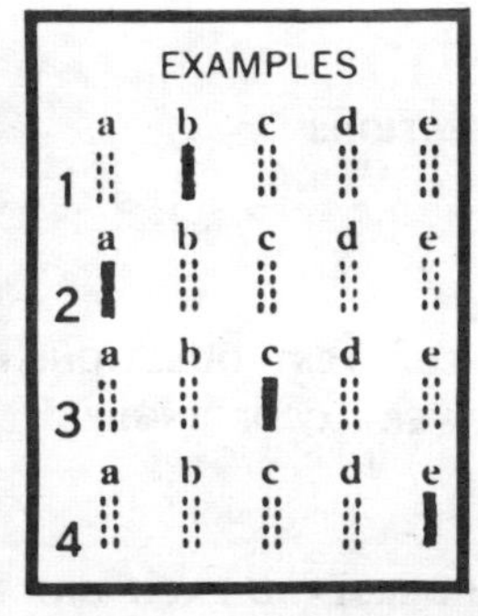

Make only ONE mark for each answer. Additional and stray marks may be counted as mistakes. In making corrections, erase errors COMPLETELY. Make glossy black marks.

Your answer sheet is the only one that reaches the office where papers are scored. For this reason it is important that the blanks at the top be filled in completely and correctly. The proctors will check this, but just in case they slip up, make certain yourself that your paper is complete.

Many exams caution competitors against making any marks on the test booklet itself. Obey that caution even though it goes against your grain to work neatly. If you work neatly and obediently with the test booklet you'll probably do the same with the answer sheet. And that pays off in high scores.

THE GIST OF TEST STRATEGY

- APPROACH THE TEST CONFIDENTLY. TAKE IT CALMLY.
- REMEMBER TO REVIEW, THE WEEK BEFORE THE TEST.
- DON'T "CRAM." BE CAREFUL OF YOUR DIET AND SLEEP ... ESPECIALLY AS THE TEST DRAWS NIGH.
- ARRIVE ON TIME . . . AND READY.
- BRING THE COMPLETE KIT OF "TOOLS" YOU'LL NEED.
- CHOOSE A GOOD SEAT. GET COMFORTABLE AND RELAX.
- LISTEN CAREFULLY TO ALL DIRECTIONS.
- APPORTION YOUR TIME INTELLIGENTLY WITH AN "EXAM BUDGET."
- READ ALL DIRECTIONS CAREFULLY. TWICE IF NECESSARY. PAY PARTICULAR ATTENTION TO THE SCORING PLAN.
- LOOK OVER THE WHOLE TEST BEFORE ANSWERING ANY QUESTIONS.
- START RIGHT IN, IF POSSIBLE. STAY WITH IT. USE EVERY SECOND EFFECTIVELY.
- DO THE EASY QUESTIONS FIRST; POSTPONE HARDER QUESTIONS UNTIL LATER.
- DETERMINE THE PATTERN OF THE TEST QUESTIONS.IF IT'S HARD-EASY ETC., ANSWER ACCORDINGLY.
- READ EACH QUESTION CAREFULLY. MAKE SURE YOU UNDERSTAND EACH ONE BEFORE YOU ANSWER. RE-READ, IF NECESSARY.

- THINK! AVOID HURRIED ANSWERS. GUESS INTELLIGENTLY.

- WATCH YOUR WATCH AND "EXAM BUDGET," BUT DO A LITTLE BALANCING OF THE TIME YOU DEVOTE TO EACH QUESTION.

- GET ALL THE HELP YOU CAN FROM "CUE" WORDS.

- REPHRASE DIFFICULT QUESTIONS FOR YOURSELF. WATCH OUT FOR "SPOILERS."

- REFRESH YOURSELF WITH A FEW, WELL-CHOSEN REST PAUSES DURING THE TEST.

- USE CONTROLLED ASSOCIATION TO SEE THE RELATION OF ONE QUESTION TO ANOTHER AND WITH AS MANY IMPORTANT IDEAS AS YOU CAN DEVELOP.

- NOW THAT YOU'RE A "COOL" TEST-TAKER, STAY CALM AND CONFIDENT THROUGHOUT THE TEST. DON'T LET ANYTHING THROW YOU.

- EDIT, CHECK, PROOFREAD YOUR ANSWERS. BE A "BITTER ENDER." STAY WORKING UNTIL THEY MAKE YOU GO.

CIVIL SERVICE AND TEST PREPARATION—GENERAL

Title	No.	Price
Able Seaman, Deckhand, Scowman	01376-1	5.00
Accountant—Auditor	00001-5	6.00
Addiction Specialist, Senior, Supervising, Principal, Turner	03351-7	8.00
Air Traffic Controller, Turner	02088-1	6.00
American Foreign Service Officer	00081-3	5.00
Apprentice, Mechanical Trades	00571-8	5.00
Assistant Accountant—Junior Accountant—Account Clerk	00056-2	6.00
Assistant Station Supervisor, Turner	03736-9	6.00
Attorney, Assistant—Trainee	01084-3	8.00
Auto Machinist	00513-0	6.00
Auto Mechanic, Autoserviceman	00514-9	6.00
Bank Examiner—Trainee and Assistant	01642-6	5.00
Battalion and Deputy Chief, F.D.	00515-7	6.00
Beginning Office Worker	00173-9	5.00
Beverage Control Investigator	00150-X	4.00
Bookkeeper—Account Clerk, Turner	00035-X	6.00
Bridge and Tunnel Officer—Special Officer	00780-X	5.00
Bus Maintainer—Bus Mechanic	00111-9	5.00
Bus Operator Conductor	01553-5	5.00
Buyer (Purchase Inspector)	01366-4	4.00
Captain, Fire Department	00121-6	8.00
Captain, Police Department	00184-4	8.00
Carpenter	00135-6	6.00
Cashier, Housing Teller	00703-6	4.00
Cement Mason—Mason's Helper, Turner	03745-8	6.00
Chemist—Assistant Chemist	00116-X	5.00
City Planner	01364-8	6.00
Civil Engineer, Senior and Supervising, Turner	00146-1	8.00
Civil Service Arithmetic and Vocabulary	00003-1	4.00
Civil Service Handbook	00040-6	1.50
Claim Examiner—Law Investigator	00149-6	5.00
Clerk New York City—Clerk Income Maintenance	00045-7	4.00
Clerk—Steno Transcriber	00838-5	5.00
College Office Assistant	00181-X	5.00
Complete Guide to U.S. Civil Service Jobs	00537-8	2.00
Construction Foreman—Supervisor—Inspector	01085-1	5.00
Correction Captain—Deputy Warden	01358-3	8.00
Correction Officer	00186-0	5.00
Court Officer	00519-X	6.00
Criminal Law Quizzer, Salottolo	02399-6	10.00
Criminal Science Quizzer, Salottolo	02407-0	5.00
Detective Investigator, Turner	03738-5	6.00
Dietitian	00083-X	5.00
Draftsman, Civil and Mechanical Engineering (All Grades)	01225-0	6.00
Electrical Engineer	00137-2	5.00
Electrical Inspector	03350-9	8.00
Electrician	00084-8	6.00
Electronic Equipment Maintainer, Turner	01836-4	6.00
Elevator Operator	00051-1	3.00
Employment Interviewer	00008-2	6.00
Employment Security Clerk	00700-1	5.00
Engineering Technician (All Grades), Turner	01226-9	6.00
Exterminator Foreman—Foreman of Housing Exterminators	03740-7	6.00
Federal Service Entrance Examinations	00528-9	5.00
File Clerk	00962-4	5.00
Fire Administration and Technology	00604-8	6.00
Firefighting Hydraulics, Bonadio	00572-6	7.50
Fireman, F.D.	00010-4	5.00
Food Service Supervisor—School Lunch Manager	01378-8	6.00
Foreman of Auto Mechanics	01360-5	4.00
Foreman	00191-7	5.00
Foreman (Tracks) T.A., Turner	03739-3	6.00
General Entrance Series, Arco Editorial Board	01961-1	4.00
General Test Practice for 92 U.S. Jobs	00011-2	5.00
Guard—Patrolman	00122-4	5.00
Heavy Equipment Operator (Portable Enginer)	01372-9	5.00
High School Civil Service Course	00702-8	4.00
Homestudy Course for Civil Service Jobs, Turner	01587-X	5.00
Hospital Attendant	00012-0	4.00
Hospital Care Investigator Trainee (Social Case Worker I)	01674-4	5.00
Hospital Clerk	01718-X	3.00
Housing Assistant	00054-6	5.00
Housing Caretaker	00504-1	4.00
Housing Inspector	00055-4	5.00
Housing Manager—Assistant Housing Manager	00813-X	5.00
Housing Patrolman	00192-5	5.00
How to Pass Employment Tests, Liebers	00715-X	5.00
Internal Revenue Agent	00093-7	5.00
Investigator—Inspector	01670-1	5.00
Janitor—Custodian	00013-9	6.00
Junior Administrator Development Examination (JADE)	01643-4	5.00
Junior and Assistant Civil Engineer	01228-5	5.00
Junior Federal Assistant	01729-5	5.00
Laboratory Aide, Arco Editorial Board	01121-1	5.00
Laborer—Federal, State and City Jobs	00566-1	4.00
Landscape Architect	01368-0	5.00
Laundry Worker	01834-8	4.00
Law and Court Stenographer	00783-4	6.00
Law Enforcement Positions	00500-9	6.00
Librarian	00060-0	4.00
Lieutenant, F.D.	00123-2	8.00
Lieutenant, P.D.	00190-9	8.00
Machinist—Machinist's Helper	01123-8	6.00
Mail Handler—U.S. Postal Service	00126-7	5.00
Maintainer's Helper, Group A and C—Transit Electrical Helper	00175-5	6.00
Maintenance Man	00113-5	5.00
Management and Administration Quizzer	01537-3	6.00
Mathematics, Simplified and Self-Taught	00567-X	4.00
Mechanical Apprentice (Maintainer's Helper B)	00176-3	5.00
Mechanical Aptitude and Spatial Relations Tests	00539-4	5.00
Mechanical Engineer—Junior, Assistant & Senior Grades	03314-2	8.00
Messenger	00017-1	3.00
Mortuary Caretaker	01354-0	4.00
Motor Vehicle License Examiner	00018-X	5.00
Motor Vehicle Operator	00576-9	4.00
Motorman (Subways)	00061-9	6.00
Nurse	00143-7	6.00
Office Assistant GS 1-4 Office Aide	00043-0	5.00
Office Machines Operator	00728-1	4.00
1540 Questions and Answers for Electricians	00754-0	5.00
1340 Questions and Answers for Firefighters, McGannon	00857-1	4.00
Operations and Maintenance Trainee	01241-2	4.00
Painter	01772-4	5.00
Parking Enforcement Agent	00701-X	4.00
Patrol Inspector	00101-1	4.00
Peace Corps Placement Exams, Turner	01641-8	4.00
Personnel Examiner, Junior Personnel Examiner	00648-X	6.00
Plumber—Plumber's Helper	00517-3	6.00
Police Administration and Criminal Investigation	00565-3	6.00
Police Administrative Aide, Turner	02345-7	5.00
Police Officer—Trainee P.D, Murray	00019-8	5.00
Police Science Advancement—Police Promotion Course	02636-7	10.00
Policewoman	00062-7	5.00
Post Office Clerk-Carrier	00021-X	4.00
Post Office Motor Vehicle Operator	01162-9	4.00
Postal Inspector	00194-1	5.00
Postal Promotion Foreman—Supervisor	00538-6	6.00
Postal Service Officer	01658-2	5.00
Postmaster	01522-5	5.00
Practice for Civil Service Promotion	00023-6	6.00
Practice for Clerical, Typing and Stenographic Tests	00005-8	5.00
Principal Clerk—Stenographer	01523-3	5.00

Title	Order	No.	Price
Probation and Parole Officer	______	01542-X	**6.00**
Professional and Administrative Career Examination (PACE)	______	03653-2	**6.00**
Professional Career Tests	______	01543-8	**5.00**
Professional Trainee—Administrative Aide	______	01183-1	**5.00**
Public Health Sanitarian	______	00985-3	**6.00**
Railroad Clerk	______	00067-8	**4.00**
Railroad Porter	______	00128-3	**4.00**
Real Estate Assessor—Appraiser—Manager	______	00563-7	**6.00**
Resident Building Superintendent	______	00068-6	**5.00**
Road Car Inspector (T.A.), Turner	______	03743-1	**6.00**
Sanitation Foreman (Foreman & Asst. Foreman)	______	01958-1	**5.00**
Sanitation Man	______	00025-2	**4.00**
School Crossing Guard	______	00611-0	**4.00**
Securing and Protecting Your Rights in Civil Service, Resnicoff	______	02714-2	**4.95**
Senior Clerical Series	______	01173-4	**5.00**
Senior Clerk—Stenographer	______	01797-X	**6.00**
Senior File Clerk, Turner	______	00124-0	**5.00**
Senior and Supervising Parking Enforcement Agent, Turner	______	03737-7	**6.00**
Sergeant, P.D.	______	00026-0	**7.00**
Shop Clerk, Turner	______	03684-2	**6.00**
Social Case Worker, Turner	______	01528-4	**6.00**
Social Supervisor	______	00028-7	**6.00**
Staff Attendant	______	00828-8	**4.00**
Staff Positions: Senior Administrative Associate and Assistant	______	03490-4	**6.00**
State Trooper	______	00078-3	**5.00**
Statistician—Statistical Clerk	______	00058-9	**5.00**
Stenographer—Typist (Practical Preparation)	______	00147-X	**4.00**
Stenographer—U.S. Government Positions	______	00031-7	**6.00**
Storekeeper—Stockman	______	01691-4	**5.00**
Structural Apprentice, Turner	______	00177-1	**5.00**
Structure Maintainer Trainee, Groups A to E, Turner	______	03683-4	**6.00**
Supervising Clerk—Income Maintenance	______	02879-3	**6.00**
Supervising Clerk—Stenographer	______	01685-X	**5.00**
Supervision Course	______	01590-X	**5.00**
Surface Line Dispatcher	______	00140-2	**6.00**
Tabulating Machine Operator (IBM)	______	00781-8	**4.00**
Taking Tests and Scoring High, Honig	______	01347-8	**3.00**
Telephone Operator	______	00033-3	**5.00**
Telephone Maintainer, Turner	______	03742-3	**6.00**
Test Your Vocational Aptitude, Gladstone	______	03606-0	**3.00**
Towerman (Municipal Subway System)	______	00157-7	**5.00**
Trackman (Municipal Subways), Turner	______	00075-9	**5.00**
Traffic Control Agent	______	03421-1	**5.00**
Train Dispatcher	______	00158-5	**5.00**
Transit Patrolman	______	00092-9	**5.00**
Transit Sergeant—Lieutenant	______	00161-5	**4.00**
Treasury Enforcement Agent	______	00131-3	**6.00**
U.S. Professional Mid-Level Positions Grades GS-9 Through GS-12	______	02036-9	**4.00**
U.S. Summer Jobs, Turner	______	02480-1	**4.00**
Ventilation and Drainage Maintainer, Turner	______	03741-5	**6.00**
Vocabulary Builder and Guide to Verbal Tests	______	00535-1	**4.00**
Vocabulary, Spelling and Grammar	______	00077-5	**4.00**
Welder	______	01374-5	**5.00**
X-Ray Technician	______	0112%-X	**3.00**

MILITARY EXAMINATION SERIES

Title	Order	No.	Price
Practice for the Army Qualification Battery	______	01301-X	**5.00**
Practice for the Armed Forces Tests	______	00063-5	**5.00**
Practice for the Navy's Basic Test Battery	______	01300-1	**5.00**
Practice for the Women's Placement Test	______	01303-6	**4.00**
Practice for Air Force Placement Tests	______	01302-8	**5.00**
Practice for Officer Candidate Tests	______	01304-4	**5.00**
U.S. Service Academy Admission Tests	______	01544-6	**4.00**